Orbis Sensualium Pictus,

A World of Things Obvious to the Senses drawn in Pictures.

The Master and the Boy.	*Magister & Puer.*
M. Come, Boy, learn to . be wise.	M. Veni, Puer, disce sa-pere.
P. What doth this mean, *to be wise?*	P. Quid hoc est, *Sapere?*
M. To understand right-ly.	M. Intelligere recte,

EDUCATIONAL MEDIA:
Theory into Practice

edited by

Raymond V. Wiman
University of Iowa

Wesley C. Meierhenry
University of Nebraska

CHARLES E. MERRILL PUBLISHING COMPANY
Columbus, Ohio   *A Bell & Howell Company*

Library of Congress Catalog Card Number: 69-11671

Standard Book Number: 675-09552-2

1 2 3 4 5 6 7 8 9 10 — 73 72 71 70 69 68

PRINTED IN THE UNITED STATES OF AMERICA

Foreword

If all of the problems that plague the organization and operation of human society were placed on a rank order of small to large or simple to complex, communication certainly would have to be included close to or at the top of this continuum. Differences in language have always been, and probably always will be a major obstacle to international understanding. But, even within a given nation where everyone ostensibly speaks the same language, regional dialects, ambiguity, idiom, colloquial expressions, and shading of meaning all take their toll in inter-group and individual relationships.

Nor is this the whole story. Communication problems are compounded as society becomes more complex. In the more simple cultures, where bloodline and prestige relationships dictate fairly routine and fixed patterns of behavior, it is not particularly difficult to learn the semantic cues and master the proper behavior responses, since these remain quite constant from generation to generation. But in societies based on greater freedom of choice and open mobility, there is no special, if indeed any security at all in patent and fixed response patterns. In the modern, especially in the highly industrialized states, all individuals and groups find themselves in environments where choices are multiple, and the cues for behavior vary from situation to situation, or even within a given situation. Modern man, in short, must learn to live in a milieu where change, tension, uncertainty, and frustration are endemic.

Moreover, it is axiomatic in societal organization, that as the industrial, financial, governmental, and even social systems become more specialized, the interdependence between individuals and groups becomes correspondingly greater. As a result, if the channels of inter-communication between these agencies break down, or even if they malfunction for an appreciable period of time, the whole complex machinery tends to slow down or halt, and the implications for cultural health are most serious and can even threaten national survival.

These phenomena are quite readily noted in the present complexity and perplexity of life in the United States. The militancy of minority groups, the disaffection between certain elements of the academic community and the current leadership in the federal government, and the impasses reached by industrial management and labor groups are only the more dramatic symptoms at the moment. Deeper within the national fabric are more subtle and perhaps more dangerous dislocations, reflecting in the disillusionment of segments of the youth population and the widening disagreements on all levels as to the revised values and moral structure the society needs to establish new directions and stability. Paradoxically, this situation exists in the nation that has reached the highest productive levels and the greatest material prosperity ever achieved. And even more paradoxical is the fact that this nation has perfected marvelously elaborate and sophisticated systems of communications.

But here lies the rub. The communication systems are complex and highly specialized in and of themselves. Actually, some of them are virtually indigenous languages, too complex and difficult to be clearly understood, much less mastered by any large portion of the population. Computers and computer science constitute a case in point. Television has become largely an entertainment medium, although some of its great educational potential has been exploited.

Obviously, the primary need lies in the development of a greater capacity within the educational complex for a complete understanding of the situation, and especially in designing some techniques for more effective use of the communication channels and devices along the whole gamut of the learning process.

There is no claim here that this book will serve this function, or anything close to it. But, it is a beginning. The editors have made what is perhaps the first attempt to review the communications problem in teaching from a truly interdisciplinary approach. They have drawn together leading people from various disciplines that contribute in rather special ways to an understanding of communication. Then, an attempt is made to produce a synthesis of the philosophies and theories involved and link these into the practical aspects of good classroom performance, especially in the design and effective utilization of materials and teaching aids.

The original idea in going to experts in the various areas and disciplines was based on the assumption that no one person could have the background and understanding to weave so many facets of specialization into a single treatise. Therefore, since communication is an interdisciplinary phenomenon, it would be most beneficial for each of the areas to be treated separately by those best qualified to do so.

As the book is read, an exciting and significant feature becomes apparent. There is a great deal in common between the areas and disciplines when focused on the problems of communication. Perhaps, this will serve as an opening wedge for further developments in the application of communications science in the solutions of some of the crises that face civilization.

Walter K. Beggs, Dean

Teachers College
University of Nebraska

Preface

Because of the nature of the audiovisual field, useful theory is
not confined to its own literature. . . . there is the literature of the
film, of photography, of the museum, of dramatization, etc.; there is
also the literature of educational method and curriculum; there is
the literature of educational psychology, of social psychology, of
social anthropology; there is the literature of art and design; finally,
and perhaps most important, there is the growing literature of communication.

—James D. Finn[*]

Human communication is related to all of the behavioral sciences.
These disciplines have often been neglected in educational media
methods courses because of too much emphasis upon the mechanical
and technical processes related to the use of media in the classroom. As
one looks at teaching and learning processes in action, it soon becomes
apparent that the communication processes involved are very complex
indeed. It is also evident that there is no single resource available for
information about communication in the classroom, or communication
anywhere for that matter.

This volume incorporates theoretical and practical considerations
drawn from a number of related disciplines. Eleven authors from such
areas as philosophy, anthropology, art, mass media, psychology, and
communications theory have contributed to this book. It is *not*, however,
just a collection of readings. Each chapter was written specifically for

[*]"Professionalizing the Audio-visual Field," *Audio-Visual Communication Review*, Vol. I, No. I (Winter, 1953), p. 14.

this publication and each author was asked to develop material from his or her particular viewpoint; not from that of the editors. Teachers will develop a greater appreciation of teaching problems and teaching strategies through an interdisciplinary approach that delves into theory and practice related to effective communication in the classroom.

Technology has reached the point where equipment can be programmed to teach students what they need to know about equipment operation and production procedures. The instructor, then, can engage the student more deeply in understanding and applying factors related to the basic processes involved in implementing learning. It is hoped that this book will provide a framework or point of departure for students in methods courses.

It is impossible to acknowledge adequately all of the people who have assisted, directly or indirectly, in the development of this text. Special acknowledgement must go, however, to Mrs. Sue Hauschild who typed drafts, labored over indexes, and ruthlessly exposed any errors as she prepared the chapters for assembly.

RVW
WCM

The Contributors*

Raymond V. Wiman

Samuel L. Becker	A. Walden Ends
Randall Harrison	June King McFee
Robert M. Gagné	Harry F. Wolcott
A. W. VanderMeer	Richard L. Darling
Donald K. Stewart	Wesley C. Meierhenry

Raymond V. Wiman is Associate Professor of Education and Director of the Graduate Program in Educational Media at the University of Iowa. He teaches undergraduate methods courses in media and graduate courses and seminars in the educational media area. His professional experience includes work at the primary, intermediate, junior high, and high school levels as well as at the college and university level. He is the author of a number of articles in the field and is educational consultant for a film series related to the teaching of audiovisual production techniques. He received his Bachelor of Arts degree from Arizona State University, his Master of Arts from San Francisco State College, and his Ed.D. from the University of Nebraska. His particular interests and research are focused on bridging the gap between theory and practice in teaching through an interdisciplinary approach to the problems involved.

---

*Biographies presented in the order in which chapters appear in this book.

Samuel L. Becker is Chairman of the Department of Speech and Dramatic Art at the University of Iowa. He is the author of books, monographs,and journal articles. These monographs and articles include some of the early research in this country in teaching by television. He has been a Fullbright professor to the University of Nottingham and recipient of research grants from the U.S. Department of Health, Education, and Welfare; The Ford Foundation; and the National Educational, Television, and Radio Center. Dr. Becker received his bachelor's, master's and Ph.D. degrees from the University of Iowa. His interests are in the areas of broadcasting, speech, and communication research. He has done post-doctoral research in sociology at Columbia University.

Randall Harrison is Director of Undergraduate Studies in the Department of Communication, College of Communication Arts, Michigan State University. He teaches graduate seminars in "message system analysis" and undergraduate courses in non-verbal communication, communication design, information theory and systems analysis. His chief research interests are in the areas of facial communication and Pictic Analysis (an examination of pictorial code). His professional experience includes work as a communications consultant to various agencies including the U.S. State Department. He received his bachelor's degree from the University of Wisconsin and his Ph.D. in communications from Michigan State University.

Robert M. Gagné is Professor in the field of educational psychology, University of California at Berkeley. He began his teaching career at Connecticut College for 'Women and, during World War II, served as an Aviation Psychologist. He returned to college teaching at Pennsylvania State University and at Connecticut College, where he also carried out a research project on the learning and transfer of skills. For eight years thereafter, he was Technical Director in two Air Force laboratories engaged in research programs dealing with learning and methods of technical training. From 1958–1962, Dr. Gagné was Professor of Psychology at Princeton University, and from 1962–65, he was Director of Research of the American Institutes for Research, where he was concerned with general supervision of research programs on human performance, instructional methods, educational objectives, design and evaluation of curricula, and instructional procedures. Dr. Gagné is the author of numerous books and journal articles. He received his undergraduate education at Yale University, and his doctoral degree in experimental psychology from Brown University.

A. W. VanderMeer is Dean of the College of Education of The Pennsylvania State University. His career as a teacher, research associate, professor and administrator, spans more than thirty years. He has been involved in a wide variety of research related to the development and utilization of educational media and is the author of numerous reports and journal articles on the research as well as in the general educational media area. He received a bachelor's degree in education from Eastern Washington State College in 1934, a bachelor's degree from the University of Washington in 1939, his master's degree from the University of Chicago in 1941, and his Ph.D. from the University of Chicago in 1943.

Donald K. Stewart is Director of Systems for Learning by Application of Technology to Education (SLATE). He did his undergraduate work in electrical engineering in television at the University of Minnesota, and his graduate work in motion picture production at the University of California. His interests are in the areas of the psychological and sociological aspects of human communication and audiovisual education. As Director of the Center for Creative Application of Technology to Education at Texas A & M University, he developed plans for a regional dial-access information retrievial system which will be implemented in several metropolitan areas within the near future. He is also editor of a newsletter and has written numerous articles on the learning-systems concept in educational media in education.

A. Walden Ends is Associate Professor of Elementary Education at the University of Georgia. His teaching and research interests center around inter-personal sensitivity training, communications, human relations, and the supervision of instruction. The focus of Dr. Ends' research is the human variable in introducing and affecting change within instructional practices. He received his bachelor's degree from San Jose State College, his Master of Arts from San Francisco State College, and his Ph.D. from Michigan State University where he completed a major in supervision curriculum development and a minor in educational television and instructional broadcasting.

June King McFee is Director of the Institute for Community Arts Studies and Associate Professor of Art Education at the University of Oregon. Her research interests are in the areas of the creative potential of adolescents and community and art studies. She has been a visiting lecturer, professor, and consultant to various universities and school districts throughout the country. She is a frequent contributer to educational publications and author of the book *Preparation for Art*. She received her Bachelor of Arts degree from the University of Washington, her Master of Arts in education from Central Washington State College, and her Ed. D. from Stanford University in 1957. Her art training was at the Amédée Ozenfant Archipenko School of Art and the Cornish School of Art.

Harry Wolcott is Associate Professor of Education and Research Associate in the Center for the Advanced Study of Educational Administration (CASEA) at the University of Oregon. His research and teaching interests are in the area of "anthropology and education," and he has done educational research in a cross-cultural setting as well as applied the prospectives in methodologies of anthropology in studying aspects of education in our own society. He took his undergraduate degree at the University of California at Berkeley and his Ph.D. at Stanford University where he completed a major in education and a minor in anthropology.

Richard L. Darling is Director of the Department of Instructional Materials in the Montgomery County Public Schools, Rockville, Maryland. He has been a teacher, librarian, and professor, as well as a school library specialist for the library services branch of the Office of Education of the U.S. Department of Health, Education, and Welfare. He is a past president of the American Association of School Librarians. He is a frequent contributer to education and library periodicals and is author of the book, *The Rise of Childrens Book Reviewing in America, 1865–1881*. He received his B.A. from Montana State University in 1950, his M.A.L.S. from the University of Michigan in 1954, and his Ph.D. from the University of Michigan in 1960.

Wesley C. Meierhenry is Assistant Dean of the Teachers College and Professor of Education at the University of Nebraska. Dr. Meierhenry is the author of numerous bulletins and articles in the field of education, with particular emphases in media, learning theory, and instruction. In addition, Dr. Meierhenry has been involved in a number of research projects related to media use and teacher competencies. He is a past president of the Department of Audiovisual Instruction, NEA, and an advisor on a number of national and state committees and commissions related to educational media. He received his B.S. from Midland College, Freemont, Nebraska and his master's and Ph.D. degrees from the University of Nebraska.

Contents

EDUCATIONAL MEDIA:
Theory into Practice

SECTION 1.

BACKGROUNDS FOR INSTRUCTIONAL COMMUNICATIONS

The Ancients writ in *Tables done over with wax* with a brazen *Poitrel*, 1. with the *sharp end*, 2. whereof letters were en- graven and rubbed out again with the *broad end*, 3.	Veteres scribebant in *Tabellis ceratis* æneo *Stilo*, 1. cujus *parte cuspidata*, 2. exarabantur literæ, rursum vero obliteraban- tur *planâ*.
Afterwards they writ *Letters* with a *small Reed*, 4.	Deinde *Literas* pingebant *subtili Calamo*, 4.
We use a *Goose-quill*, 5. the *Stem*, 6. of which we make with a *Pen-knife*, 7. then we dip the *Neb* in an *Ink-horn*, 8. which is stopped with a *Stopple*, 9. and we put our *Pens* into a *Pennar*, 10.	Nos utimur *Anserina Pen- na*, 5. cujus *Caulem*, 6. temperamus *Scalpello*, 7. tum intingimus *Crenam* in *Atramentario*, 8. quod obstruitur *Operculo*, 9. & *Pennas* recondimus in *Calamario*, 10.
We dry a Writing	Siccamus Scripturam

Introduction

Throughout history, man has constantly struggled to release himself from ignorance. He has been confronted by such basic and important questions as: Should all human beings, regardless of their economic, social, or cultural condition, have an opportunity to be educated and, thus, free? Should the outcome of learning consist only of symbols and abstractions? or are performance, understanding, reason, and other similar results desirable and appropriate?

In Chapter 1, Raymond V. Wiman provides an historical perspective. He identifies and describes the points of view of those who would make education available only to the elite, and those who would view educational outcomes broadly—depending upon the objectives of the educational activity. Seen from these perspectives, it becomes evident why improved communication techniques receive the attention given to them by each succeeding generation.

In addition to the impact of media on formal educational programs, there is also the impingement of mass media on our society. Anyone involved in education must be aware of and informed about the background of learners in order to understand their motives, desires, and ambitions. In Chapter 2, Samuel Becker identifies and discusses a series of questions concerning the attitudes and concepts which are developed as a result of radio, television, and other forms of mass communication. This chapter is an analytic one, assisting the reader to gauge the extent to which different forms of media stimulate, shape, or confirm the thinking of a society.

3

CHAPTER ONE

An Historical View of Communication in the Classroom

Raymond V. Wiman

In order to develop a perspective for the future, one must look to the past for guidance. In this complex civilization where rapid change has become a way of life and the body of knowledge doubles every few years, it is not surprising that the persistent demands of the present make the past seem less important than it really is. History tells us where we are, how we got there, and perhaps, where we want to go. Without any systematic documentation of man's cumulative experience or methods for the transmission of this body of knowledge from one generation to the next, man would be doomed to repeat his life cycle

over and over again with little change. The study of history is, among
other things, a study of man's mistakes. These mistakes have been repeated to some degree in every generation, but with variations, and
with slow but sure progress that often has been achieved in the face of
outright hostility to new ideas. The old ways are known and comfortable; many people resist ideas and technological devices because they
tend to disturb the status quo. This seems particularly true in education. Socrates, for instance, in a dialogue with Phaedrus said of the
written word:

> You who are the father of letters, from a paternal love of your own
> children have been led to attribute to them a quality which they
> cannot have; for this discovery of yours will create forgetfulness in
> the learners' souls, because they will not use their memories; they
> will trust to the external characters and not remember of them-
> selves . . . they will be the hearers of many things and will have
> learned nothing. . . .[1]

The idea that men could learn truth from the written word was contrary to Socrates' notion that, in addition to a theoretical understanding of something, the learner must have first-hand experience or he
could never know more than his teacher—in this case, the manuscript.
After listening to a discourse written by Lysais and read to him by
Phaedrus, Socrates commented sarcastically, "I can only infer that I
have been filled through the ears, like a pitcher, from the waters of another. . . .[2] This "pouring-in" concept has been applied to and by teachers of every age. It was applied first to manuscripts, then to books, and
currently to newer educational media. Many educational concepts discussed in the Greek Classics have their counterparts in contemporary
education. The basic idea of programed learning for instance, can be
found in the dialogues of Plato (Meno) where Socrates teaches an il-
literate attendant using a teaching technique that is defined today as
linear programed learning; one of several types of programed learning
under investigation at the present time.

Perhaps, before delving further into past history, it might be well
to define more precisely what kind of person the schools should produce—the ultimate objective of education. I would like to propose that
the ultimate objective of education is to produce creative, rational,
stable members of society. In other words, education should develop in
the student a growing awareness of the personal, physical, and political

---

[1] Benjamin Jowett, trans., *The Dialogues of Plato* (Chicago: Encyclopaedia
Britannica, 1952), pp. 138–139.

[2] *Ibid.*, p. 119.

world in which he lives; an ability to communicate effectively with others artistically as well as verbally; and finally, education should enable him to develop those skills necessary for earning a living in his chosen area of competence. Thus, rationality should not be here equated with conformity. Conformity should be fostered only to the extent necessary to produce law-abiding members of society. Even more important, education should prepare the student to participate intelligently in democratic procedures so necessary in a republic. Uniformity or sameness cannot be considered a valid educational objective either; uniformity in education is the nemesis of creativity—a creator of mediocrity. Education should be designed to aid each student in the development of his own personality and his unique talents and abilities. Opportunity should be provided for the student to learn, to experiment, to determine the extent of his personal resources, and to come to terms with himself in relation to the society in which he lives. All too often, such opportunities are denied students because of the "system"—a system still based, in many respects, on instructional techniques at least 500 years old. Meaningful learning situations should involve each student as a person, participating actively rather than passively in what is going on around him. Educational emphasis should be upon the effective utilization of knowledge, rather than on the collection and storage of information that remains relatively unexamined and unprocessed by the brain in which it is stored. In order to accomplish these objectives, it is not necessary to discard entirely either traditional or current methods of instruction; all that is traditional is not bad, nor is everything that is new necessarily good. Education today is an amalgamation of both traditional and current educational thought; ideally, it should represent the best that can be drawn from both.

In primitive societies, the task of directing the formal education of the young was often the responsibility of a shaman or witch doctor. Formal instruction usually involved teaching the rituals of the tribe— rituals of puberty, fertility, marriage, birth, death, religion, and so on. The tribe transmitted its heritage, traditions, taboos, and culture to the young through symbolic ceremonials, by example, and through stories told over and over again so that they would be passed on without change from one generation to the next. Masks, totems, paintings, stone carvings, statues, and other vestiges of prehistoric life have provided contemporary man with enough information to trace faint outlines of the cultures, religious beliefs, and superstitions of his ancestors.

Even before man had a defined culture, he left traces of his existence. Crude axes, spear points, and knives found in Africa provide the earliest known indications of man's existence and development. Man alone makes tools designed to fit specific needs and to give him more control over his environment. The chronicle of man has been compiled in part by the tools he has left behind, or the tools he is now using; witness the Stone Age, the Bronze Age, the Atomic Age. More important, however, and the deciding factor in man's progressive development of tools, is his communicative power: the ability to transmit abstract ideas first one to another, and eventually across time and space. The bow and arrow, the wheel, and the discovery of fire represent minor advances when weighed against the development of language and, eventually, the alphabet. Smoke signals and drums were the primitive telegraph; perhaps they were the first agreed upon abstractions from which man could interpret meaning. Pictures and symbols painted and inscribed on the walls of caves in southern France and in Spain represent some of the earliest known efforts of man to preserve his rituals and culture for those to follow. Early paintings, stone carvings, and hieroglyphic inscriptions evolved slowly into various forms of picture writing and, eventually, into abstract symbols which had specific meanings. In the Far East, picture writing evolved rather literally into a set of several thousand symbols, each with its own meaning. Many of the modern characters are so similar in form to the original picture writing that they can be traced back to their early counterparts.

Picture writing in the Western world followed another track and developed into a set of finite symbols which, when combined in various sequences, could represent an infinite variety of meanings. Man now had the means whereby his accumulated knowledge could be recorded and collected, first on stone and clay, then on animal skins, and later, on paper. Libraries of manuscripts began to develop, and information could be stored and transported with comparative ease. When the total body of knowledge and the population were relatively small, libraries of manuscripts were probably adequate, but as the known world, the population, and the store of knowledge all began to expand, the needs of the society could no longer be met by manuscripts, since each had to be copied by hand. The dissemination of knowledge was restricted by a lack of adequate copies convenient to the growing group of scholars. This situation, in a sense, forced man to invent a new tool: printing. At first, hand-written manuscripts, charts, and maps were carefully duplicated on flat blocks of wood or stone and reproduced in small quantities on crude printing presses. This process proved to be too slow and cumbersome, and, in the fifteenth century, the idea of movable type made of individual letters carved on blocks of wood was conceived. The invention of movable type finally brought together three products of man's technical ingenuity: paper, movable type, and the printing press. All of these elements had been discovered many years earlier in China and Korea. Paper and ink were known to the Chinese in the first century A.D.; block printing was in use by 450 A.D.; movable type was invented sometime between 900 and 1450 A.D. The spread of knowledge in the Far East was, and is, severely restricted by technical problems involving the use of an alphabet made up of several thousand characters.

In the Western world, the alphabet and technology were finally brought together in a combination that was the beginning of a chain reaction in the communication of knowledge that is still going on, fed by the ever-inventive minds of a growing host of literate people.

Man moved rapidly into the reading and writing world created by printing. As learning could be pursued independently, the body of knowledge began to expand. The move to books was accomplished almost instantly after the invention of printing. Access to man's accumulated knowledge fostered the steady growth of technological communications and transportation devices. About 1500, only fifty years after the invention of printing with movable type, Rabelais wrote, "I see robbers, hangmen, freebooters, tapsters, ostlers, and such like, of the very rubbish of the people, more learned now than the doctors and preachers of my time."[3]

Technological advances in communication have far outdistanced all of man's other achievements. The Gutenburg Bible was printed in 1456; one hundred fifty-five years later (1621) the first news sheet was printed; in 1731, the magazine made its appearance; and in 1814, steam was used as a source of power for printing presses. The telegraph, invented in 1844, finally released the spread of information from dependence upon available surface transportation. In the next century, the communications devices known today were developed, and man moved from a horse-drawn world to the exploration of outer space.

For education, the advent of books brought problems as well as solutions. According to Marshall McLuhan (whose ideas will be discussed further in Chapter 3), "it established the divorce between literature and life."[4] Some long-standing problems were only intensified, such as the relative values of learning and understanding. In an essay on pedantry, Montaigne wrote, "Knowledge is not so absolutely necessary as judgment; the last may make shift without the other, but the

---

[3] Sir Thomas Urquhart and Peter Matteux, trans., *Francais Rabelais: Gargantua and Pantagruel* (Chicago: Encyclopaedia Britannica, Inc., 1952), p. 82.

[4] Merton Babcock, ed., *Ideas in Process* (New York: Harper and Brothers, 1958), p. 402.

other never without this. For as the Greek verse says, 'To what use serves learning, if the understanding be away.' "[5]

Schoolmasters were quick to utilize books in their classes. The book combined easily with existing oral traditions and though the oral tradition did not give way entirely, the book became the schoolmaster's idol; the teaching of Latin and Greek his purpose. Education became a synonym for instruction in these two languages; persons reading and speaking only their native tongue were not considered educated by "the scholars." The classical scholars, interested in the Classics alone, eschewed new knowledge. They ignored new ideas and inventions such as the telescope, because telescopes were not known in the ancient world. Thus, learning for many students became an almost futile exercise with words; a trial rather than an adventure. Of the classrooms of his day, John Amos Comenius (1592-1670) wrote with bitter insight:

> They are the terror of boys and the slaughter houses of minds—places where a hatred of literature and books is contracted, where ten or more years are spent in learning what might be acquired in one, where what ought to be poured in gently is violently forced in and beaten in, where what ought to be put clearly and perspicuously is presented in a confused and intricate way, as if it were a collection of puzzles—places where minds are fed on words.[6]

Traditional schoolmasters perceived their role as that of a fountain of knowledge, and viewed the students as little more than empty containers to be filled full of facts, information, and words. Young scholars were required to learn by heart, whether or not anything was understood about the facts or words learned. Here was the "pouring-in" theory brought up again; many more would question it in years to come. Rabelais noted that "it would be better for a boy to learn nothing at all than to be taught such-like books by such-like masters."[7] Montaigne wrote:

> We only labour to stuff the memory, and leave the conscience and the understanding unfurnished and void. Like birds who fly abroad to forage for grain, and bring it home in the beak, without tasting it themselves, to feed their young; so our pedants go picking knowledge here and there, out of books, and hold it at the tongue's end, only to spit it out. . . .[8]

[5] Charles Cotton, trans., *Montaigne: The Essays of Michel Eyquem de Montaigne* (Chicago: Encyclopaedia Britannica, Inc., 1952), p. 59.

[6] S. S. Laurie, *John Amos Comenius* (New York: C. W. Bardeen, 1892), p. 29.

[7] Robert Herbert Quick, *Essays on Educational Reformers* (New York: D. Appleton and Co., 1897), p. 508.

[8] Charles Cotton, *op. cit.*, p. 57.

Comenius set the stage for many reforms in education with his criticisms of curriculum and methods. He has received credit as the author of the first illustrated textbook for children. The book, *Orbis Pictus*, was first published in 1657 or 1658. It was translated into many languages and remained an outstanding publication for well over a century. Each of the illustrations in the book (see section openings of this text for examples) served as the basis for lessons that dealt with religion, science, mathematics, and politics. In addition, there were lessons of a practical nature such as breadmaking, brewing, and gardening. In the preface, Comenius explained how the book should be used to develop reason and understanding rather than memory:

I. Let it be given to children into their hands to delight themselves withal as they please, with the sight of the pictures, and making them as familiar to themselves as may be, and that even at home before they be put in school.

II. Then let them be examined ever and anon (especially now in the school) what this thing or that thing is, and is called, so that they know not how to name, and that they can name nothing which they cannot shew.

III. And let the things named them be shewed, not only in the picture, but also in themselves; for example, the parts of the body, clothes, books, the house, utensils, etc.

IV. Let them be suffered also to imitate the picture by hand, if they will, nay rather, let them be encouraged, that they may be willing; first, thus to quicken the attention also towards the things; and to observe the proportion of the parts one towards another, and lastly to practice the nimbleness of the hand, which is good for many things.

V. If anything here mentioned cannot be presented to the eye, it will be to no purpose at all to offer them by themselves to the scholars; as colors, relishes, etc., which cannot here be be pictured out with ink. For which reason it were to be wished, that things rare and not easy to be met withal at home, might be kept ready in every great school, that they may be shewed also, as often as any words are to be made of them to the scholars.

Thus at last this school would indeed become a school of things obvious to the senses, and an entrance to the school intellectual.[9]

---

[9] Charles Hoole, trans., *Comenius: Orbis Pictus* (New York: C. W. Bardeen, 1887), pp. xviii–xix.

Comenius was a man of the future—a true pioneer in educational thought and practice. In his own time, however, he was noted more for textbooks such as the *Orbis Pictus* and *Janua* than for his major treatise on education, *The Great Didactic*, which remained in manuscript form over one hundred and fifty years after his death. "Didactics," as explained by Comenius, "is the art of good teaching. (In Greek *didasko* means 'I teach'; *didaktos*, 'one who has been taught'; *didaktikos*, 'apt at teaching,' that is, 'one who knows how to teach.')"[10] Even today his writings have a contemporary flavor; for instance, in Chapter 16 of *The Great Didactic*, Comenius outlined nine teaching principles based upon the imitation of nature:

1. Nature observes a suitable time.

2. Nature prepares the material, before she gives it form.

3. Nature chooses a fit subject to act upon, or first submits one to a suitable treatment in order to make it fit.

4. Nature is not confused in its operations, but in its forward progress advances distinctly from one point to another.

5. In all the operations of nature development is from within.

6. Nature, in its formative processes, begins with the universal and ends with the particular.

7. Nature makes no leaps, but proceeds step by step.

8. If nature commence anything, it does not leave off until the operation is completed.

9. Nature carefully avoids obstacles and things likely to cause hurt.[11]

In *The Great Didactic*, Comenius discussed each principle; his treatment is interesting and worthwhile, containing ideas that are pertinent today, and that reach into the future as well.

Thus far, two concepts of education had begun to develop: the concept of formal discipline or Faculty Psychology; and the concept of learning as experiences gained through the senses. Faculty Psychology was based upon the idea that the mind is made up of "faculties" which, like the muscles of the body, must be exercised if they are to be developed and trained properly. Logic and will (or self-discipline) for instance, were looked upon as desirable qualities and, therefore, it was felt that students should be taught subjects which developed logically and which required a certain amount of self-discipline to learn. A

---

[10] Vladimir Jelinek, trans., *The Analytical Didactic of Comenius* (University of Chicago Press, 1953), p. 96.

[11] M. W. Keatinge, *Comenius* (New York: McGraw-Hill Book Company, Inc., 1931), pp. 54–72.

thorough and rigorous exercise of the scholars' faculties was the school-master's primary objective. Anything that could be learned without causing the student a certain amount of anguish or suffering was considered to be without merit, as it would not "exercise the faculties." In essence, any subject matter that would develop and exercise the faculties was acceptable, whether or not the student learned anything useful from the subject matter being studied. John Locke, an eighteenth century English philosopher, has been credited by some as supporting, if not fathering, the idea of Faculty Psychology or formal discipline as an educational method, perhaps because he discussed and used the term "faculties" a great deal in his *Essay Concerning Human Understanding*. While Locke was not always consistent in his proposals, the underlying theme of this essay seems to place him outside the formal-discipline camp. On the development of ideas he wrote:

> All ideas come from sensation or reflection. Let us then suppose the mind to be, as we say, white paper, void of all characters, without any ideas:—How comes it to be furnished? Whence comes it by that vast store which the busy and boundless fancy of man has painted on it with an almost endless variety? Whence has it all the *materials* of reason and knowledge? To this I answer in one word, from EXPERIENCE. In that all our knowledge is founded; and from that it ultimately derives itself. Our observation employed either, about external sensible objects, or about the internal operations of our minds perceived and reflected on by ourselves, is that which supplies our understandings with all the *materials* of thinking. These two are the fountains of knowledge, from whence all the ideas we have, or can naturally have, do spring.[12]

Locke also discussed education as a process of *habit formation* in a treatise entitled *Some Thoughts Concerning Education*. One method of habit formation described is that of repeated practice for the purpose of committing certain material to memory, so that the information learned could be recalled automatically and accurately. Certainly, this particular concept represented the focus of educational efforts in both England and America for many years. The following is an example of an argument by Goold Brown favoring formal discipline. He scorned innovations with a classic display of rhetoric in his *Grammar of English Grammars*, first published in the 1850's:

> The vain pretensions of several modern simplifiers, contrivers of machines, charts, tables, diagrams, vinicula, pictures, dialogue,

---

[12] Quoted in *Locke, Berkeley, Hume*, Vol. 35 of *Great Books of the Western World*, Robert Maynard Hutchins, Editor in Chief (Chicago: Encyclopaedia, Britannica, Inc., 1952), p. 121.

familiar lectures, ocular analysis, tabular compendiums, inductive exercises, productive systems, intellectual methods, and many various new theories, for the purpose of teaching grammar, may serve to deceive the ignorant, to amuse the visionary, and to excite the admiration of the credulous, but none of these things has any favorable relation to that improvement which may justly be boasted as having taken place within the memory of the present generation. The definitions, and rules which constitute the doctrines of grammar, illustrated, and applied; and in the expression, arrangement, illustration and application there may be room for some amendment; but no contrivance can ever relieve the pupil from the necessity of committing them (definitions and rules) thoroughly to memory. The experience of all antiquity is added to our own, in the confirmation of this; and the judicious teacher, though he will not shut his eyes to a real improvement, will be cautious of renouncing the practical lessons of hoary experience for the futile notions of a vain projector.[13]

The evils of an instructional method, which for many resulted in learning without understanding, could be found in most schools of the times. Even today, there are those favoring formal discipline as an effective method of instruction.

Two more eighteenth century Europeans deserve mention before moving to education in the United States. One is Jean Jacques Rousseau, a brilliant but unstable French philosopher-writer; the other, Johann Henrich Pestalozzi, a Swiss educator. Rousseau was not a teacher. He expressed his concept of what education should be for the aristocracy (in his opinion, the poor did not need an education) in his educational treatise *Emile*, published in 1762. Since Rousseau (1712-1778) preceded Pestalozzi by some thirty years, his *Emile* had a definite effect on the thinking of Pestalozzi. In essence, Rousseau relied upon directed experience as the method of teaching. He viewed teaching as a one-to-one relationship between pupil and tutor, with the tutor guiding the pupil into meaningful learning situations without the pupil realizing that the learning was being guided. Rousseau believed that the pupil should "learn by doing" whenever possible and use lectures only when learning by doing was completely out of the question. He saw education as a process of unfolding that which is enfolded in the young. Early teaching, according to Rousseau, should often consist of nothing more than protecting the innate good enfolded in the young from evil, error, and vice until that good could unfold. Rousseau and

---

[13] Goold Brown, *Grammar of English Grammars*, 10th ed. (New York: William Wood and Co., 1884), pp. 107–108.

his English counterpart, Locke, considered education as a process of habit formation. The examples given by Rousseau in *Emile* are nothing more than habit formation for useful purpose.

Pestalozzi, whose educational thought was later espoused by Horace Mann, read *Emile* and actually tried Rousseau's theories in educating his own son. He soon found that some of them would not work, but he was not disenchanted. Eventually, Pestalozzi established schools and set a pattern for education that was adopted widely.

Pestalozzi has been called a "school teacher of the ages." He devised arithmetic tables, and spelling tablets with letters and numbers that slid in and out of the tablet edge. If he could not use real objects in his teaching, he would substitute a model or a picture. Books were used to supplement experience and to provide material and facts that were not available by any other means. He was a critic of symbolism, believing that all of the senses should be brought into play whenever possible in the teaching-learning transaction. Seeing or telling alone was not enough: "The mere sight of an object does not satisfy a child, he must handle it, weigh it, smell it, taste it and examine it in all of its parts, in order to gain a complete idea of it."[14] Pestalozzi, in his attempts to "wheel the educational car of Europe upon another track,"[15] attracted the attention and respect of teachers throughout the Western world. Oddly enough, the pattern for Pestalozzian schools in Switzerland has been enshrined so rigidly that lunch is not served because Pestalozzi said nothing about lunch in his writings. Obviously, his perceptors lacked any educational insight or philosophy of their own. Pestalozzi was continually searching for, and trying out, new ideas and teaching methods. One wonders what he would think of such a literal, long-standing interpretation of his ideas.

As the New World became settled, schools were established. It was natural that the educational practices of the Old World would be transplanted, if for no other reason than the emulation of observed teaching practices by those educated in Europe and England. Here too, the knowledge of Latin and Greek became the mark of an educated person. This tradition persisted into the latter half of the nineteenth century, and strong defenses for the teaching of these subjects abounded.

Benjamin Franklin, whose mind sought in all directions, cited the need for a meaningful curriculum in his *Proposals Relating to the Education of Youth in Pensilvania* [sic], published in 1749. He pro-

---

[14] Herman Krusi, *Pestalozzi* (New York: Wilson Hinkle and Co., 1875), p. 161.
[15] *Ibid.*, p. 152.

posed that an academy (the forerunner of today's high school) be
chartered and its library furnished with maps, globes, mathematical
instruments, scientific experimental equipment, and prints and drawings of machines and buildings. Of the curriculum to be taught, Franklin wrote:

> . . . it would be well if they could be taught every thing that is use-
> ful, and every thing that is ornamental: But Art is long, and their
> Time is short It is therefore propos'd that they learn those Things
> that are likely to be most useful and most ornamental. Regard being
> had to the several Professions for which they are intended.[16]

Drawing was included in the proposed course of studies for both mechanics and gentlemen. "*Drawing,*" according to Franklin, "is a kind of
Universal Language, understood by all Nations. A man may often express his ideas, even to his own Countrymen, more clearly with a Lead
Pencil or Bit of Chalk, than with his Tongue."[17] This basic mode of
communication is neglected in contemporary schools. Drawing is a
skill; once the skill has been mastered, those with special talent can
go beyond to produce "art." Look again at Comenius' encouragement
to let children copy the pictures in *Orbis Pictus* in order to learn skills
of observation and drawing.

Franklin came from a typical tradesman's family of the time. Born
in 1706, the tenth son of Josiah Franklin, he showed early promise and,
while his brothers were "apprenticed out," he was put in a grammar
school at the age of eight. Though he did well, his father withdrew
him from the school after a short time because of the expense, and because the classical education received by the pupils did not fit them for
much of anything after graduation. For a time, Franklin was tutored by
a master in writing and arithmetic, but he quit at the age of ten and was
apprenticed in the printing trade.

In later years, recognizing the need for a less formal education that
prepared students for something besides the ministry, Franklin proposed that a more realistic appraisal be made of the needs of youth, and
that the opportunity for education be extended to the "common folk."
His proposals eventually were carried out and gave added stature and
strength to the idea of universal education. Long after Franklin's death,
his gift of 116 books to the town of Franklin, Massachusetts contributed

---

[16] William Pepper, *Benjamin Franklin: Proposals Relating to the Education of
Youth in Pensilvania* [*sic*] (Philadelphia: University of Pennsylvania Press, 1931),
p. 11.

[17] *Ibid.,* p. 12.

to the intellectual development of the most commanding figure in public education in the early nineteenth century, Horace Mann. Mann's early education was sketchy and intermittent, but once he had learned to read, he made good use of this small library of books.

Horace Mann entered Brown University in 1816, and after his graduation in 1819, stayed on for several years as a "tutor." He eventually became a lawyer, a legislator, and in 1837, the first secretary of the Massachusetts State Board of Education. During the next twelve years, he prepared a series of annual reports on education which were widely read and which had a profound effect upon education in the United States. Copies of these reports can be found in many libraries and are well worth the time spent reviewing them. Mann's insights into the problems of learning were, like Comenius', far ahead of his time. Rote learning was then an accepted teaching method and, according to a report of the Boston Survey Committee, floggings in a representative school of four hundred averaged sixty-five per day. Mann advocated the elimination of flogging, more effective methods of teaching, consolidated school districts, better school housing, better training for teachers, and many other reforms. Selected portions of his reports are presented here; they are perhaps just as timely today as when they were written.

From his Second Annual Report in 1838 on the subject of reading with understanding:

> I have devoted especial pains to learn, with some degree of numerical accuracy, how far the reading in our schools is an exercise of the mind in thinking and feeling, and how far it is a barren action of the organs of speech upon the atmosphere. My information is derived, principally, from the written statements of the school committees of the different towns—gentlemen who are certainly exempt from all temptation to desparage the schools they superintend. The result is, that more than eleven twelfths of all children in the reading-classes, in our schools, do not understand the meaning of the words they read; that they do not master the sense of their reading-lessons, and that the ideas and feelings intended by the author to be conveyed to, and excited in, the readers mind, still rest in the author's intention, never having yet reached the place of their destination. . . . It would hardly seem that the combined efforts of all persons engaged, could have accomplished more, in defeating the true objects of reading.[18]

---

[18] Horace Mann, *Lectures and Annual Reports on Education* (Cambridge: Published for the Editor, 1867), pp. 531–532.

In his seventh report Mann, reporting on European schools, commented on learning without understanding as follows:

> I have seen schools in which four or five hundred children were obliged to commit to memory, in the Latin language, the entire book of Psalms and other parts of the Bible, *neither teachers or children understanding a word of the language they were prating.*[19]

Later on in this same report he wrote of education in Holland and a teaching-training situation with meaning.

> In Holland, I saw what I have never seen elsewhere, but which ought to be in every school,—the actual weights and measures of the country. These were used, not only to as a means of conveying useful knowledge, but of mental exercise and cultivation. . . . It is easy to see how much more exact and permanent would be the pupil's knowledge of all weights and measures, obtained in this way, than if learned by heart from dry tables in a book, and also how many useful and interesting exercises could be founded upon them by a skillful teacher.[20]

After a discussion of uses and rote learning of the tables, Mann said: "Having learned the tables by rote, the words have long ago vanished from the mind, and the ideas were never in it."[21]

Mann saw teaching as a profession—one which required skills beyond a knowledge of subject matter. His report for 1839 includes a thoughtful discussion of teacher qualifications, portions of which are excerpted in the following paragraphs. His use of the term "aptness to teach" must have come from Comenius' *Didactic*.

> 1st. One requisite is a knowledge of Common-school studies. Teachers should have a perfect knowledge of the rudimental branches which are required by law to be taught in our schools. They should understand, not only the rules, which have been prepared as guides for the unlearned, but also the principles on which the rules are founded,—those principles which lie beneath the rules, and supersede them in practice, and from which, should the rules be lost, they could be framed anew. Teachers should be able to teach *subjects*, not manuals merely.
>
> This knowledge should not only be thorough and critical, but it should be always ready at command for every exigency,—familiar like the alphabet, so that, as occasion requires, it will rise up

---

[19] Horace Mann, *Annual Reports on Education* (Boston: Horace B. Fuller, 1868), p. 239 (italics added).

[20] *Ibid.*, pp. 274–275.

[21] *Ibid.*, p. 275.

in the mind instantaneously, and not need to be studied out with labor and delay. . . .

The leading, prevailing defect in the intellectual department of our schools is a want of thoroughness,—a proneness to be satisfied with a verbal memory of rules, instead of a comprehension of principles, with a knowledge of the names of things, instead of a knowledge of the things themselves; or, if some knowledge of the things is gained, it is too apt to be a knowledge of them as isolated facts, and unaccompanied by a knowledge of the relations which subsist between them, and bind them into a scientific whole. That knowledge is hardly worthy of the name, which stops with things, as individuals, without understanding the relations existing between them. The latter constitutes indefinitely the greater part of all human knowledge. For instance, all the problems of plane geometry, by which heights and distances are measured, and the contents of areas and cubes ascertained, are based upon a few simple definitions which can be committed to memory by any child in half a day. With the exception of the comets, whose number is not known, there are but thirty bodies in the whole solar system. Yet, on the relations which subsist between these thirty bodies is built the stupendous science of astronomy. How worthless is the astronomical knowledge which stops with committing to memory thirty names! . . .

For these and similar considerations, it seems that the first intellectual qualification of a teacher is a critical thoroughness, both in rules and principles, in regard to all the branches required by law to be taught in the Common Schools; and a power of recalling them in any of their parts with a proptitude and certainty hardly inferior to that with which he could tell his own name.

2d. The next principal qualification in a teacher is the *art of teaching*. This is happily expressed in the common phrase, *aptness to teach*, which in a few words comprehends many particulars. The ability to acquire, and the ability to impart, are wholly different talents. The former may exist in the most liberal measure without the latter. It was a remark of Lord Bacon, that "the art of well-delivering the knowledge we possess is among the secrets left to be discovered by future generations." Dr. Watts says, "There are some very learned men who know much themselves, but who have not the talent of communicating their knowledge." Indeed, this fact is not now questioned by any intelligent educationist. Hence we account for the frequent complaints of the committees, that those teachers who had sustained an examination in an acceptable manner failed in the schoolroom through a want of facility in communicating what they knew. The ability to acquire is the power of understanding the subject-matter to be learned, and

what, in the natural order, is the next step he is to take. It involves
the power of discovering and of solving at the time the exact difficulty by which the learner is embarrassed. . . .

Aptness to teach includes the presentation of the different parts
of a subject in a natural order. If a child is told that the globe is
about twenty-five thousand miles in circumference, before he has
any conception of the length of a mile or of the number of units in
a thousand, the statement is not only utterly useless as an act of
instruction, but it will probably prevent him ever afterwards from
gaining an adequate idea of the subject. . . .

Aptness to teach, in fine, embraces a knowledge of methods and
processes. These are indefinitely various. Some are adapted to
accomplish their object in an easy and natural manner; others in
a toilsome and circuitous one; others, again, may accomplish the
object at which they aim with certainty and dispatch, but secure it
by inflicting deep and lasting injuries upon the social and moral
sentiments. We are struck with surprise on learning, that, but a
few centuries since, the feudal barons of Scotland, in running out
the lines around their extensive domains, used to take a party of
boys, and whip them at the different posts and landmarks in order
to give them a retentive memory as witnesses in case of future
litigation or dispute. Though this might give them a vivid recollection of localities, yet it would hardly improve their ideas of
justice, or propitiate them to bear true testimony in favor of the
chastiser. But do not those who have no aptness to teach sometimes
accomplish their objects by a kindred method?

He who is apt to teach is acquainted, not only with common
methods for common minds, but with peculiar methods for pupils
of peculiar dispositions and temperaments; and he is acquainted
with the principles of all methods whereby he can vary his plan
according to any difference of circumstances. The statement has
been sometimes made, that it is the object of Normal Schools to
subject all teachers to one inflexible, immutable course of instruction. Nothing could be more erroneous; for one of the great objects
is to give them a knowledge of modes as various as the diversity of
cases that may arise, that, like a skilful pilot, they may not only
see the haven for which they are to steer, but know every bend in
the channel that leads to it. No one is so poor in resources for difficult emergencies as they may arise as he whose knowledge of
methods is limited to the one in which he happened to be instructed. It is in this way that rude nations go on for indefinite
periods, imitating what they have seen, and teaching only as they
were taught.

3d. Experience has also proved that there is no necessary connection between literary competency, aptness to teach, and the

power to manage and govern a school successfully. They are independent qualifications; yet a marked deficiency in any one of the three renders the others nearly valueless.[22]

Mann emphasized again and again the need for teaching for understanding rather than for rote learning of isolated facts. He returned to the problem of teaching and learning once again in his report for 1845. On building a frame of reference for learning he wrote:

> . . . The competent teacher adopts this method in regard to all the studies pursued in his school. He shows the relation between what is present and visible, and what is distant and unseen. Physical geography can never be learned, unless the child is first led to form adequate conceptions of space, when he can assign locality to objects, and give arrangement to all the facts he learns. History can never be learned unless the learner has adequate conceptions of past time,—of successive centuries along whose years and decades he can distribute and arrange the events which history brings under his notice.[23]

Mann did not believe that all students could profit by the same curriculum. He foresaw the development of a broader curriculum based upon the needs, abilities, and interests of all students. An interesting facet of his reports is his awareness of unintended learnings gained by students, as discussed in the third report dealing with "aptness to teach" and again in the ninth report quoting from an arithmetic text of the day:

> . . . as a specimen of the utter oblivion into which a love of intellectual acuteness and skill may throw the moral relations of a subject, I quote the following question from a modern arithmetic:
>
> A sea-captain on a voyage had a crew of thirty men, half of whom were blacks. Being becalmed on the passage for a long time, their provisions began to fail; and the captain became satisfied, that, unless the number of men was greatly diminished, all would perish of hunger before they reached any friendly port. He therefore proposed to the sailors that they should stand in a row on deck, and that every ninth man should be thrown overboard until one-half of the crew were thus destroyed. To this they all agreed. How should they stand *to save the whites?*
>
> Doubtless this question was prepared by the author, and has been laboriously studied by thousands of pupils, without any distinct contemplation of the fiendish injustice and fraud which it

---

[22] *Ibid.*, pp. 58–63.
[23] *Ibid.*, p. 488.

involves, but only with admiration for the ingenuity which origi-
nated, and for the talent that can solve it; and yet the idea which
the question has lodged in the mind may become the parent of a
fraud as base if not appalling as its prototype.[24]

The subject of unintended learnings in the classroom is further discussed in Chapter 9. It is, perhaps, a bit disconcerting to realize that
everything a teacher does or says in the classroom comes under the
scrutiny of the pupils, and that many things are learned without being
consciously taught.

Horace Mann was representative of a number of educators of his
time, such as Michigan's John Pierce and Connecticut's Henry Barnard.
Mann's dedication to American education is reflected in his own words
given in an address two months before he died in 1859. "I beseech you
to treasure up in your hearts, these, my parting words: *Be ashamed to
die until you have won some victory for humanity.*"[25] He made his total
commitment to education at the age of forty-one by giving up a lu-
crative law practice and a respected place in politics to become secretary of Massachusetts' first State Board of Education. His friends im-
plored him not to take the position but he replied, ". . . the interests of
a client are small compared with the interests of the next generation.
Let the next generation, then, be my client."[26]

This commitment is representative of the dedication that good
teachers must require of themselves. One cannot become an outstanding teacher without making such a commitment.

As noted earlier, many of Mann's pronouncements have meaning
today, perhaps because education moves so slowly. For example, the
problem of consolidating small school districts is still with us. Rote
learning, formal discipline, and teacher brutality became the target of
a number of writers in the nineteenth century; in America the most
notable of whom was Samuel Clemens (Mark Twain). Clemens obviously supported the schools. In an address at the Berkeley Lyceum in
New York in 1900 he said:

> We believe that out of the public school grows the greatness of
> a nation.
> It is curious to reflect how history repeats itself the world over.
> Why I remember the same thing was done when I was a boy on the

---

[24] *Ibid.*, pp. 489–490.
[25] Horace Mann, *Educational Writings of Horace Mann, Vol. V* (Boston: Lee
and Shepard, publishers, 1891), p. 254.
[26] Burke A. Hinsdale, *Horace Mann and the Common School Revival in the
United States* (New York: Charles Scribners' Sons, 1898), p. 114.

Mississippi River. There was a proposition in a township there to discontinue public schools because they were too expensive. An old farmer spoke up and said if they stopped the schools they would not save anything, because every time a school was closed a jail had to be built.

It's like feeding a dog his own tail. He'll never get fat. I believe that it is better to support schools than jails.[27]

Samuel Clemens' support of the teachers in the schools was quite another thing. In vivid word pictures he aptly pointed out the need for changes in teaching methods and the necessity to teach for understanding. Regarding the rote memorization of historical dates and facts he wrote:

Dates are hard to remember because they consist of figures; figures are monotonously unstriking in appearance, and they don't form pictures; they form no pictures so they give the eye no chance to help.[28]

In a discourse on "English as She is Taught," Twain wrote that "American students' memories were well stocked, but not their understandings." He noted further that a student's head might as well be crammed with brickbats as with "obscure and wordy rules" which are not understood.[29] In *Tom Sawyer*, he described how the prizes went to the students with well-stocked memories and an ability to please the schoolmaster.

The late 1800's saw the beginning of a new ferment in education. William James was considered by many to be the first educational psychologist. In his *Talks to Teachers*, published in 1899, he had this to say about rote memorization and understanding:

The more accurately words are learned, the better, if only the teacher make sure that what they signify is also understood. It is the failure of this latter condition, in so much of the old fashioned recitation that has caused that reaction against "parrot-like reproduction" that we are so familiar with today. A friend of mine, visiting a school, was asked to examine a young class in geography. Glancing at the book she said: "Suppose you should dig a hole in the ground, hundreds of feet deep, how should you find it at the bottom,— warmer or colder than on top?" None of the class replying, the teacher said: "I'm sure they know, but I think you didn't ask the

---

[27] Mark Twain, *Mark Twain's Speeches* (New York: Harper and Brothers, 1910), p. 146.

[28] Mark Twain, *What is Man?* (New York: Mark Twain Co., 1917), p. 141.

[29] *Ibid.*, pp. 36–37.

question quite rightly. Let me try." So, taking the book, she asked: "In what condition is the interior of the globe?" and received the immediate answer from half the class at once: "The interior of the globe is in a condition of *igneous fusion.*"[30]

Following close on James' heels came John Dewey, who mounted a new attack on traditional educational practices. Dewey saw education *as life,* not as preparation for life. He felt that meaningful education must involve the student to such an extent that he learned by doing; that originality and initiative were to be cultivated, rather than submission and obedience.

Up to this time, the spoken word and the book were still the main instruments of instruction. The blackboard represented the only major innovation accepted in the schools. Early blackboards were constructed of smooth boards painted black. For many years, if a teacher wanted a blackboard, he had to make it himself; commercially manufactured blackboards were not generally available until the latter half of the ninteenth century.

The motion picture, first demonstrated by Thomas Edison in 1894, was accepted much more readily than the blackboard. Fifteen years after the first film showing, more than a thousand films were available for educational purposes, and the superintendent of the New York City schools was recommending that motion picture projectors be installed in the New York schools. Of educational films Edison said:

> I firmly believe that the moving picture is destined to bear an important part in the education of the future. One may devote pages to the descriptions of the processes of nature to be learned by rote in the schools. Suppose instead that we show to the child the stages of that process in nature—the cocoon itself, the picture of the cocoon unfolding, the butterfly actually emerging. The knowledge which comes from actually seeing is worthwhile. The geography which comes from travel is better than the geography of the books: The next thing to travel is following the same things through the moving picture.[31]

Technology and educational thought had arrived at a point where education could begin to accept technological devices as useful aids in the teaching-learning process; the assimilation of such devices into the teaching-learning situation has moved with ever-increasing ra-

[30] William James, *Talks to Teachers* (New York: Henry Holt and Co., 1900), p. 150.

[31] Leon Gutterman, ed., "The Wisdom of Thomas A. Edison," *Wisdom,* Vol. 35, November, 1960, unpaged.

pidity. This does not mean that the teacher can let a machine do the teaching—far from it— but mechanical devices have proven useful aids in the effective communication of abstract ideas. Some routine teaching tasks can be performed more effectively by machines, thereby releasing the teacher for more important teaching functions.

For all that has been written, for all that has been said, learning without meaning still persists. The perfect combination has not been found. In view of our increasingly complex society, perhaps a perfect system will never be developed. Bel Kaufman, in her poignant book about teaching in New York City, writes of learning without understanding. Frustration is mirrored by her mythical students in response to the question, "What did you learn from English?"

> In my 16 year life span so far I've had my share of almost every type of teacher but one I shall ne'er forget was in elementary (6th grade) because with her I had to watch my peas and ques. She was so strict she gave us homework every night and tried to pound it into our heads but its the way she did the pounding that makes her different. She took a real interest and brought out our good and bad points. She stayed in every day after school so we could come in and ask her questions about the work. She militarized us and sometimes whacked us but for all her strictness a strange thing happened at the end of the term: every one gathered around her and kissed her.
>
> But high school seems harder, speeches, speeches, that's all we hear.
>
> (Signed) Dropout[32]

Certainly the teacher's attitude toward the subject and toward the student is also communicated to the student, whether or not on purpose; witness the following:

> What I learned in English is to doodle. It's such a boring subject I just sat and doodled the hours away. Sometimes I wore sunglasses in class to sleep.
>
> (Signed) Doodlebug[33]

And so we find that the "pouring-in" process is still with us, and that some educational methods have not changed materially over the years. Still, progress has been made. Education for the "common folk" has become a reality, and educational opportunities are being extended further and further all the time. We should not expect educational thought and practice to advance in the same way, or at the same rate, as has

---

[32] Bel Kaufman, *Up the Down Staircase* (Englewood Cliffs, New Jersey: Prentice-Hall, Inc., 1964), p. 76.

[33] *Ibid.,* p. 77.

scientific knowledge. Perhaps it is good that some areas of human knowledge such as art, music, philosophy, and religion accumulate more slowly. The measured pace of growth in these areas provides stability and security on which to base thought and action. If progress is too fast, it becomes difficult to establish rational patterns for progress. If progress is too slow, the possibility of stagnation exists.

It is estimated that scientific knowledge is doubling every decade or so, and possibly the pace will accelerate. Scientists have been willing to quickly discard obsolete theory and practice, whereas educators have not been so avid in accepting and promulgating change. If the scientific advances of the past fifty years were wiped out tomorrow, we would hardly recognize the world we live in, but if all progress in educational practice during the past half-century were forgotten, the change would be minimal. Will it be possible to erase the next fifty years of educational advances without changing education materially? I think not. Education is on the verge of momentous changes; perhaps most important will be an ever-growing awareness of the need to know everything possible about effective communication in the classroom. Learning to communicate should permeate the entire teacher-education program, so that teachers will know, not only how to acquire knowledge, but also how to impart that knowledge effectively to others, utilizing all of the devices and techniques at their command. Technological devices are designed to assist teachers, but if their use is not well planned, they may only implement the "pouring-in" process, and thus, defeat the purpose for which they are created. If, on the other hand, we apply knowledge about human communication in the teaching-learning process and make full use of instructional materials and equipment, we might say, as did Comenius, ". . . thus at last this school would indeed become a school of things obvious to the senses, and an entrance to the school of intellectual."[34]

---

[34] Charles Hoole, *op. cit.*, p. xix.

CHAPTER TWO

The Impact of the Mass Media on Society

Samuel L. Becker

As far back as the development of printing, every major innovation in the mass media has been heralded by pronouncements in the popular and educational press that the savior of education has arrived and, conversely, pronouncements have been made that the executioner of culture and the other benefits of education is here.[1] This speculation

---

[1] One of the many examples of the latter is the assertion by J. B. Priestly, "We spend billions on education, only to have the good work—if it is good work—rapidly undone by the mass communication experts, waiting to pounce on the boys and girls as they come out of school." *New York Times,* October 4, 1953, Sec. 2, p. X15.

For an excellent history of the claims and counter-claims which have accompanied each media innovation since the beginnings of the silent film, see Robert Edward Davis, "Response to Innovation: A Study of Popular Argument about New Mass Media" (Unpublished Ph.D. dissertation, University of Iowa, 1965).

has been accompanied by surprisingly little research. Of course, most
of the effects of the media are difficult to assess. Some of the long-range
effects on attitudes, on culture, and on social structure may be assess-
able only through the methods of the social historian. Even with these
methods, one cannot *pinpoint* causal relationships because media
change develops slowly amidst a complex web of social change. It is
only one of the threads. Some scholars say that it is not even meaningful to talk about the impact or effects of the mass media; that it is more
meaningful to ask how various individuals and institutions *use* the
media. This is the "functional" approach. However, an acceptance of
this view is as misleading as a total acceptance of media as all-powerful
change agents. A mass medium is both an index and agent of change;
it is used by people, but it also affects those who use it—and perhaps
even those who do not. A modern society is impossible without the
mass media, and the mass media cannot operate except in a modern
society.

To consider all of the effects of the media is beyond the scope of
this paper. I shall concentrate, then, upon those effects which I believe
are most relevant to the educator. The term "effects," as I am using it,
should not be taken to indicate a causal relationship necessarily. In
some cases, it will concern the ways in which the media are used and
concomitant adjustments in the rest of our behavior; in other cases,
the effects of content transmitted by the media will be considered, or
the effects of the media themselves, independent of content. This last
is an important distinction that too many persons overlook. In any of
the cases to be considered, one must avoid equating the effect of the
media with the direct effect of a serum administered with a hypodermic
needle. All media effects are mediated by a myriad of factors such as
the prior knowledge, habits, interests, and attitudes of the audience,
and the social-cultural milieu in which the communication process
occurs. The same film has different effects on different people, and
the same medium has a different impact on two basically different cultures. The reader must keep this in mind in regard to the generalizations about media impact that follow.

EFFECTS OF NEW MEDIA ON THE OLD

The rise of each new medium of communication obviously results in
some loss of power for the old. One of the latest examples of this is
that, in spite of the fact that radio stations are making more money
today than ever before, they have never regained the status they lost

with the advent of television. One sees this reflected in the professional broadcasting associations, both commercial and educational. Though radio broadcasters far outnumber television broadcasters in these associations, they believe themselves to be poor country cousins. One also sees it reflected in the publicity which each gets in the print media. Though the Kennedy-Nixon "Great Debates" were on both radio and television, the discussion of the events in the press were centered on the telecasts, rather than on the radio broadcasts.

Old media are affected by the new when it is discovered that the new satisfy or serve some of the functions of the old better. For example, television cut deeply into the audience of movie houses. Radio saved itself only by serving needs which television could not, and by adapting the receiving apparatus so that it could literally follow one wherever he went—into the kitchen, the barn, the beach, or the automobile. In one sense, the educational film industry is doing the same thing by moving away from the type of subject matter which is being accepted by television, and toward the short, single-concept film in a cartridge which is much more flexible than educational television can possibly be. The Hollywood motion picture industry, however, has not yet found new functions to serve, other than prerecording television programs. Hollywood was completely dedicated to serving an entertainment function with light drama. Light drama is now provided by television without apparent cost to the audience and without the effort of "going out" to the movie house. A few film-makers seem to be attempting to find other functions to serve by dealing with more serious topics for a minority audience whom television does not adequately serve.

Broadcasting, both radio and television, has usurped much of the information-giving functions of the print media and even of face-to-face communication. The print media, as a result, have changed their emphasis in two ways: First, by an increasing attempt to cover stories which cannot be covered with microphone or camera and, second, and probably more important, by an effort to do more interpretation, trying to give order and meaning to the mass of complex facts with which the citizen is assailed. This second emphasis has probably always been a function of face-to-face communication, as individuals have turned to those whose opinions they respect for help in interpreting and ordering information, and, most important, deciding what to do about that information. Again, as first the print media and then, even more, the electronic media have taken the information-distribution function away from the opinion leaders, the leaders' organizing and guidance functions have probably increased in importance.

EFFECT OF THE AUDIENCE ON THE MEDIA

Before considering the impact of the media on their audiences, it should be noted that there is also an important influence in the other direction. Whenever one attempts to reach very large audiences (as most of the media in this country must), he becomes—in a very real sense—a captive of those audiences. The tastes and interests of selected audiences set limits within which a medium must operate to remain in business. The more expensive the production and distribution of a particular medium product is, the more attention must be paid to the "mass" audiences. And, as the costs of production and distribution rise, the producer must set his sights on larger and, by definition, less select audiences. The implication of this is that, in the United States and other countries in which the bulk of the media are not subsidized, they must serve an entertainment function in order to obtain the capital needed to support their other functions.

It is probably safe to say that more of the matter printed fifty to seventy-five years ago was intellectually challenging than is true today. The reason is that the literate audience was comparatively small and select and the total volume of printed matter was less. Today, with almost universal literacy in the United States, the market for mediocrity is much greater. Thus, the supply is greater. In absolute terms, there is more "good" material being printed now than fifty to seventy-five years ago, but it is less visible because of the flood of material for the literate but non-intellectual. In other words, the percentage of intellectuals does not rise in direct proportion to the growth in literacy.

The audience has another effect on the media which, though indirect, is probably much more important to an understanding of mass-communication processes. The personality traits of the audience members, their educational backgrounds, prior information, attitudes, interests, social positions, even areas of residence within a community or within the country create what we might call a set of screens. These screens differ for each individual in the population, so that different media products "get through" to each individual; those that get through are distorted indifferent ways for different individuals; and those that get through and are perceived similarly by different individuals, tend to be remembered in different ways. These are the phenomena which are generally labeled "selective exposure," "selective perception," and "selective retention." Evidence of the precise ways in which these screens operate is given in a study by Kaufman.[2] She discovered many

---

[2] Helen J. Kaufman, "The Appeal of Specific Daytime Serials," in Paul F. Lazarsfeld and Frank Stanton, eds., *Radio Research 1942–1943* (New York: Duell, Sloan and Pearce, 1944), pp. 86–107.

of the audience factors which determine the type of women exposed to the broadcasts of different daytime serials, and the way in which those exposed interpret what they hear.

THE MEDIA AND DIFFUSION OF INFORMATION

In 1920, *Colliers* magazine gave credit to the infant motion picture industry which, it said,

> . . . transformed insular creatures into cosmopolitans, putting a magic telescope to the vision of the farmer boy, townsman, and city hemmed-in folks. The movies have opened minds, and with them opened, people are forced to keep ahead of the intelligence thus awakened, and the imagination thus aroused.[3]

Similar claims have been made for radio and, more recently, for television. The evidence on this growth of knowledge, however, presents a far more complex picture.

It is clear that certain types of information are transmitted to more people more quickly than could possibly be the case without the mass media. Somewhat spectacular examples are:

1. The diffusion of information about the power failure and consequent blackout in the New York City area in 1965. The transistor radio is credited with a major role in averting disaster by bringing information to all who were, both literally and figuratively, in the dark.[4]

2. The almost instantaneous diffusion of information about the assassination of President John F. Kennedy to all parts of the world.[5]

3. The even more rapid diffusion in this country of information about the assassination of the President's assassin. Individuals in all parts of the country were eye-witnesses to the macabre drama as it was carried on television.

There are many more general examples which indicate the importance of the mass media to the diffusion of information. Consider that less than fifty years ago, seeing and hearing the President of the United States speak was an event which highlighted the lives of some of our

---

[3] *Colliers*, February 28, 1920, p. 16. Quoted in Davis, p. 63.
[4] *New York Times,* November 11, 1965, pp. 1, 40.
[5] Bradley S. Greenberg and Edwin S. Parker, eds., *The Kennedy Assassination and the American Public* (Stanford, Calif.: Stanford University Press, 1965). See especially pp. 89–146.

grandparents and great-grandparents. It was an experience that was shared by few of their fellow citizens. Rare is the citizen today who has not welcomed the President into his living room, courtesy of one of the television networks! Data from the polls in 1960 indicate that roughly eighty per cent of the population of the United States heard or saw at least one of the Kennedy-Nixon debates.[6]

For modern man, it is difficult to realize that, until recently, almost the sole source of information for the masses about the varieties of experience that lay beyond the limits of their personal lives was interpersonal communication. A major source of information for the elite was the book—in large part, the novel. Today, we take for granted the fact that adults obtain much of their information through the popular press and the electronic media. We tend not to be aware of the implications of this change.

Traditionally, the availability of information varied greatly among men. Thus, their pictures of the world to which they responded varied greatly. The mass media, and especially the electronic media which depend less on receiver skills, have made an increasing proportion of existing information available to all. Some traditional patterns of leadership have, in turn, been affected. (This will be considered further in the section on the effect of the media on social structure.) In a very real sense, space and time have been altered also. As one writer has noted, the new limits are not obvious, nor it is now clear what "authentic" experience is.

> Direct personal experience becomes indistinguishable from the vicarious, the compelling secondhand version, when the doings of the outer world are brought to us on television, as they happen. We know at the same moment as the astronaut whether his shot is successful. It is not only real life; it is real time.[7]

This is not to say that the media transmit events without distortion. There is bias in the selection of events to be covered, and distortion of those events which are selected. Most readers, listeners, and viewers accept as a truism that the media cover the events that they do because these events are news. "All the News That's Fit to Print" reads the masthead of the *New York Times*. Audience members fail to realize that such assertions are tautological; the events covered are news *solely*

---

[6] Elihu Katz and Jacob J. Feldman, "The Debates in the Light of Research: A Survey of Surveys," in Sidney Kraus, ed., *The Great Debates* (Bloomington: Indiana University Press, 1962), p. 190.

[7] Judith Wheeler, "The Electronic Age," *Saturday Review of Literature,* June 4, 1966, p. 22.

because they are printed in newspapers or broadcast on radio or television.

We have been conditioned by the media to accept as fact that bad news is news; good news is not news. The way in which individuals, especially individuals in other countries, perceive the "reality" of desegregation in the United States is an excellent illustration of this point. Media coverage tends to give the impression that trouble accompanies almost every effort at desegregation. The front pages and the headlines of newspapers do not accurately reflect the national, or even the southern situation where a large portion of the desegregation in schools and other civil rights advances are proceeding quietly. A striking, but far from isolated, example is seen in two reports concerning the effect of desegregation on the Washington, D. C. public schools. A report by a House of Representatives subcommittee stating that trouble resulted from this desegregation and recommending that segregation should be reinstated received front-page play in most newspapers. A contradictory report by the assistant superintendent of Washington schools, indicating that integration had gone well in the District, was buried on inside pages, if it was printed at all. Even the *New York Times* handled these two stories in this way.[8] This treatment of the news does not reflect racial prejudice on the part of newsmen; it reflects, rather, their definition of news, for we see them act in the same way for many types of stories.

This equating of news with conflict or, at times, with entertainment, is seen throughout the news media in coverage of all aspects of public affairs. Even when the Kennedy Foundation presented awards in December, 1962 to a group of scientists for their outstanding contributions to the prevention of certain types of mental retardation, the press gave better coverage to the jokes which Adlai Stevenson told at the dinner than to the important scientific news. Reading the account in many newspapers, it would be impossible to tell what the dinner was about; the awards were not even mentioned. The jokes were more "newsworthy" than the scientific research which had deep meaning to the fifteen or twenty million persons in the United States who live in families in which there is a mentally retarded individual and to the many more who will someday be in such a family.[9]

Not only does the audience get a distorted picture of reality because of the selectivity of the media in covering events, but also be-

---

[8] Walter Spearman, "Racial Stories in the News," in Walter Spearman and Sylvan Meyer, *Racial Crisis and the Press* (Atlanta, Ga.: The Southern Regional Council, 1960), pp. 12–15.

[9] Unpublished study in the files of the author.

cause the requirements of each medium result in a "shaping" of each event that is covered. Few newspaper stories are organized in an accurate time sequence. Newspaper stories tend rather to follow a pyramid arrangement, with the most spectacular part of the story first and the details on which the story is based last—where many readers never see them. In broadcasting, every event, no matter what its nature, must be constantly interesting so that the attention of the audience will be held. The result, to cite a trivial example, is that there never has been a dull baseball game on radio. An extended example of how television has distorted an important public event is the report of a study by Lang and Lang.[10] When General MacArthur was relieved of his Korean command by President Truman and returned to this country, the media gave ample coverage to his progress across the country. By the time he arrived for the MacArthur Day Parade in Chicago, audience members expected an exciting and unusual event. The Langs placed observers along the parade route. What they reported was compared with the images which were transmitted by television. Though observers on the scene found little excitement and relatively small crowds, the television viewer, because of the selection of pictures and the announcer's commentary, received the impression of wildly cheering and enthusiastic crowds. Thus, the often-heard statement that the mass media are "neutral"—that they are merely conveyor belts which transmit whatever one feeds onto them—is misleading. Clearly, each medium of communication imposes some of its own form upon that which it transmits.

> The barbecue-Chautauqua favored the oratorical elder statesmen and was especially susceptible to emotional and demagogic exploitation. Radio put a high premium on a pleasing voice and accent. Television . . . has created its own symbolic language: certain shorthand stereotypes which carry a maximum audio-visual message at a minimum cost.[11]

Though we think that we perceive some of these differences in symbolic language among the media, and though we act upon these perceptions, experimental verification of them to date is limited. One of the few experimental studies that I know about is more interesting for what it suggests than for what it proves. This is a study which a colleague and I did a number of years ago to study the interaction between type of political speaker and medium. We obtained film recordings

---

[10] Kurt Lang and Gladys Engel Lang, "The Unique Perspective of Television and Its Effect: A Pilot Study," *American Sociological Review*, XVIII (1953), pp. 3–12.
[11] Harvey Wheeler, "TV Technique," *Nation*, November 5, 1960, p. 343.

of three *Meet the Press* television programs: one with Senator Robert Taft, one with Governor Tom Dewey, and one with Senator Richard Russell. At the time of our study, all were possible Presidential candidates for 1952. We had nine groups of college students: one to *view* the program with each candidate, one to *listen* to the sound track of each program (as though it were a radio program), and one to *read* the script of each program. We found attitudes toward Senator Russell went up no matter which medium was used. In general, these Iowa students were unfamiliar with Russell prior to the experiment and so initial attitudes were unusually low. With Senator Taft, radio made little difference; attitudes went down for those who saw him on television, attitudes went up for those who read his statements in the script. For Governor Dewey, the opposite effect was found. Again radio made little difference; attitudes became more favorable for those who watched him on the program, attitudes became less favorable for those who read what he said. Interesting questions are raised about the symbolic language of each of these media which, apparently, works to the advantage or disadvantage of different speakers. Some of these differences are quite subtle, I believe. Others are more obvious, and fairly clear even from casual observation of the contemporary scene.

In addition to the media "shaping" the messages which they transmit, they are sometimes responsible for changing the event itself. Consider, for example, the changes which have occurred in public speaking as the means of transmission have changed.

Radio was hardly out of swaddling clothes before the need for some new type of political speaker was recognized. By 1928, the death knell had been sounded for "the spellbinder, gesticulating, pounding, striding up and down, stirred to frenzy by the applause of his audience" who, up to then, had been considered the great vote-getter. The *New York Times* had this to say of the 1928 campaign:

> Almost a funeral procession for the old-fashioned spellbinder, it is less important to sway crowds than to be able to send a voice quietly into a million or ten million homes and speak convincingly to men and women sitting by their own firesides.[12]

As radio continued to develop, the "conversational style" developed with it. How much of this was due to radio, and how much to an already existing trend is difficult to say. It is probable that radio's effect on the public acceptance of this new style of delivery was simply to accelerate and legitimize the trend. In any case, it clearly had an effect.

---

[12] *New York Times,* October 28, 1928, Sec. 10, p. 1.

Another event which the mass media are credited with changing is the national political convention. Radio, for example, was at least partially responsible for the smooth and apparently harmonious atmosphere of the 1928 Democratic national convention. In 1924, radio had allowed the nation to listen for the first time as the Democratic party leaders fought over condemnation of the Ku Klux Klan and over a Presidential nominee. The nation heard the fight between the Klan forces and their opposition. And for seventeen days, the nation listened to the monotonous drone of 103 successive ballots before a compromise candidate, J. P. Morgan's lawyer, John W. Davis, could be nominated. Four years later, it took only one ballot for the Democrats to nominate Al Smith.[13] Clearly, the Democratic party leaders were determined not to have their family squabbles overheard by the nation. Twenty-eight years later, history was repeated, with emphasis this time on the visual show rather than the aural. Walter Cronkite has said that the 1952 conventions were "the last to maintain the spontaneity of the normal manipulations of party politics in this country."[14] Some aspects of the 1952 convention broadcasts bored the audience, thus worrying network executives; other aspects showed the parties in a poor light, thus worrying party leaders. The result was a political face-lifting. "The National Committees of both parties started issuing guides to behavior for the delegates. They even established 'schools' that offered short dramatic courses on keeping one's eye—and mind—on the camera."[15] Anything that might have bored the audience or revealed too much political manipulation was swept out of view. The platform was packed with entertainers. The result is that, "instead of being candid eyewitnesses to this aspect of democracy, we have become spectators to a staged extravaganza."[16] Even as early as 1952, convention sites were selected with television coverage in mind. In that year, Convention Hall in Chicago was chosen by the parties, rather than the much larger Chicago Stadium, primarily because the former was more suitable for television. With this choice, party chieftains gave up roughly six thousand seats. One observer has noted that this surrendering of large blocks of tickets for a politician is roughly the equivalent of having to donate a goodly portion of blood.[17]

---

[13] Samuel L. Becker and Elmer W. Lower, "Broadcasting in Presidential Campaigns," in *The Great Debates,* pp. 29–30.

[14] Walter Cronkite, "Television and the News," in *The Eighth Art* (New York: Holt, Rinehart and Winston, Inc., 1962), p. 229.

[15] *Ibid.,* p. 230.

[16] *Ibid.*

[17] *New York Times,* June 15, 1952, Sec. 2, p. X9.

The existence of newspapers across the country led President Woodrow Wilson to hold the first White House news conference over fifty years ago, on March 15, 1913.[18] He saw these conferences as an opportunity to express his points of view more clearly to the electorate through the newspapers. As other mass media developed and were brought into the news conference, its character changed. During Franklin D. Roosevelt's years, the conference remained an informal interchange between President and reporters, wherein the latter could ask any question and usually get a response. They could probe and discuss, and get a feel for the President and his ideas and he, in turn, could get a feel for them and their ideas. This now has changed. Perhaps it was inevitable as news from our nation's capitol became of greater interest throughout the world. However, the change seemed most evident as first film and then live television was introduced. The President is now on a stage and everyone has become an actor. The President has even resorted to planted questions at times.[19]

This changing of the event which broadcasters cover is not always a chance affair, nor are the changes manipulated only by politicians or others who want to appear in a favorable light. There are times when the broadcasters set about the change of such events very consciously; and this is not necessarily bad. It is important, however, that we be aware of these occurrences if we are to understand either mass communication or politics in this latter half of the twentieth century. One example of this conscious attempt to alter the political campaign scene is the series of Kennedy-Nixon debates of 1960 which, without question, would never have taken place if it had not been for broadcasting and the broadcasting leaders who promoted it. Without these debates, it is likely that Richard Nixon would have become President.

Thus, one of the effects of the mass media in effecting information diffusion is that the information diffused is biased in certain ways. The input to the media is selective in the events covered. Those that are covered are shaped to fit each particular medium. This, again, is a selective process in part, but also a distortion process. The existence of the media also change the event covered, as well as the message about the event, simply because they are there (somewhat like the "indeterminacy" principle of quantum mechanics). Sometimes media presence leads to the event being changed because the persons involved in the event wish to project a different image over the media, and sometimes

---

[18] Ray Stannard Baker, *Woodrow Wilson, Life and Letters* (Garden City, New York: Doubleday, Doran and Co., 1931), IV, p. 229.

[19] *The Daily Iowan,* January 29, 1966, p. 2.

because media personnel become more than observers and transmitters; they become actual participants in the event.

In spite of the various kinds of information distortion, statistics on the exposure of people to information about public affairs, such as election campaigns, make it appear that the mass media have a strong and positive effect on both knowledge and interest in these matters. I mentioned earlier the eightly per cent of the population of the United States that heard or saw at least one of the Kennedy-Nixon debates in 1960. I am also reminded of the story which former Republican National Chairman Leonard Hall has told about the state of Maine. Maine was always a Republican state. People were born Republicans, so they went to the polls and voted Republican. Then, suddenly, they voted for some Democrats. Hall says that he asked an elderly Maine resident about what had happened. "Well," was the response, "we can't do anything with this television. Our children were brought up to think that Democrats had horns. Now they see them on television and realize some of them don't have horns a-tall."[20]

Though this story and the data from 1960 are impressive, they may be misleading if we assume that they indicate a *general* increase in knowledge and interest in public affairs brought about by broadcasting. It seems likely that interest and knowledge in national affairs, such as Presidential elections *have* increased, but at the expense of interest and knowledge of state and local affairs, such as congressional, state, and local elections. This is evident when one tries to get an audience for a senatorial candidate during an election campaign. It is very difficult. It is also evident in the decline of the political club, once the rallying point and training ground for local candidates, and a place where local issues could be hotly debated.[21] Two of the world's most imaginative and insightful sociologists, Paul Lazarsfeld and Robert Merton, have even hypothesized that the media sometimes contribute to political apathy and inertness, rather than to interest and action. This they call the "narcotizing dysfunction" of the media. They note that as an individual devotes more time to the media, he has less time to devote to organized social action. His involvement with politics, for example, becomes intellectualized, rather than action-oriented. As Lazarsfeld and Merton say:

> He comes to mistake *knowing* about problems of the day for *doing* something about them. His social conscience remains spotlessly clean. He *is* concerned. He *is* informed. And he has all sorts of ideas

[20] Leonard W. Hall, "How Politics is Changing," in J. M. Cannon, ed., *Politics U.S.A.* (Garden City, New York: Doubleday, 1960), pp. 107–108.
[21] *Ibid.*

as to what should be done. But after he has gotten through his dinner and after he has listened to his favored radio programs [or viewed his favorite television programs] and after he has read his second newspaper of the day, it is really time for bed.[22]

Considering our behavior from this viewpoint, one is bound to have second thoughts about the claims of the broadcasters that the electronic media are leading us to a social and political utopia. However, asserting that the media have a narcotizing dysfunction—even when it is done by such distinguished scholars as Lazarsfeld and Merton— does not make it so. Perhaps the hypothesis is sound; perhaps it is not. Without question, it is important and needs to be tested. The best evidence for this hypothesis so far comes from a study by Wiebe,[23] who explored public reactions to the televised Kefauver hearings on crime and corruption in New York City. The purpose of the hearings was to arouse public concern and to reduce apathy. Wiebe found that after the broadcasts more people said that they were concerned, but there was little evidence that apathy was reduced, for few respondents reported taking any actions to improve the situation.

Though the Wiebe study does not completely confirm the narcotizing dysfunction hypothesis, its findings are consistent with the hypothesis. I have not been able to find evidence that is contrary to the hypothesis. However, the Wiebe study shows only that the media do not lead to more action; it does not show that the media lead to *less* action. Therefore, we must conclude tentatively that the media do not increase participation in public affairs. On the other hand, there is no strong evidence that they have decreased overall participation in such affairs.

A major result of the faster and wider diffusion of information about events is that national or even international issues are made out of what were once local or regional issues. In this way, the media are contributing to the power of the central government and, particularly, of the chief executive. Prior to the development of the electronic media in particular, which, in turn, created what Woodrow Wilson called "national information" and "national opinion," Presidential powers in the United States tended to increase during periods of national crisis such as war or national depression, whereas Congressional powers increased relatively during other periods. Broadcasting has tended to

[22] Paul F. Lazarsfeld and Robert K. Merton, "Mass Communication, Popular Taste and Organized Social Action," in Wilbur Schramm, ed., *Mass Communications,* (Urbana: University of Illinois Press, 1960), p. 502.
[23] G. D. Wiebe, "Responses to the Televised Kefauver Hearings: Some Social Psychological Implications," *Public Opinion Quarterly,* XVI (1952), 179–200.

focus the attention of national audiences upon local or regional issues, literally making them into national crises. Examples are the problem of school integration in the South and unemployment in Michigan and Illinois. These problems are thrust upon the nation-wide scene by the mass media and, therefore, upon the President. In this indirect way, broadcasting has pushed the President further up the pole of political power, relative to the Congress,[24] and has contributed to the increasing power of the federal over the state and local governments (though it is far from the only force acting in this direction in either case).

The effect of this information which we get through the mass media is greatest when we have no direct experience with an object or event which the media cover. One study with first-grade children has shown that it is possible, through the mass media, to establish stereotyped images of social reality, for example of taxi drivers, where a child's normal experience has not previously provided contrary or conflicting information. But in areas of experience, where family and community experiences have already established strong image patterns in a child (for example, of the father, teacher, etc.), mass media apparently will not dislodge or destroy them.[25]

Most of us have had the experience of discovering that young children learn some things from the mass media—jingles from radio, commercials from television. At least they learn to identify brand names and brand packages. However, our evidence indicates that this learning is highly specific, with little transfer. That is to say, children who have viewed television regularly in the home do not appear to have acquired greater skill at learning new words—no greater *general* "reading readiness."[26] Both the Schramm and Himmelweit studies confirm the fact that children just beginning school who have been exposed to television have a larger vocabularly than children not exposed. However, by the time the viewers and non-viewers have been in school a few years, these vocabularly differences are erased.[27] Though youngsters say that they learn many things from television, and that it helps them in school by giving them ideas for themes or

---

[24] For a fuller discussion of broadcasting's contribution to Presidential power, see Samuel L. Becker, "Presidential Power: The Influence of Broadcasting," *Quarterly Journal of Speech*, XLVII (1961), 10–18.

[25] Alberta Engvall Siegel, "The Influence of Violence in the Mass Media Upon Children's Role Expectations," *Child Development*, XXIX (1958), 35–56.

[26] "Toward More Effective Educational TV: A Pilot Study of the Effect of Commercial TV on the Verbal Behavior of Pre-School Children" (Urbana: University of Illinois, Institute of Communications Research, December, 1958, dittoed).

[27] Wilbur Schramm, Jack Lyle, and Edwin B. Parker, *Television in the Lives of Our Children* (Stanford, California: Stanford University Press, 1961), pp. 86–88.

topics to talk about,[28] there is no evidence to validate these claims. This may be an area in which further research would be fruitful.

MEDIA IMPACT ON ATTITUDES

[Movies] encourage goodness and kindness, virtue and courage.[29]

The movies are so occupied with crime and sex stuff and are so saturating the minds of children the world over with social sewage that they have become a menace to the mental and moral life of the coming generation.[30]

These quotations exemplify the range of claims made about the effects of the various media on the attitudes of their audiences. The evidence is clear that most of such claims grossly overstate the case. Those who make such claims have apparently generalized the impact of the mass media on purchasing behavior to an impact on attitudes, or on voting behavior, or on basic values. These critics have failed to notice the essential difference among these various types of effects. When influencing purchasing behavior, the media are reaching an audience which is already interested in buying cigarettes, or soap, or some other product. This is an audience that tends to have no strong tie to one brand, and the various brands have little to distinguish them from each other. The important thing is to make the brand name salient, so that when one thinks of buying soap, for example, he instantly associates the felt need with the brand name. On the other hand, with voting behavior, or most other sorts of beliefs or behaviors for which individuals tend to have longer learning histories and which, in general, are most ego-involving, evidence indicates that the media have far less effect. This is not to say that they have *none*. Such a broad statement is obviously unfounded. The first generalization that we can make, on the basis of existing evidence, is that the impact of the mass media tends to be in *inverse* proportion to the importance to the audience of the issue involved.

Closely related to the variable of importance, though not necessarily identical, are the variables of degree to which one's attitude is structured, and the amount of relevant knowledge one has. Here, too, evidence indicates that the mass media have relatively greater impact when an attitude is unstructured or when an individual possesses

---

[28] *Ibid.*, p. 58.

[29] *World's Work*, March, 1913, p. 40. Quoted in Davis, p. 142.

[30] *Christian Century*, January, 1930, p. 110. Quoted in Davis, p. 231.

little relevant knowledge. Peterson and Thurstone,[31] for example, have found that the attitudes of junior and senior high school students who had little exposure to either Negroes, Chinese, or Germans, could be influenced by motion pictures. The anti-Negro film, *Birth of a Nation*, resulted in a striking increase in hostile attitudes, which was still apparent in sixty-two per cent of the cases five months after exposure to the film. Viewing a pro-Chinese film and a pro-German film resulted in more favorable attitudes toward these groups. Kraus,[32] more recently, found that rather simple dramatic films which featured a mixed cast of white and Negro characters could change attitudes of high school students who, again, had had relatively little exposure to Negroes. There is similar evidence from the study which I mentioned earlier that shows television's influence on stereotyping by children.[33] None of this would be especially important, except that the picture which youngsters get from the mass media about the world with which they have little direct experience is a distorted picture. As Barcus noted, after reviewing some 1700 studies of mass media content, "the media world is a white man's world. Not only is it white, it is a white American world."[34] Barcus found this to be true both in terms of the number of characters and their preferred status. He also found this bias to be consistent in movies, television, comics, and magazine fiction. Not only were minority groups badly underrepresented, relative to their true proportion in our population, they tended to receive unfavorable treatment as well. Though Barcus does not report the fact, there has been some change in media content in recent years, especially in the treatment of the Negro. Negroes are being shown more in non-stereotyped roles, both in advertisements and in dramas. Though they are probably not yet seen in anything approaching what would represent their proportion in the population, distinct progress is being made. And from what we know of learning theory, and from the aforementioned studies of stereotyping, this should have a positive effect on attitudes toward this minority group.

Research indicates pretty clearly that if those who are exposed to media messages which alter their attitudes do not find support for

[31] Ruth C. Peterson and L. L. Thurstone, *Motion Pictures and the Social Attitudes of Children* (New York: Macmillan, 1933).

[32] Sidney Kraus, "Modifying Prejudice: Attitude Change as a Function of the Race of the Communicator," *Audio Visual Communication Review*, X (1962), 14–22.

[33] Siegel, *loc. cit.*

[34] Francis Earl Barcus, "Communication Content: Analysis of the Research, 1900–1958 (A Content Analysis of Content Analysis)" (Unpublished Ph.D. dissertation, University of Illinois, 1959), p. 262.

these new attitudes in their interpersonal contacts or among their reference groups (the groups to which all of us look for cues as to how to behave or for support in our attitudes), they will quickly discount the messages. In other words, mass media messages seldom, if ever, are a sufficient cause of attitude change. They rather tend to interact with a complex series of other influences and predispositions.

In some cultures at least, and under some conditions, the media themselves can provide social suport for attitudes newly acquired through other means. The evidence is even clearer that those individuals who often provide this support (the so-called opinion leaders) receive much of their information and ideas from the mass media. Findings of this sort have led Katz and Lazarsfeld to coin the phrase, "two-step flow of communication."[35] The point is that the mass media of communication do not usually have a direct effect on the behavior of audiences, but rather tend to supply opinion leaders with the information which they use, in turn, to affect others.

Another type of attitude change is that related to the acceptance of a new idea or a new practice, such as the use of hybrid seed corn, certain health practices, or perhaps even birth control. For this sort of change, interpersonal communication has been shown to be relatively more important than the mass media, but the latter also play a critical role. As Katz[36] has indicated, when such changes are broken down into phases, we get a clearer picture of the function of the mass media in the change process. For example, we can break the diffusion process into the following phases:

Phase 1. An individual becomes aware of an innovation.

Phase 2. He becomes interested in it.

Phase 3. He considers trying it.

Phase 4. He tries it.

Phase 5. He decides to continue doing it.

Evidence indicates that mass communication, in general, is more influential in the early phases of the process, while interpersonal communication is more influential in the later phases. Thus, mass and interpersonal communication are complementary, each playing a major role at different stages of the change process.

---

[35] Elihu Katz and Paul E. Lazarsfeld, *Personal Influence, the Part Played by People in the Flow of Mass Communications* (Glencoe, Ill.: The Free Press, 1955).

[36] Elihu Katz, "Communication Research and the Image of Society: Convergence of Two Traditions," *American Journal of Sociology*, LXV (1960), 435–440.

Those who have studied the process by which new ideas or practices are accepted have also found that the so-called "innovators" —those who accept a new idea early—are more likely to have been influenced by the mass media than those who accept the idea later. The latter, again, are more likely to be influenced directly by other people whom they know.

In this section on media impact on attitudes, I have concentrated upon situations in which individuals have unstructured attitudes and/ or little knowledge about the attitude object. As I indicated earlier, where individuals have strong or ego-involved attitudes (as they do toward much of the content of the mass media), the media have little impact. The major reason for this limited impact appears to be what we might call the law of consistency. (This is what Heider calls "Balance theory."[37] Festinger calls "Dissonance theory,"[38] and Osgood and Tannenbaum call the "Congruity hypothesis."[39]) This is the pressure within individuals to be consistent—to keep attitudes consistent, to keep their cognitions consistent, and to keep their cognitions consistent with their attitudes. For example, an anti-Semitic attitude and the knowledge that some Jews are good people are inconsistent. An individual with such an attitude who is confronted with such knowledge must do something to avoid or reduce this inconsistency. If his attitude is not strongly held, he might change it. More likely, he will either avoid the information, misperceive or reinterpret or deny the fact, or he will conveniently forget the fact. These are what have been labeled selective exposure, selective perception, and selective retention. These are the psychological processes which sharply limit the often laudable efforts of people in the mass media to change destructive attitudes. For example Lazarsfeld,[40] who was one of the first to note the phenomenon of selective exposure, has described the incident of the radio series which was designed to better human relations. Each program told about a different nationality and the things it had contributed to American culture. It was hoped that the series would help to teach tolerance of other nationalities. The only problem was that the audience for each program turned out to be mainly from the

[37] Fritz Heider, *The Psychology of Interpersonal Relations* (New York: John Wiley and Sons, Inc., 1958).

[38] Leon Festinger, *A Theory of Cognitive Dissonance* (Evanston, Ill.: Row Peterson and Co., 1957).

[39] Charles E. Osgood and Percy H. Tannenbaum, "The Principle of Congruity in the Prediction of Attitude Change," *Psychological Review*, LXII (1955), 42–55.

[40] Paul F. Lazarsfeld, "The Effects of Radio on Public Opinion," in Douglas Waples, ed., *Print, Radio, and Film in a Democracy* (Chicago: University of Chicago Press, 1952), p. 69.

national group which was being discussed. Thus, there was little chance to teach tolerance or anything else because selective exposure resulted in an audience which already highly approved of what was being said. Another example of this phenomenon was the study done of the effects of the motion picture *Gentlemen's Agreement* on anti-Semitism. When one compared only the post-viewing attitudes of those who had gone to see the film with the attitudes of persons who had not seen the film, there were great differences. The average attitude of those who had seen the film was much less anti-Jewish than that of the latter group. The researchers would have concluded that the film had great impact, except that they also had attitude measures for the movie-goers before they had seen the film. These data showed clearly that those who chose to see *Gentlemen's Agreement* tended to be more favorable to Jews *initially*. Those on whom the film might have had the greatest impact, avoided it.[41]

The classic case of selective perception is that described by Kendall and Wolfe.[42] This was the study in which a series of cartoons featuring a very unattractive individual displaying his prejudices against minority groups was shown. The purpose was to show the stupidity of bigots. However, those at whom the cartoons were aimed—those who were highly prejudiced—tended to misperceive the point of the cartoons. Some with very strong prejudices even perceived the purpose of these cartoons as being to encourage prejudice.

There are a great many studies in which we can see evidence of the selective retention phenomenon; the tendency to remember the things which are consistent with our attitudes and to forget those which are not consistent. An example is Taft's study of Negro boys who, over a period of time, tended to forget the parts of a message about a Negro baseball player which were unfavorable to Negroes but remembered the parts which were favorable.[43]

Having noted these points about selective exposure, perception, and retention, we must avoid the erroneous conclusion that the media, therefore, have no effect on these strong attitudes. The conclusion is rather that those who disagree with a persuasive message *tend* not to expose themselves to it or, if exposed, *tend* to misperceive the

[41] Charles Y. Glock, "Some Applications of the Panel Method to the Study of Change," in Paul F. Lazarsfeld and Morris Rosenberg, eds., *The Language of Social Research* (Glencoe, Ill.: The Free Press, 1955), pp. 243–244.

[42] Patricia L. Kendall and Katherine M. Wolfe, "The Analysis of Deviant Cases in Communications Research," in Paul F. Lazarsfeld and Frank N. Stanton, eds., *Communications Research, 1948–1949* (New York: Harpers, 1949), pp. 152–179.

[43] Ronald Taft, "Selective Recall and Memory Distortion of Favorable and Unfavorable Material," *Journal of Abnormal and Social Psychology,* IL (1954), 23–28.

point or, if they perceive the point correctly, *tend* to forget that which is contrary to their prior attitudes. We must keep in mind that this means *some* who disagree with a mesage do expose themselves to it, do perceive it correctly, and do remember it. One of the important research jobs remaining to us is to study these so-called deviant cases to a greater extent, to find the conditions which cause them to deviate from the norm. Such findings will add immeasurably to our understanding of the mass media's impact on attitudes.

MEDIA IMPACT ON CULTURE

One of the questions which has interested scholars of communication, since at least the beginnings of the age of mass communication, is the effect which changing modes and media of communication have upon our culture. In considering this question, it is important first to recognize two facts. One is that this sort of causal relationship is impossible to establish with much certainty; historical data have severe limitations for the establishment of such relationships. There are too many factors which are confounded with the introduction of various media. To name only a few, innovation in media use has generally been accompanied by urbanization, an increase in literacy, and, often, even political changes. If anything, the evidence indicates a type of reciprocal relationship: certain levels of urbanization and literacy both facilitate and make necessary the development of mass communication and, once a mass communication system exists, it facilitates urbanization and further developments in literacy. A modern society is impossible without mass media. They are essential for the marketing of mass-produced products, both for diffusing information about such products and for establishing common tastes in style and type. In other words, the media are both indices and agents of cultural change.

The second fact to keep in mind as we consider the question of whether the media have an effect on our culture is that the question is, in a very real sense, tautological, for the media are an important part of our culture. Thus, any change in the media or in the pattern of media use, by definition, is a change in our culture.

Having noted these facts, there are still obviously some important unanswered questions. To what extent do the media, as they are operated in the United States, affect our tastes? To what extent do they hinder or aid the development of art products of greater artistic merit? Was Reinhold Niebuhr correct when he saw the effect of television as "a further vulgarization of our culture"?[44] Or is Neibuhr one of the disenchanted members of the intelligentsia of whom Paul Lazarsfeld speaks? These people fought and won the battle for shorter working hours and better wages for the American laborer, hoping that the workers would spend some of this extra money and time at Columbia University, only to find that they spent the time instead with the Columbia Broadcasting System. These are emotion-laden questions for most of us. I will try to examine them as objectively as I can.

> In general, cultural traits diffuse outward from the point of origin *along the most-used lines of communication* and contact; and those traits that are *objectively superior* or that come from a *more powerful or prestigious source* are especially likely to be taken over.[45]

These are the generalizations about cultural change which Berelson and Steiner believe can be made up on the basis of existing studies in the behavioral sciences.

It is certainly clear, even from casual observation, that the mass media, by facilitating communication, facilitate the diffusion of culture through space and time. The effects here are analogous to those of other mass-production industries or mass-marketing chain stores. These organizations have made a *greater variety* of products available to the average person but, conversely, have made pretty much the *same* choices available to all. Thus, social class, education, size of community, or part of the country (or perhaps even part of the world) have little effect on styles of clothing available in local stores to the average person, or the kind of music or drama to which one can expose himself at the local cinema, or on one's radio or television receiver. The exchange of records, films, and television programs between Great Britain and the United States has created a common culture. We see the same phenomenon in the fashion industry. Though international fashions are not a completely new phenomenon, they were once the exclusive province of the wealthy who moved physically back and forth among the continents. They are now the province of everyone. One travels to Paris via the mass media to learn what is being worn there and then buys the latest Paris fashions at Macy's in New York or Marx and Spencer in London or at comparable stores in other parts of the world. The elite "BBC speech" is slowly becoming the common dialect of Great Britain, just as General American has become more

---

[44] *Time,* February 7, 1949, p. 70. Quoted in Davis, p. 225.
[45] Bernard Berelson and Gary A. Steiner, *Human Behavior: An Inventory of Scientific Findings* (New York: Harcourt, Brace & World, Inc., 1964), p. 653 (italics added).

generally accepted in the United States since it became the standard pronunciation for most network radio and television announcers in this country. As the mass media increase the communication between our countries, we expect these two dialects to slowly merge.

Thus, Berelson and Steiner's first generalization, that "cultural traits diffuse outward from the point of origin along the most-used lines of communication," and my corollary generalization that, as these lines increase and extend, cultural products and practices can no longer remain the special province of a particular class or region or time, appear to be clearly supported. On the other hand, Berelson and Steiner's second generalization, that "those traits that are objectively superior or that come from a more powerful or prestiguous source are especially likely to be taken over," appears to me to be highly questionable. Unless one defines "objective superiority" and "powerful and prestiguous sources" circularly; i.e., by considering any trait that is adopted as necessarily superior, or the source that it came from necessarily powerful or prestiguous, this generalization cannot be supported. Judged by the media products to which most members of the American public expose themselves, there is little question that objective superiority has little effect on popular taste. The extent to which the mass media are responsible for the level of taste that exists is quite another question however. To what extent do the media follow taste? To what extent do they lead taste? The answer is probably that they do some of both, though hard evidence of either (especially evidence that the media lead taste) is hard to acquire. Historically, there is certainly no evidence that the media have lowered taste, for the taste of the "masses" has never been high. If anything, it is probably higher today than it ever was. Conversely, one cannot attribute this probable raising of taste to media influence, for the change has been accompanied by developments other than the growth of the media, most especially the extended formal education of most people who thus, presumably, learn more about literature, music, art, and theatre. The school orchestra, a relatively recent innovation in most schools, undoubtedly has had some influence on interest in certain types of music. Also, increased wealth and leisure for a larger proportion of the population are probably important factors in the development of taste. As Lazarsfeld and Merton pointed out:

> The effective audience for the arts has become historically transformed. Some centuries back, this audience was largely confined to a selected aristocratic elite. Relatively few were literate. And very few possessed the means to buy books, attend theatres, and travel to the urban centers of the arts. Not more than a slight fraction, pos-

sibly not more than 1 or 2 per cent, of the population composed the effective audience for the arts. . . .

Some forms of music, drama, and literature now reach virtually everyone in our society. . . . [But] the great audiences for the mass media, although in the main literate, are not highly cultivated. . . .

Whereas yesterday the elite constituted virtually the whole of the audience, they are today a minute fraction of the whole.[46]

Clearly, the majority of today's audience for whom the arts are available, choose art products that are less demanding. They prefer a western to *Death of a Salesman,* Norman Rockwell to Renoir, Lerner and Lowe to Wagner. On the other hand, attendance at museums, opera houses, and art museums has soared in the past decade or two. More people attended concerts in 1962 than went to all of the major and minor league baseball games.[47] The book has become a "mass medium" in a very real sense, in part because of the paperback revolution. The sale of books increased tenfold from 1950 to 1960.[48] This is roughly twice as high a rate of growth as population growth can account for.[49] The circulation of "high-brow" magazines has more than doubled since World War II.[50]

The role of the mass media in stimulating this involvement with the arts is clearly considerable. No individual can like something or want something if he does not know it exists. The mass media have helped to make the bulk of the public aware of a great variety of arts and entertainments. (Whether the media could have made the public aware of an even broader range is another question.) As Leonard Bernstein reported, after an extremely successful cross-country tour of the New York Philharmonic:

> In Las Vegas, whose cultural opulence doesn't always run in traditional channels, and where no major symphony had performed before, a hall holding 7,000 was jammed. . . . These people were well aware of the Philharmonic. I doubt if awareness of the Philharmonic extended much beyond the Hudson 50 years ago.[51]

---

[46] Paul F. Lazarsfeld and Robert K. Merton, "Mass Communication, Popular Taste, and Organized Social Action," in Bernard Rosenberg and David Manning White, eds., *Mass Culture* (Glencoe, Ill.: The Free Press, 1957), pp. 466–468.

[47] *Concert Music USA* (New York: Broadcasting Music, Inc., 1961). Quoted by Frank Stanton, *Books and Television* (New York: New York Public Library, 1963), p. 9.

[48] "Currents," *Publishers' Weekly,* CLXXVII (May 9, 1960), 10.

[49] Dan Lacy, "The Economics of Publishing," *Daedalus,* XCII (1963), 47.

[50] Leo Bogart, *The Age of Television* (New York: Frederick Ungar, 1956), p. 140.

[51] Reported by Frank Stanton in a speech at Dartmouth College, November 26, 1962.

The New York Philharmonic's *Young People's Concerts,* carried on television, made the orchestra a familiar group in homes across the country. When the Philharmonic opened Lincoln Center in New York in 1961, almost 26,000,000 persons saw or heard some part of the two-hour concert on television.[52] Another mass medium which is contributing to an increased interest in music is the phonograph recording. The record industry sold in excess of 25,000,000 classical, long-playing records in 1962.[53] The mass magazines also play a role in familiarizing the public with the arts. *Life,* for example, publishes excellent color reproductions of some 500 art pictures a year.[54] After Henry James' *The Turn of the Screw* was dramatized on television, the entire Modern Library edition of the book was sold out.[55] Radio has widened public appreciation of good music by making it more readily available to more people.

I am not saying that the mass media changed people from art-haters to art-lovers, or even that they created active seekers-after-art from people who were totally oblivious to the arts before. Quite the contrary. The evidence indicates that those who were affected had either a prior propensity in this direction or that other forces were pushing them toward this new behavior.

> The importance of the radio as a source of music . . . lies in its ability to make other influences effective. The radio is seen to have its greatest success with those individuals who possess some basic predisposition toward listening. The main importance of the radio does not lie in its direct ability to create interests, but in its effectiveness as a follow-up for forces quite detached from it.[56]

The media here, as in some of the attitude areas, seem to be energizers, rather than change agents. This however does not change the basic point that there would be fewer people exposing themselves to these esthetic experiences, either first-hand or through the media, if the media had not existed.

Critics of the mass media not only berate the effects of the media on audience tastes, they also complain that a type of Gresham's Law has operated, so that the flooding of the market with mass art has driven out the class art. This point of view is difficult to reconcile with

---

[52] *Ibid.*

[53] Alvin Toffler, "A Quantity of Culture," *Fortune,* LXIV (November 1961), 127.

[54] Stanton, 1962.

[55] Stanton, 1963, p. 11.

[56] Edward A. Suchman, "Invitation to Music," in Paul F. Lazarsfeld and Frank N. Stanton, eds., *Radio Research 1941* (New York: Duell, Sloan and Pearce, 1941), pp. 172–173.

the statistics which I cited earlier on museum and concert attendance, reading and record purchases. Clearly, because there are more art products being produced, we must expect that the *average* quality of these products has gone down. But are there fewer high-quality symphonies being created proportionately to the total population? Fewer high-quality plays? novels? paintings? These are impossible questions to answer with certainty. Underlying all of these questions is the basic question of standards. What are the standards by which one labels an art product as "good" or "bad"? As "mass" or "class"? Whose standards are they? Is "good" art that which serves a need of the people as indicated by their use of it or preference for it? Or is "good" art that which passes muster with some authority? I do not have the answer to these questions, but I do believe that those who claim that standards are declining have an idealized picture of the past. When they point, for example, to the decline of the theatrical road show, they neglect to consider the quality of those shows. Toby and Susie shows have declined, as have the other second-rate road shows, but there are more good repertory theatres in America than there ever were before. As White indicates,[57] not only should we compare American mass media to Shakespeare's theatre, we should compare them to the bear-baiting entertainments which were popuar in the Elizabethan age.

In addition to the idealization of the past, another factor in the perception of a decline in the arts or of culture in America is that there is less diversity of culture today than there was in earlier years; there is less difference among groups. The media, working together with universal education, have contributed to the more rapid assimilation of these groups into the American culture. Even when a group maintains some semblance of its own culture, it has knowledge of and access to the general culture of the country and more quickly assimilates it with its own. Thus, the unique "folk cultures" once so common throughout the United States are more difficult to find now, or at least to recognize.

Though the mass media have not had a negative effect upon our culture (as a matter of fact quite the opposite), it is possible that they could have a more positive effect. The precise ways in which this could be accomplished within our present mass communication system needs to be studied. This may well be one of our most important media research needs at the present time.

---

[57] David Manning White, "Mass Culture in America; Another Point of View," in Bernard Rosenberg and David Manning, eds., *Mass Culture* (New York: The Free Press of Glencoe, 1957), p. 14.

MEDIA IMPACT ON SOCIAL STRUCTURE

I indicated earlier that the mass media took many of the kinds of information (art, styles, etc.) to which only the privileged classes had access previously and made them available to all. This revolution began in the sixteenth century with the perfection of printing. This media impact was limited by literacy, however, until the development of photography, the motion picture, and, especially, radio and television. As the speech, dress, and knowledge of the Colonel's Lady and Rosie O'Grady became virtually indistinguishable, class lines began to waver and disappear. As the mass media made information equally available to a wider and wider circle of the population, the base of power widened from the few to a larger and larger group. This shift in power was recognized early in the development of the media. The licenser of the Press in London noted it as early as 1680.

> A newspaper makes the multitude too familiar with the actions and councils of their superiors and gives them not only an itch but a kind of colorable right and license to be meddling with the government.[58]

As late as 1958, Lerner[59] found evidence that radio and the motion picture were changing leadership patterns in the Middle East. In the villages, the grocer with a radio or the bus driver who has seen movies brings news from the outside world. These innovators are listened to. They become the new opinion leaders. There is evidence from a study of broadcasting and politics in Great Britain[60] that radio and television are changing the power structure of the political parties in that island country. Though elections are completely local (constituency), the mass media (and especially the broadcasting media) are essentially national. In addition, the broadcasting media tend to personalize the political parties in the image of the party leaders. Thus, the national leaders are gaining in strength relative to the other members of Parliament. This has happened to such an extent that one finds speakers and newspaper editorials in Great Britain inveighing against the trend toward "Presidential-type" elections. This phenomenon in Great Britain is related to the previously mentioned relative gain in the power of the President over the power of the Congress in this country.

---

[58] Roger L'Estrange, Licenser of the Press, London, 1680. Quoted in unpublished paper by Harry Ashmore, n.d.

[59] Daniel Lerner, *The Passing of Traditional Society* (New York: The Free Press of Glencoe, 1958).

[60] Samuel L. Becker, "Broadcasting and Politics in Great Britain," *Quarterly Journal of Speech*, Vol. 53 (February, 1967), 34–43.

In the modern societies, with an ever-increasing level of technology, there is a great deal of mobility—both social and spatial. The mobility is both effect and cause of urbanization, the disintegration of family ties, and the questioning of traditional religious faiths. These faiths and family relationships and interpersonal relationships within the small community were the cement which held society together. The media have become, to a large extent, the new cement for the modern society. The process by which they do this societal cementing has been described by Lasswell:

> (1) The surveillance of the environment; (2) the correlation of the parts of society in responding to the environment; (3) the transmission of the social heritage from one generation to the next.[61]

So it is no accident that the mass media have developed first and fastest in those countries with the highest technology and, thus, the greatest capability and the greatest need for these forms of communication.

Probably the most provocative hypothesis concerning the impact of the mass media on social structure is one that has been advanced by Lerner.[62] It grew out of his study of the role of communication in the social changes of developing countries. His hypothesis is that the media provide the people of these countries with the capacity to conceive of situations and ways of life quite different from those which they have experienced. This is an important state for social change. Until men can conceive of something different from their existing situation, it is difficult for them to become sufficiently motivated to change. It should be noted also that, assuming the hypothesis is confirmed, it would indicate again the special importance of radio, television, and the motion picture as opposed to the print media in much of the world. The visual and aural media are able to leap the barrier of illiteracy and bring information and ideas to those to whom interpersonal communication was, until recently, their only medium to the world outside their immediate experience. Data gathered by Lerner and others indicate that this is, indeed, what is happening.

Considering the impact which the mass media have had upon us, and considering our failure to recognize this impact by appropriate

---

[61] Harold D. Lasswell, "The Structure and Function of Communication in Society," in Lyman Bryson, ed., *The Communication of Ideas* (New York: Cooper Square Publishers, 1964), p. 38.

[62] Daniel Lerner, "Comfort and Fun: Morality in a Nice Society," *The American Scholar*, XXVII (1958), 153–165.

additions to or adjustments in our school curricula, the following parable seems to be the most relevant conclusion to this chapter.

The story is told of an ancient tribe whose people lived a comfortable and unchanging existence. The children of the tribe were brought up in the traditions of their fathers and were taught how to fish in clear streams and how to hunt the sabre-toothed tiger. Then the snows came and the streams became muddy and the sabre-toothed tiger moved south. But the tribe preserved their traditional ways. They cleared a small part of the stream so that the children could continue to fish, and they stuffed a tiger's head so that they could learn to hunt. Then a radical young tribesman approached the council and asked why, instead, the children were not taught to fish in muddy streams and hunt the polar bear, which had recently begun to ravage the villages. But the council was angry. "We have always taught how to fish in clear streams and how to hunt the sabre-toothed tiger. These are the classical disciplines. Besides," they added, "the curriculum is overcrowded."[63]

---

[63] Stuart Hall and Paddy Whannel, *The Popular Arts* (New York: Pantheon Books, 1964), p. 1.

SECTION 2.

THE INTELLECTUAL
SYNTHESIS

A *Book*	*Liber,*
as to its outward shape,	quoad exteriorem form**am**
is either in *Folio*, 1.	est vel in *Folia*, 1.
or in *Quarto*, 2.	vel in *Quarto*, 2.
in *Octavo*, 3.	in *Octavo*, 3.
in *Duodecimo*, 4. either	in *Duodecimo*, 4.
made to open Side-wise, 5.	vel *Columnatus*, 5.
or *Long-wise*, 6.	vel *Linguatus*, 6.
with *Brazen Clasps*, 7.	cum *Æneis Clausuris*, 7.
or *Strings*, 8.	vel *Ligulis*, 8.
and *Square-boſses*, 9.	& *angularibus Bullis*, 9.

Within are *Leaves*, 10. with two *Pages*, sometimes divided with *Columns*, 11. and *Marginal Notes*, 12.

Intùs sunt *Folia*, 10. duabis *Paginis*, aliquando *Columnis*, 11. divisa cumq; *Notis Marginalibus*, 12.

Introduction

Communications, learning, instruction and other similar terms embrace many complex ideas. In Section 2 which follows, the authors have dealt with these matters in a thorough and comprehensive manner.

In the chapter on "Communication Theory" by Randall Harrison, the various fields and disciplines contributing to an understanding of communication (he includes among others psychology, sociology, anthropology, philosophy, political science, psychiatry, and even engineering) are identified. Harrison presents the major communication models along with appropriate discussion of the strengths and weakness of each of them. He also discusses communication from the standpoint of "message" and "receiver" systems; in this context, it would appear to be quite similar to "teaching" or "instruction."

Robert Gagné's considerable practical experience with newer instructional developments is evident in his chapter on "Learning and Communication." Gagné begins by pointing out that he does not consider the terms "communication" and "instruction" to be synonymous, but rather that he considers instruction to be the broader term. Gagné places heavy emphasis upon the necessity of identifying or categorizing learning outcomes. He suggests, for example, that there are at least seven categories of learning outcomes including S-R connections, discriminations, motor chains, verbal chains, concepts, principles, and strategies. He then suggests that an important part of the design for learning consists of the selection of appropriate stimuli or experiences, including media, in order to make possible the fulfillment of the learning objective. At the conclusion of his chapter, Gagné presents a series of steps to be followed in the development of effective learning situations.

A. W. Vandermeer, in his chapter on "Educational Philosophies and Communication," begins by suggesting that there is not a direct application from either philosophy or psychology to the making of instructional decisions, but that the relation is rather one of methods and processes to be followed. The reader, however, is stimulated to believe that most instructional decisions have direct philosophical antecedents. For example, if the philosophic position taken is that knowledge is fixed, then emphasis is placed upon the content, and the major function of instruction is to assemble this content in proper scope and sequence to be presented most effectively to the learner generally in groups. If, on the other hand, knowledge is considered important only in terms of its usefulness to an individual at a particular time and place, then the emphasis is placed on the learner as an individual, or as a member of a small group. Thus, current questions about "process," inquiry," "discovery," and "inductive reasoning" have answers which are basically philosophic.

In the final chapter in this section, Donald Stewart approaches the questions of communication, learning, and instruction from the vantage point of a systems engineer. He suggests that there is a difference between an industrial system which is a "man-machine system," and an educational system where the emphasis is upon a "learning system." He emphasizes the need to begin with clear specification of objectives in behavioral form, followed by certain systematic steps leading to the development of an instructional sequence. The schema which he suggests has many similarities to the proposals of Gagné. The prescriptions which Stewart makes are also similar to those which would be followed in the development of programed instruction materials.

Section II provides the reader with a number of views as to how learning takes place. It is evident that some of these views conflict, some are neutral, and some are supportive of others. The reader is urged to formulate his own models, drawing upon the theories and philosophies identified and described by the authors.

CHAPTER THREE

Communication Theory

Randall Harrison

Modern communication theory springs from a variety of intellectual fountains: psychology, sociology, anthropology, philosophy, political science, psychiatry, and even electrical engineering—as well as the professional communication areas such as speech, English, journalism, radio and television, and cinema. There is, in fact, no single communication theory, just as there is no single psychological theory. Rather, we find a flow of research and theorizing, bound by a concern with symbolic behavior.

As we examine the mainstream of communication research today, we can see clear traces of the intellectual tributaries that fed this growing interdisciplinary river; a turbulent new river, in constant ferment, with mixtures never before seen, with unexpected new findings bubbling to the surface.

SCIENTIFIC THEORIES

A scientific theory, in its purest form, is a distillation of the complex data of life into its crystal essence. The theory is a set of statements, including some lawlike generalizations. The statements must be deductively related. And some of the statements should be empirically testable. (61)

Unfortunately, in the social sciences today, we do not have many fully formalized, well-articulated scientific theories to gladden the heart of a rigorous philosopher of science. We do have some partially formalized theories and numerous probes which may eventually escalate into full-fledged scientific theories.

In communication, especially, we have been blessed (though some scholars say plagued) with a plethora of "models." In the philosophy of science, a model has a somewhat ambiguous standing. (13, 14, 19, 67) Some equate model with theory. Others see "model" as a broad umbrella, covering everything from visualized ignorance to tolerably well-formalized scientific theories.

COMMUNICATION MODELS

For the most part, today's popular communication models are first steps toward theory—initial cuts into a complex and dynamic process. The typical model pinpoints key elements—crucial variables that must be considered if we are to understand communication. The model always selects; it cannot consider all of the elements that might be encompassed. Further, a model abstracts; it moves up from the concrete until it finds an inclusive term like "source," which blankets the teacher, the actor, the reporter, etc.

Having sorted out the crucial components of the communication process, the model usually specifies organization; that is, how the elements are inter-related. Finally, particularly in the predictive models, we find propositions about the process itself. Beyond laying out the elements and their structure, the model explicates the dynamics; it details the operations. It predicts: If this variable changes from this state to that state, then that variable will change also.

Aristotle and Lasswell: Who Says . . . ?

Three centuries before the Christian era, Aristotle outlined a primitive communication model when he said that rhetoric had three major components: (a) the speaker, (b) the subject, and (c) the person addressed. He went on to specify that the third, the audience, was most important in shaping the message.

In this century, political scientist Harold Lasswell elaborated on Aristotle's sparse verbal model. To adequately describe a communication system, Lasswell concluded, one must ask:

Who

Says *What*

In which *Channel*

To *Whom*

With What *Effect?* (43)

This model provided the launch pad for Lasswell's probes into political communication, propaganda, and political symbolism—some of the pioneering communication research in social science.

Shannon and Weaver: Signals and Noise

Lasswell's work in the 1930's was followed by theorizing from quite another sector in the 1940's. Claude Shannon's wartime work culminated in "information theory," and Warren Weaver, writing in *The Mathematical Theory of Communication,* provided a visual model of Shannon's communication system. (65) (Fig. 3-1)

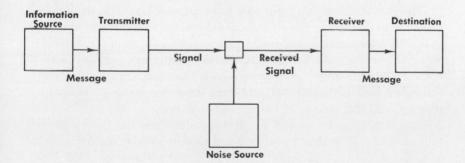

FIGURE 3-1.   *A General Communication System: The Shannon and Weaver Model* (Adapted from *The Mathematical Theory of Communication* by C. E. Shannon and W. Weaver, 1963. Copyright by University of Illinois Press.)

The Shannon-Weaver model comprises five key components: (1) an information source, which produces a message; (2) a transmitter, which transforms the message into a signal suitable for transmission; (3) a channel, which carries signals from transmitter to receiver; (4) the receiver, which reconstructs the signal into a message; and (5) the destination, the final consumer of the message.

The model introduces a final—and novel—component: the noise source. Shannon recognized that communication always takes place in the face of "noise," interference, and the natural tendency toward deterioration. A key problem for Shannon's theory was: How do you most efficiently overcome noise? How much redundancy is necessary so that the receiver can successfully reconstruct a message from signals decimated by noise?

Weaver saw three levels of communication problems: Level A, the technical problem; how accurately can the symbols of communication be transmitted? Level B, the semantic problem; how precisely do the transmitted symbols convey the desired meaning? Level C, the effectiveness problem; how effectively does the received meaning affect conduct in the desired way? For Weaver, Shannon's theory was clearly directed at Level A, with strong implications for Level B and C.

Others have humanized Shannon's admittedly mechanical model. The words "encoder" and "decoder" have replaced "transmitter" and "receiver." Boxes for "semantic noise" have been added to the box for "channel noise." But perhaps more important, the Shannon-Weaver visual model provided an impetus for the visual modeling of the 1950's and 1960's.

The guts of Shannon's theory are not captured, however, in Weaver's visual representation. The visual model isolates components and diagrams their organization. But the process of this system is detailed in Shannon's mathematical formulas. He demonstrated a unique way to measure "information," and armed with this measurement he sliced through a host of traditional problems involving coding, channel capacities, and the design of communication systems. While Shannon's original focus was on electrical telecommunication, the theory proved to have wide applicability and diffused rapidly into such diverse fields as biology, optics, sociology, psychology, and physiology. (16)

Hovland: Attitude and Communication

While Shannon was generating information theory, psychologist Carl Hovland was immersed in attitude research for the armed services. His findings propelled him into a large-scale postwar study of communication and persuasion. (33) To guide his research, Hovland adopted a classificatory model. (34) (Fig. 3-2) Laid next to the Shannon-Weaver model, the Hovland scheme highlights the proliferation of variables needed to predict effects in human communication.

Hovland was primarily interested in predicting attitude change, although for him this included opinion, perception, affect, and action change. He noted that in any communication situation, observable communication stimuli could be grouped into characteristics of the content, the communicator, the media, and the situation. He suggested that

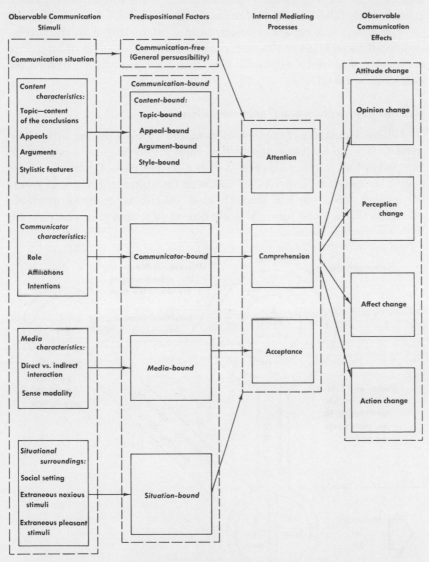

FIGURE 3-2.   *The Hovland Model of Communication and Attitude Change* (Adapted from *Personality and Persuasibility* by C. I. Hovland, 1959. Copyright by Yale University Press.)

individuals might differ in their predispositions toward communication stimuli. Some, for instance, might be influenced by communicator-bound factors while others might be affected more by media-bound factors. And among media characteristics, some might prefer visual stimuli while others might prefer aural cues.

The observable communication stimuli, interacting with the predispositional factors, lead to the internal mediating processes of attention, comprehension, and acceptance. These, in turn, lead to the observable communication effects.

Gerbner: Perception and Communication

Where Hovland's communication model focuses on the attitudinal output, George Gerbner designed a model which gives emphasis to the perceptual input. (23) (Fig. 3-3) Stated verbally, Gerbner's model says: (1) Someone (2) perceives an event (or statement) (3) and reacts (4) in a situation (5) and through some means (6) to make available materials (7) in some form (8) and context (9) conveying content (10) with some consequences.

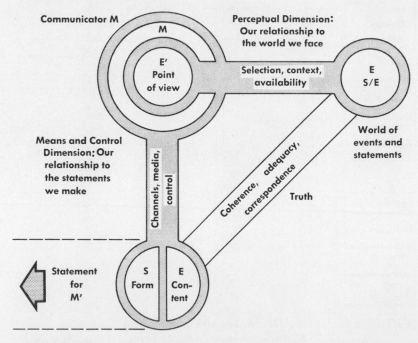

FIGURE 3-3.   *The Gerbner Interaction Model of Communication*

Central to the communication process, for Gerbner, is the message. This is the social act which makes possible inferences about events not directly observed. Gerbner is therefore interested first in the perceptual dimension—the communicator's viewpoint, his relationship to the world he sees. Next, he is interestd in the "means and control dimension"— the relationship between the communicator and the statements he makes. Finally, he is concerned with the correspondence between event and statement—the truth dimension. The statement, of course, becomes an event in the perceptual field of another communicator.

Berlo: S-M-C-R

One of the most widely used communication models is the S-M-C-R model, developed by David Berlo. It is simple and versatile, yet it subsumes an enormous background of behavioral science theory and research. S-M-C-R stand for the four key components—source, message, channel, receiver. (8) (Fig. 3-4)

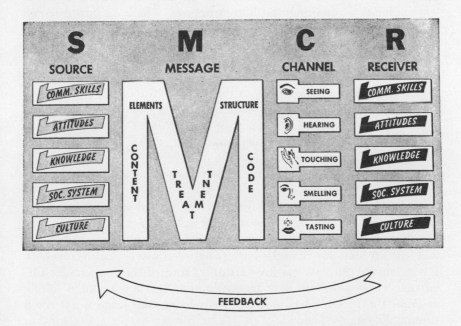

FIGURE 3-4. *Berlo's* S-M-C-R *Model of Communication* (From *The Process of Communication* by D. K. Berlo. Copyright © 1960 by Holt, Rinehart and Winston, Inc. Reprinted by permission of Holt, Rinehart and Winston, Inc.)

Source. To predict the source's effectiveness, we will want to know about (a) his communication skills, (b) his attitudes, (c) his knowledge, (d) his social and cultural context. First, is he literate? Does he have the skill to create pictures? to manipulate language? Next, what are his attitudes toward his receiver? toward his subject? toward himself? Third, what is his knowledge level? Does he know his subject matter? his receiver? himself? Finally, what are the roles and norms that shape his communication behavior? Does he speak as a member of a political group? a religious group? a professional group? Does he start from certain cultural assumptions, such as the American values of individualism and progress? Or does he come from a culture where progress is rare, where kinship is stronger than self?

Message. A message has content—the what's-it-about? And this content appears in some code—English or French, picture or word. The source selects contents and codes and weaves them into his treatment, his style, and his tone. Content, code, and treatment can be analyzed on various levels. At each level, elements can be isolated. These elements are organized into structures, which, in turn, become elements at the next highest level of analysis. The written English code has letters for elements; these elements combine into words. At the next highest level, these words become elements which, in turn, combine into sentences.

Channel. The message reaches the receiver through some channel. It may be "natural"; one of the sense modalities, seeing, hearing, touching, smelling, tasting. And it may be an "artificial" channel, such as television, radio, newspaper, telephone. One implication of the model is that more than one channel may be used at once. The selection and patterning of these channels may affect the total communication outcome.

Receiver. Like the source, the receiver has communication skills, attitudes, knowledge, and a social-cultural context. Each may contribute to his capacity as a receiver. In addition, for each category, we may wish to examine the relationship between source and receiver. If, for instance, both have positive attitudes toward the topic under discussion, communication may be facilitated. Or, if the source falsely assumes the receiver has common knowledge, the stage is set for a communication breakdown.

Feedback. In recent presentations of the model, Berlo includes the important concept—feedback. The source's message to the receiver typically elicits some behaviors, and some of these become available as messages which can be fed back to the source. On the basis of this information, the source may modify his successive messages. In a dynamic communication situation, of course, two individuals may shift rapidly back and forth between source and receiver roles. In fact, in conversation, an individual usually plays both roles at once, sending verbal messages through the air while receiving visual messages about the hearer's reactions.

Westley and MacLean: Mass Media

Bruce Westley and Malcolm MacLean, Jr. elaborated on the roles communicators can play. Their model is especially helpful in analyzing the complex media, where teams of communicators mold the message. (73) (Fig. 3-5) A four-stage model, the Westley-MacLean design grows out of an earlier model by Newcomb (53) in which Person *A* transmits something about an Object *X* to Person *B*.

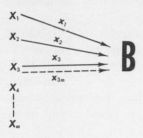

Stage I: Receiver *B* selects from objects of orientation.

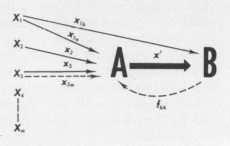

Stage II: Communicator *A* selects and abstracts for Receiver *B*.

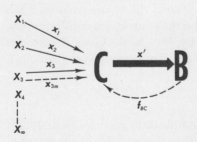

Stage III: Non-purposive Communicator *C* extends Receiver *B*'s environment.

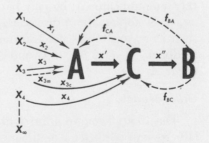

Stage IV: Receiver *B*, as in the classroom or mass media audience.

FIGURE 3-5. *The Westley-MacLean Model* (Adapted from "A Conceptual Model for Communications Research" by B. H. Westley and M. S. MacLean, *Journalism Quarterly*, Winter, 1957.)

Stage I. Westley and MacLean first show Receiver *B* selecting from the objects of orientation—labeled X_1 through X_{infinity}—in his sensory field. Not all objects are selected; for example, X_4. The selections are based, in part, on *B*'s needs and problems. The objects reach the receiver in abstracted form, represented by the small x's—x_1, x_2, x_3. And some or all may come via more than one sense; for example x_3 and x_{3m}.

Stage II. Westley and MacLean next introduce Communicator *A*, who selects and abstracts *X*'s, transmitting them as Message *X'* to Receiver *B*. Communicator *A* has an intent; he not only wishes to transmit *X*'s, he wants to structure the receiver's perceptions. He would like to influence *B*. The objects of orientation may or may not be in *B*'s direct sensory field. For example, information about X_1 is transmitted directly; i.e., x_{1b}, and indirectly, x_1, through *A*. Finally, Receiver *B* provides feedback, f_{BA}, to Communicator *A*. He may or may not intend to modify *A*'s behavior with this feedback.

Stage III. As an alternative type of communicator, Mr. *C* is introduced. Communicator *C* selects and abstracts objects of orientation which definitely are not in the normal sensory field of Receiver *B*. In the Westley-MacLean model, Communicator *C* is seen as "non-purposive." He extends Receiver *B*'s environment, but he does not intend to influence *B*. The selections *C* makes for Receiver *B* are based in part on the feedback, f_{BC}, from *B*.

Stage IV. In its final complex form, the model simulates the situation that might be found in the mass media or the classroom. Receiver *B* gets messages, x'', from Communicator *C*, a reporter or a teacher. *C* gets information from three sources: He has messages, x', from purposeful Communicator *A*; he may have additional direct information, such as x_{3c}, on topics Mr. *A* discusses; and he may incorporate information, such as x_4, on topics not transmitted by Mr. *A*. Receiver *B* provides feedback, f_{BC} and f_{BA}, to *C* and *A*. *C* similarly provides feedback, f_{CA}, to Mr. *A*.

Other Models

The 1950's brought a flurry of communication models. Bettinghaus (10) reviewed thirteen of them, including the sociologically oriented Riley and Riley model. (49) More recently, Miller (51) has discussed models, including Kelman's (40) model of opinion change, and a model emphasizing non-verbal communication.

In the 1960's, the era of general model building seemed to wane. Scholars turned attention to special problems within the communication process. Mathematical modeling became more important, and computer simulation began in earnest. Attempts were made, for instance, to simulate interpersonal communication, the diffusion of information through a population, an audience's choice of television programs, and legislators' communication before a vote.

Summarizing the implications of the general models reviewed so far: (a) The communication process is complex; (b) The modeler typically isolates key components, such as the source, message, channel, and receiver; (c) Depending on his interests, the modeler isolates the characteristics, or variables, important to each component—for example, the source's attitudes and knowledge; (d) The modeler may try to specify the possible states of each variable—e.g., high or low knowledge for the source, positive or negative attitudes for the receiver; (e) He moves finally toward stating relationships—e.g., high source knowledge leads to high receiver attitude.

In the next two sections, we will focus in on message systems and receiver systems, examining the theorists who have modeled these aspects of the communication process.

MESSAGE SYSTEMS

Message systems can be defined within or between; that is (a) within the system of components, such as code, content and treatment, which make up a message, or even among sets of messages, as in an audiovisual presentation; and (b) between the message and the source, or between the message and receiver, or between the message and the referents encoded.

Morris: Semiotic

An early attempt to logically organize the study of message systems can be found in Charles Morris' semiotic, the science of signs. (52) As formulated by Morris, semiotic has three domains: (a) syntactics, the study of sign-to-sign relationships; (b) semantics, covering sign-to-referent relationships; and (c) pragmatics, roughly sign-to-interpreter relationships. The relationship between a sign and its referent exists, of course, in the mind of interpreter. Thus, we really have three overlapping spheres: Pragmatics includes semantics and syntactics; semantics includes syntactics. (Fig. 3-6)

For Morris, each area of semiotic can be sub-classified as pure, descriptive, or applied. Pure semiotic develops a metalanguage to talk about signs, while descriptive semiotic analyzes actual signs, and ap-

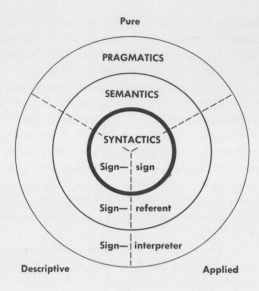

FIGURE 3-6. *Morris' Semiotic: Pragmatics, Semantics, Syntactics*

plied semiotic uses knowledge about signs to accomplish various purposes. Communication theorists have been interested in each area. They have tried to develop more precise vocabularies for talking about codes. They have been interested, for instance, in content analysis, with actual signs. And they have examined the effective use of signs for a variety of goals.

Codes: Patterned Stimuli

We will broach the subject of signs by first discussing codes and code systems. What is necessary for a code to exist? First, we need some stimulation which is above the sensory threshold of some receptor. Next, we need variation, or a pattern, in the stimulation. A constant noise provides no information. If we can turn it off and on, it has information-carrying potential. If we can vary its pitch, we may be on our way to music.

Finally, we need a set of agreements that certain variations in the patterned stimuli will refer to objects and events outside the code. We may decide that three dots and a dash will stand for the letter "V." Or, Secret Agent Triple-Naught may arrange a code: "When I draw the blind, you close in."

Miller (50) has noted that humans seem able to handle around seven elements at a time. When elements proliferate, we begin to "chunk," or re-code. A complex code system, like human language, is enormously complex and efficient. It handles tremendous amounts of information and operates at several levels at once. While language has received the most attention, we are coming to realize that man uses many code systems, frequently without ever consciously learning the code.

Code Systems

Each of the fundamental motor acts, such as uttering or scratching, can produce patterned stimuli, usable as a code system. Martin Krampen has organized a set of motor acts showing the code systems arising out of each act. (Fig. 3-7) Each has a basic code element, such as the phoneme, and these elements combine into structures, such as the morpheme, which become elements at the next highest level of analysis.

Linguistics, now more than a century old, is most advanced. Kinesics, now in its third decade, has made substantial gains, particularly through the research of Ray Birdwhistell. (11) An area like pictics is relatively new, and some of the code systems are virtually unexplored.

Fundamental motor act	Basic (differential) unit produced	Combined into	Studied by	Typical art or skill
uttering	phoneme	morpheme	linguistics	poetry
scratching	glyph	glytomorph	glyptics	writing
	pict	pictomorph	pictics	drawing
molding	plasm	plastomorph	plastics	sculpture
building	technem	technomorph	tectonics	architecture
moving	kine	kinemorph	kinesics	dance
sound	tone	melos	melodics	music
touch	hapton	haptomorph	haptics	fondling
produce smell	ozone	aroma	aromatics	perfumery
produce taste	edon	edomorph	edetics	cooking

FIGURE 3-7.   *Code Systems: Patterned Stimuli*

In addition to the ten suggested by Krampen, Edward Hall argues that time and space can be patterned into code systems. (29, 30) He calls the study of space "proxemics." Both can be organized into isolates, sets, and patterns, comparable to the phonemes, morphemes, and syntax of spoken language.

Krampen's analysis permits us to re-examine communication systems in terms of the codes used. (Fig. 3-8) For instance, the label "audio-visual communication" suggests a channel orientation. Of greater theoretic interest may be the variety of ways information can be encoded in A-V communication.

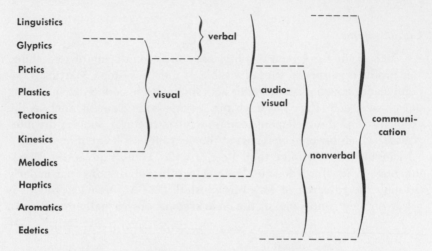

FIGURE 3-8.   *Communication Systems Based on Code Divisions*

Multiple Codes: Interband Congruence

Given multiple codes, or even one complex code, it becomes possible to create messages which are simultaneously redundant—or conflicting. Osgood and Sebeok (55) speak of communication "bands," such as the linguistic band, the kinesic band, and the situational-manipulational band. Between-band organization can provide information which agrees, disagrees, or is essentially independent.

Ruesch and Kees (62) discuss "meta-communication"—communication about communication. In other words, in each message there is information about some referent; there is also information about the message and how it should be interpreted. The source may encode cues which tell the receiver: "This is important." "Listen especially to this." "This is kidding; don't take it seriously." In multi-code communiques, of course, meta-communication may flow in a separate code.

Figure 3-9 illustrates the pairing of a simple linguistic morpheme—
"now"—with three different face pictomorphs. The faces lead us to reinterpret the "now." For Face I, it seems to be: "Now—Oh Boy!" For
Face II: "I mean do it *now!*" Face III is, itself, a complex message. It
contains the smile of Face I, a cue of happiness, plus the frowning
brows of Face II, a menacing cue of anger. Used simultaneously in one
face, the cues no longer seem simply happy or simply angry. (See also
Fig. 7-1.)

FIGURE 3-9.   *Interband   Organization: A   Linguistic   Morpheme plus a Face Pictomorph*

In the three illustrations, the between-band organiation is essentially complementary. Different information is provided by each code.
It is like a smiling face saying, "I'm thinking of Liz." Without the
smile, you wouldn't know how he feels about Liz. But without the
statement, you wouldn't know what is making him smile.

In addition to complementary organization, bands can be redundant. A smiling face says, "I'm happy." Or the bands can be in conflict,
providing different and countermanding information. A smiling face
says: "You rascal!" The various alternatives mean that a great deal of
uncertainty can be absorbed—or stimulated. Hence, the amount of information transmitted can vary greatly.

Codes and Capacity: Information Theory

In information theory, Shannon provided some major breakthrugs
on problems of coding and channel capacities. To get at least some
flavor of Shannon's thinking, we might note that for Shannon a "bit" of
information is that which reduces uncertainty by one-half.

In Fig. 3-10, we can see that choosing between two equally probable alternatives, I and II, involves one bit of information. Choosing between four equally probable alternatives—*A, B, C,* or *D*—involves two bits. Choosing between eight alternatives involves three steps, or three bits of information. Uncertainty increases as the number of alternatives increase. And uncertainty increases if alternatives are equally probable. (A 50-50 situation is more uncertain than a situation where the chances are 90-10.)

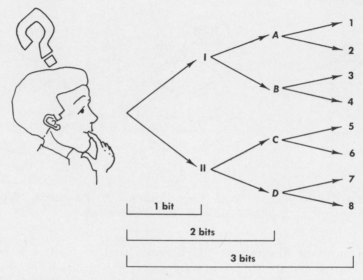

FIGURE 3-10.   *An Information "Bit" Reduces Uncertainty by One-Half*

Building on his definition of information, Shannon was able to calculate the capacity of communication channels, compute the information and relative redundancy within a message, and provide some surprising theorems about how best to encode information for a noisy channel. He noted, for instance, that as a code, written English is about 50 per cent redundant. You could knock out every other letter and, with enough patience, a receiver could reconstruct your message. Taylor (68), has used this idea to develop "cloze" procedure, a test for readability. He blanks out every fifth word and the receiver's ability to correctly replace the missing word is an index of reading ease.

Code-Referent: Iconicity

The relationship between a code element and its referent is usually arbitrary. We say "horse." The French say "cheval." Spaniards say "caballo." Each is equally adequate—as long as the users of the code agree. But for some codes, such as pictures, the relationship between element and referent is "natural" rather than arbitrary. This is known as the iconicity dimension.

Morris suggests that a sign be called iconic if it has some of the properties of the thing it represents. The power of the iconic sign, for Morris, lay in the receiver's ability to respond directly to the properties presented.

Ruesch and Kees (62) speak of iconicity in terms of analogic and digital codification. The analogic symbol is similar, in proportions or relations, to the idea, event, or thing encoded. Digital codes are meanwhile discrete and deal with arbitrary step intervals. They give numbers and the phonetic alphabets as prime examples. For them, the coding systems have sharply different potentials, especially in coding aspects of time and space.

The psychologist James Gibson (24) talks of iconicity in terms of "degrees of fidelity." The full fidelity "surrogate by projection" presents to the eye the same sheaves of light that the original would present. A "surrogate by convention" does not. It stands for something in the same way a license plate "stands for" the car it was assigned to.

Edgar Dale's "cone of experience" deals with the coding of information along an iconicity dimension. (17) Writers like A. Korzybski (42), Wendell Johnson (37), and S. I. Hayakawa (31) have similarly wrestled with the implications of coding objects and events into abstract symbols.

One point frequently overlooked in discussions of iconicity is that a code element can be like its referent in many different ways. Iconicity involves "leveling," the dropping of some cues, but it also involves "sharpening." Some cues are heightened and even distorted, as in a caricature.

Code-Receiver: Sign, Signal, Symbol

People receive a vast number of stimuli every day. We might say that man's environment "communicates" to him constantly. The sun "communicates" its warmth. The car "communicates" its noise, its odor. But usually we find it convenient to distinguish between those stimuli that speak for themselves, and those that have communication value; i.e., mean something beyond themselves.

Morris calls these communication stimuli "signs," and he distinguishes two kinds: signals and symbols. A signal stands for something else in the way smoke stands for fire. It is a stimulus which heralds some other event. Meanwhile, a symbol is more explicitly encoded, and stands in place of its referent. The word "fire," or a picture of a fire, stands in place of the actual flames.

Code Preference: Visualizers and Verbalizers

The British scholar, Berkeley, once became interested in the creative processes of great men. He asked some of his well-known peers how they visualized things; for instance, a year. To his amazement, he found that some of his friends thought him quite mad; they had none of the visualizing facility he had. He concluded that there must be "visualizers" and "verbalizers."

Continual anecdotal evidence supports Berkeley's notion, but this dimension of encoding and decoding remains somewhat cloudy. Yale psychologist Leonard Doob (20) spent much energy exploring the reported "photographic memories" of primitive African tribes. Enthused at first, Doob now feels this "eidetic" ability is a will-o-the-wisp which is to elusive for firm observation.

Earlier, Victor Lowenfeld (46) developed his theory of the "haptics" and the "optics." The former are touch-oriented, while the latter are visualizers. He operationalized the types in terms of the pictures they drew, and he suggested that they had different needs in art education.

Perhaps some of the firmest evidence on the issue comes from analyses of intelligence tests. Louis Guttman, for instance, has made a facet analysis of intelligence which indicates two major dimensions. The first is an inductive versus a deductive type of ability; in other words, the capacity to generalize to a rule from a set of examples, as opposed to being able to apply a rule.

The second dimension deals with the code used: verbal, numerical, or pictorial-geometric. Some individuals, of course, are adept with all three codes. Others may be high in one, but low in the remaining codes.

In another line of research, psychologist Jeffery Shapiro recently developed a test which appears to distinguish linguistically oriented individuals from non-linguistic types. The test was developed out of face pictomorphs, such as those illustrated in Fig. 3-9. The face is paired with a caption, and an individual's response indicates whether he is giving more weight to the words or to the picture.

While great individual differences probably exist, some writers have argued that a particular culture may shape verbalizers as opposed to visualizers or haptics. It's been argued, for instance, that the Puritan tradition was very word-oriented. Pictures were considered evil; there was a systematic attempt, in clothing and furnishings, to provide minimal sensory stimulation. In Catholic cultures, meanwhile, extensive sensory involvement existed through incense, stained glass, statuary, organ music, and so on. Starting from a somewhat different premise,

Marshall McLuhan makes a similar inference about the shaping of decoding processes.

The Medium as a Message: McLuhan

Marshall McLuhan (48) argues: "The medium is the message." At one level, this suggests that the content of the message is less important than the way in which it's received. McLuhan, a student of Harold A. Innis, takes a long historical view. Innis (35) used to take a crabby delight in pointing out that words often turned out to be less important than the materials they were written on. Papyrus, for instance, revolutionized the social control of ancient Egypt, putting the priests in command.

In modern time, McLuhan argues that radio permitted Adolf Hitler to take command. And, according to McLuhan, we understand all too little the implications of the electronic revolution going on around us. We have moved, he says, from the pre-Gutenberg period, to the point where man is again returning to a tribal village, this time on a world scale.

McLuhan sees technological development as an extension of man. A shovel extends man's arm. A bow-and-arrow extends his reach in another way. Clothing extends his skin. An auto extends his legs. Similarly, new communication technology extends man. The telephone extends his voice and hearing. Writing does the same; but it also extends his memory. With computers, McLuhan feels that we may be extending man's central nervous system, changing the way he can sense and think about his universe.

McLuhan suggests that the print media encourage man to think in a linear, segmented fashion, whereas the electronic media surround man in a mosaic. He further argues that some media, like movies, are "hot," while other media, like television, are "cool": A hot medium extends one sense in "high definition," which, he says, means being well filled with data. He even sees countries as being "hot" and "cold": The backward countries are cool; the developed countries are hot. In McLuhan's writings, the theme "classroom without walls" reappears as he argues that this generation needs to study the "grammar of its media" as well its content. (15)

RECEIVER SYSTEMS

Receiver systems, like message systems, can be defined within or between: (a) the psychological, symbolic processes within a receiver; and (b) the sociological, interaction processes among sets of receivers.

Perception: Structure and Function

Perception is an enormously complex human process. And it is an important process to anyone interested in multiple-channel communication as is noted in Chapters 6 and 9. Fortunately, an increasing number of good books are appearing on the subject. (2, 6, 12, 25, 71, 72) We will point here to merely two sets of factors which have dichotomized perceptual phenomena: structural and functional factors.

The structure of the stimuli and the perceptual equipment of the receiver lead to certain impressions. Some stimuli are perceived as figure, distinct from surrounding ground. This, of course, suggests patterned stimuli, the basic requirement for a code. The Gestaltists in particular have pointed to those characteristics of the stimuli (proximity, common movement, closure) which lead to the perception of a coherent form.

Meanwhile, social psychologists have been interested in the impact of emotions, moods, needs, and desires on perceptual processes. A hungry man sees food in an ambiguous stimulus. A valued object, like a coin, is judged larger than it is. So is a threatening object. These and other findings have led psychologists to the conclusion that the internal states of the individual play a surprisingly important role in what and how the receiver will perceive.

Arousal: Berlyne

A stimulus, once past the perceptual threshold, speeds through the central nervous system to the cortex of the brain for interpretation. On its way, however, it feeds information to the reticular arousal system, a column of nerve cells in the lower brain. This system, it now appears, plays a crucial role in activating the individual, in attention, in alertness. It may, in fact, be the heart of all emotions; what are usually called emotional states may be periods of high arousal overlain with cognitions which are pleasant, fearful, sad, and so on.

Berlyne (9) relates the arousal system to attention, which, in turn, can be related to learning. Of interest to the communicator, Berlyne has spelled out some of the stimulus conditions which lead to arousal. He notes first that moderate rates of arousal may be most efficient. With extreme arousal, the individual goes into shock; with too little arousal, he becomes inattentive. Berlyne sees the following as determinants of attention: (a) high-intensity stimuli; (b) color; (c) indicating stimuli—a pointing finger, a verbal, "Now hear this!"; (d) novelty; (e) surprisingness; (f) complexity, uncertainty, and incongruity; (g) conflict. The last four categories are especially important in arousal.

Novelty, for instance, depends not only on the unusualness of the stimulus, but also on how long it has been since a similar stimulus was received. In general, the opportunity for novelty, surprisingness, complexity, and conflict would seem to multiply with multiple codes and multi-bands.

Meaning: Early Views

The symbolic process is at the heart of man's ability to communicate, and communication theorists have been vitally concerned with the problem of meaning. Under what conditions, and why, should some pattern of stimulation come to "mean" some other pattern of stimulation?

The early mentalistic view, as represented by Ogden and Richards (54), said simply that something becomes a sign of some referent if it gives rise to the idea or thought of that referent. Behavioral psychologists, of course, wanted to know why this was. In the tradition of Pavlovian conditioning, the substitution view was suggested: A sign, through conditioning, comes to elicit the same reactions in the individual as the real referent would. Obviously, however, the sign does not elicit all of the same reactions. The word "fire" does not evoke the same responses as the actual flames.

This led to the dispositional view, articulated by Charles Morris. (52) In essence, this view says: A pattern of stimulation becomes a sign if it produces in the individual a "disposition" to make any of the responses previously elicited by the actual referent. Psychologists like Charles Osgood (56) have since tried to boil the ambiguity out of the term "disposition."

Osgood: Representational-Dispositional

As an explanation of the meaning process, Osgood has suggested the representational mediation hypothesis. Wired-in reflexes, such as the knee-jerk response to a tap on the patella, lock reactions unfailingly to certain stimuli. In symbolic behavior, however, a stimulus sets off a pattern of small, internal responses, which, through learning, become the internal stimuli for other, perhaps overt, responses. The response chain can in effect be unlinked if other internal stimuli impinge.

Osgood's representational-dispositional model (Fig. 3-11) shows three levels of meaning, or response. Let's begin with 1. This is the perceptual phase. At the message level, a set of signs, $[s]$, has been presented to the individual. At the sensory- and motor-skill level, S indicates the stimulus as perceived by the person. It may not be identi-

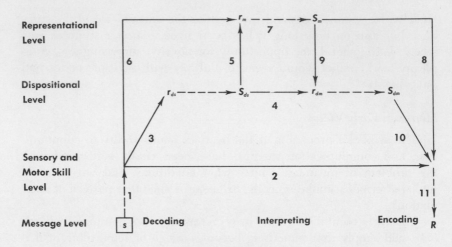

FIGURE 3-11. *Osgood's Representational-Dispositional Model* (Adapted from *The Process and Effects of Mass Communication* by Wilbur Schramm, 1954. Copyright by University of Illinois Press.)

cal with the message sign, but S, as perceived will now determine further responses.

For some stimuli, we have automatic, habitual responses which take virtually no thinking. In fact, in some tasks, like tying shoe laces, thinking about it may interfere with a chain of behavior. In the model, 2 represents this direct, habitual link at the sensory-motor level.

At the highest level, the stimulus may move, through 6, to the representational plane where it elicits a small internal response, r_m. This response, in turn, moves through 7 to initiate an internal, mediational stimulus, S_m, which triggers through 8 a response, r. This response may lead to an overt response, R, through 11. An example would be a message encoded in response to the original message.

Between the representational level and the sensory-motor level is what Osgood calls the dispositional level. This is the level of learned integrations: attitudes, values, sets, expectations. In many instances, a stimulus sets off a chain of responses at the dispositional level, such as 3 through 4 through 10. The first line of a familiar poem leads us almost automatically to say the second line.

We may, however, monitor the meaning of that line of poetry, seeing new representations that we did not see before. In this case, stimulation passes through 5, through 7, and perhaps back down through 9. Let us apply the model to a simple example.

If s is the first word in a written sentence, the response at the sensory-motor level may be to move the eyes horizontally to the right to pick up the next word. If the first word is "Red . . ." this may be interpreted on the representational level as a color, a certain known hue, a range in the light spectrum. At the dispositional level, the word "Red . . ." may create the expectation that the next words will be "white and blue." In addition, red may have some associations, such as warm, vibrant, dramatic.

From the Osgood model, we can see that the receiver may be responding at several levels simultaneously. With complex messages, particularly with several codes and multiple sensory channels, the response process can become extremely complex. In certain learning tasks, of course, we may be trying to teach the receiver to respond to a complex set of stimuli simultaneously and on several levels.

Meanings: Denotative, Connotative, Structural

The major varieties of meaning have been classified: denotative, connotative, and structural. Words (or for that matter, pictures) denote objects, events, and conditions. The word "mother" points to a woman who has a specific kinship relationship to another human; the word can be used to denote a particular person. But "mother" also has strong connotative associations. People are likely to feel it's a strong, active, positive word.

Finally, we know that the word "mother" is a certain type of word. It is used in a certain way in sentences. We know that with "mother" we use "is" and not "are." Words, in short, have structural significance; they play roles in the larger organization. Some words, of course, are strongly denotative. *Chair, ball, house* would be examples. Other terms —such as *beauty, democracy, dishonor*—tend to be strongly connotative. And many words—*but, of, from*—are largely structural.

What has been said of the verbal code applies also, of course, to the pictorial code. A caricature can denote a politician. It can also stimulate connotations; the politician can be made to look like a hero or a bum. Pictures, too, have structural rules—within a single picture, and between pictures, as in a comic strip or a motion picture. The pictorial element which is large and overlapping other elements is seen in the foreground. The film shot that dissolves is seen as being in a different time or place than the succeeding shot.

Semantic Space

In one of the most extensive empirical studies of meaning ever made, Osgood and his associates found three main dimensions of what they called "semantic space": the evaluative, potency, and activity factors. Figure 3-12 illustrates these three dimensions. The evaluative dimension is defined by polar adjectives such as "good" and "bad." Potency is defined by such scales as strong-weak and hard-soft. The activity dimension is anchored by scales like active-passive and excitable-calm.

To measure meaning, Osgood uses the "semantic differential." With this instrument, an individual can indicate his meaning for any concept. In Fig. 3-12, we have the concepts "mother" and "coward" repre-

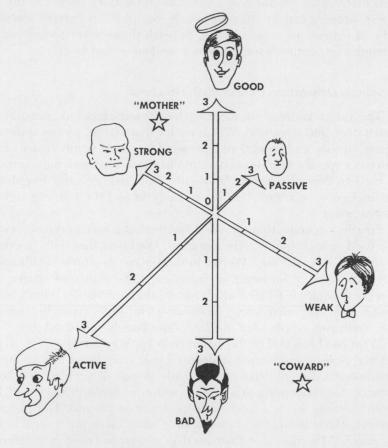

FIGURE 3-12. *Semantic Space: Evaluative, Potency, and Activity Dimensions of Meaning*

sented in semantic space. "Mother" is seen as good, strong, and active. "Coward" is seen as bad, weak, and passive.

Using the semantic differential and the concept of semantic space, Osgood and his associates have also developed the "principle of congruity." Given an individual's meaning for two concepts, Osgood can predict what meaning will arise when the concepts are paired. This has been especially useful where the concepts are a communicator and his subject. Osgood can predict the impact, on both the source and his topic, when a positive source makes a favorable statement about a negative subject, or vice versa.

Cognitive Systems: Equilibrium

Osgood's principle of congruity parallels the thinking of other theorists; in a cognitive system there will be a strain toward equilibrium or consistency. (57) Newcomb observed this equilibrium phenomenon in his A-B-X model. If Source A is liked by Receiver B and Source A makes favorable comments about some object X, Receiver B is under pressure to think favorable of X. (53) Fritz Heider (32) and Leon Festinger (22) elaborated their own consistency theories.

Festinger called his a "theory of cognitive dissonance." He noted that any decision is likely to cause dissonance; a choice of one alternative means giving up the advantages of the other alternative. He predicted that in a dissonant condition, an individual might increase his information-seeking. Festinger found, for instance, that new car buyers may increase reading ads for their own brand of car—*after* buying.

Milton Rokeach (59) explored "belief congruence" within his theory of the open and closed mind. He theorized that an individual's belief system might be visualized as three concentric circles. (Fig. 3-13) The inner circle of primitive beliefs include the individual's unquestioned beliefs about himself and his universe; for instance, what his name is. Authority beliefs specify the authority figures the individual follows, and peripheral beliefs include all the other beliefs held by the individual.

Of interest to the communicator, Rokeach suggested that some belief systems are "closed" and some are "open." The closed system places strong reliance on authority; may have low tolerance for dissonance; does not discriminate well among disbelief systems (beliefs other than its own) and; finally, may practice "isolation," holding conflicting beliefs apart so they are never examined together. In communication, the closed individual may have trouble discriminating

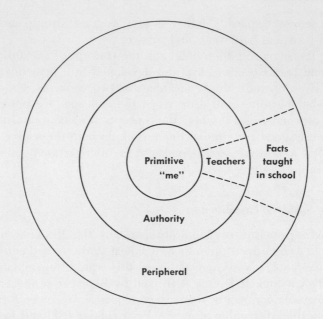

FIGURE 3-13. *Rokeach: Belief Systems and the Open and Closed Mind*

meta-communication from content; information about the source will strongly influence response to the message.

Mapping the Receiver's System

Rokeach developed a scale to index one aspect of a receiver's cognitive system. Osgood's semantic differential provides another way to map a receiver's system and changes in that system over time. Other psychologists, like George Kelly (39), have innovated additional ways to map what Kelly called an individual's "personal construct system." A continuing theoretic problem, however, is the process of mapping the receiver's symbolic system and measuring changes that occur during communication.

Linking Receivers: External Systems

The S-M-C-R model points to the social-cultural context, and a broad array of research underscores its importance. We might ask first if it makes any difference how communicators are linked together. In a series of experiments, Bavelas (7), Leavitt (44), and others (28) or-

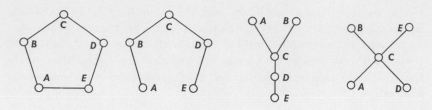

FIGURE 3-14.   *Communication Nets: The Circle, Chain, Y, and Wheel*

ganized communicators into various patterns, such as the circle, the chain, the Y, and the wheel. (Fig. 3-14)

In the circle, communicator *A* could only pass messages to *B* and *E*. *B* could communicate with *A* and *C*, and so on around the circle. In the wheel, *C* held the central spot and could communicate with everyone else; they, however, could only communicate with *C*. The various nets were then given simple problems to solve.

The different linkages affected accuracy, total activity, the emergence of a leader, and the satisfaction of group members. In general, the circle and the wheel were most different, with the chain and the Y falling between. The circle tended to be active, leaderless, unorganized, often inaccurate, and yet was enjoyed most by its members. In the wheel, *C* tended to emerge as leader and he enjoyed his role, but other members were distinctly less satisfied. The wheel tended to be stable, well organized, less active, and less erratic than the other networks.

Social Dimensions: Roles

A man in his role of employer may talk one way to an employee. The same man, in his role as father, may talk in quite a different way to his son; he may even use different language. Communication theorists have long been intrigued with the various roles that can be played in the communication process, such as the "gate-keeper" role (45), or the "opinion-leader" role (38). Other theorists have elaborated role theory (60, 63), and have examined the consequences of "role conflict" and "role communication." (27)

In small-group research, Robert Bales (5) suggested that distinct communication roles may emerge. He hypothesized that as a group works on a problem, a task leader is likely to emerge: an individual who actively asks questions, clarifies objectives, and gives answers. But as a group moves toward task-solution, internal frictions are likely to arise.

Unless socio-emotional needs are met, the group may fly apart. So another role emerges: the socio-emotional leader who gives praise, releases tension, and soothes ruffled feathers. Sometimes one individual plays both roles, but in the family, for instance, the father often plays the task-leadership role, while the mother assumes socio-emotional leadership.

Social Dimensions: Norms

If a group is asked to judge an ambiguous stimulus, norms will develop that are quite firm—though they may be totally inaccurate. (66) These norms, once rolling, exert enormous pressure on group members. (4) If, for instance, a naïve member hears everyone in the group report an incorrect observation, he is under tremendous pressure to deny his own senses and report what everyone else did.

If a group member deviates from group norms, communication to that member will typically increase. (21) Finally, however, communication to the deviant will be cut off. In effect, he's ejected from the group. When a group is under attack, of course, norms become more rigid and members have less freedom to deviate.

Norms may vary in the amount of deviation allowed, and in the sanctions levied. Jay Jackson (36), for instance, used the classroom as an example. (Fig. 3-15) The group, probably led by the teacher, can express approval, illustrated by the scale from +3 to −3. The norm could concern any classroom behavior, but Jackson used as an example the number of times a student is expected to communicate during a class period.

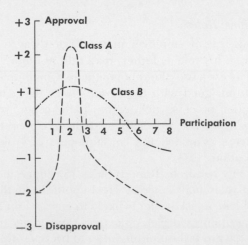

FIGURE 3-15. *Jackson: A Diagram of Classroom Norms*

In Class *A*, each student is expected to participate twice and he meets with high approval if he does. If, however, he participates less than twice, or more than twice, he meets with rather sharp disapproval. In Class *B*, meanwhile, the range of permitted behavior is broader, and the approval or disapproval is not as extreme.

Diffusion Through a System

We can observe the diffusion of a message, a new idea, or an innovation through a population, and learn much about the communication process. Rumor studies, for instance, focus on what happens to a message as it passes from communicator to communicator. (58) Typically, the message is subjected to a process of leveling, sharpening, and assimilation. Some elements drop out. This gives the remaining elements increased importance, and frequently they are elaborated even further. In addition, the message may be assimilated to the beliefs, attitudes, and expectations of the communicators. The message becomes systematically distorted until it "makes sense."

Mass media theorists have long been concerned with the diffusion that takes place between media and mass audiences. At first, a widely held assumption favored a "one-step" flow; the media were presumed to have a direct and uniform effect on the public. (18) Later research indicated that individuals varied widely in their response to the media. Their exposure patterns, their reference groups, their individual beliefs and experiences substantially modified the impact of the media.

A "two-step flow" seemed a better hypothesis. The mass media fed key opinion-leaders, who in turn informed their followers. (41) This hypothesis was sounder than the concept of a one-step flow, but recent research indicates that this hypothesis, too, is an oversimplification. (70) Depending on the topic, and depending on a variety of receiver characteristics, the mass media are used in a complex variety of ways. (26)

Everett Rogers (58) hypothesized that in the adoption of an innovation, mass media may be particularly important at the early, "awareness" stage. At the later evaluation and trial stages, interpersonal communication may be more significant. Rogers categorized receivers into innovators, early adopters, early majority, late majority, and laggards. The characteristics and the interaction patterns of each category have been studied across a broad range of innovations, and across several cultures.

SYNTHESIS

Figure 3-16 attempts to sort out and integrate some of the ideas that we have examined thus far.

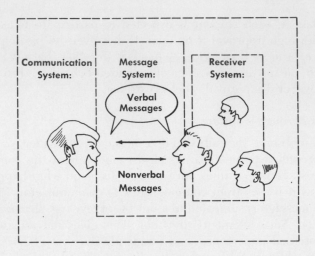

FIGURE 3-16. *The Communication Systems: A Partial Model*

As with any system, we may wish to raise questions about the viability and success of the system itself. Does it, for instance, have cohesion? Have the communicators developed, or maintained, positive attitudes toward each other? Are there other constraints or rewards which will keep them interacting? (69) Is the system stable? or is it likely to be reorganized? Is the system productive? Is it effective? If this is a teaching situation and the decoder's recall is the most important output, is that the variable that is indeed changing? How efficient is the system? Is the decoder's recall changing with a minimum expenditure of the encoder's resources and energy?

Decoder outputs include immediate message responses: attention, comprehension, acceptance, recall, and use. Outputs also include longer-range changes in skills, beliefs, and so on. The decoder responses may give rise to feedback which can be picked up by the encoder. This helps him to shape further messages.

Some of the factors which impinge upon the decoder's reception and interpretation of the message include perceptual factors, arousal, levels of meaning, attitudes, beliefs, and finally, interacting with these, roles and norms. A similar set of factors pattern the communication behavior of the encoder as well.

Many facets of the communication process have been omitted in this discussion. We have skimmed lightly over problems that are significant for the theorist and the practicing communicator. We have, however, reviewed some of the major currents of contemporary theory and perhaps, pointed a few routes for further exploration.

REFERENCES

1. Ackoff, R. L. "Towards a Behavioral Theory of Communication," *Management Sciences*, 1958, 4, (3), 218–234.

2. Allport, F. H. *Theories of Perception and the Concept of Structure*. New York: Wiley, 1955.

3. Allport, G. W. and L. J. Postman. "The Basic Psychology of Rumor," in E. E. Maccoby, T. M. Newcomb, and E. L. Hartley, eds., *Readings in Social Psychology*. Holt, New York: 1947, pp. 54–65.

4. Asch, S. E., "Effects of Group Pressure upon the Modification and Distortion of Judgments," in E. E. Maccoby, T. M. Newcomb, and E. L. Hartley, eds., *Readings in Social Psychology*. New York: Holt, 1947, pp. 174–183.

5. Bales, R. F. "Task Roles and Social Roles in Problem-Solving Groups," E. E. Maccoby, T. M. Newcomb, and E. L. Hartley, eds., *Readings in Social Psychology*. New York: Holt, 1947, pp. 437–447.

6. Bartley, S. H. *Principles of Perception*. New York: Harper, 1958.

7. Bavelas, A. "A Mathematical Model for Group Structures," in A. G. Smith, ed., *Communication and Culture*. New York: Holt, Rinehart & Winston, 1966, pp. 216–222.

8. Berlo, D. K. *The Process of Communication*. New York: Holt, Rinehart, & Winston, 1960

9. Berlyne, D. E. *Conflict, Arousal and Curiosity*. New York: McGraw-Hill, 1960.

10. Bettinghaus, L. P. "Communication Models," in *Research, Principles, and Practices in Visual Communication*. Washington, D.C.: National Education Association, 1960, pp. 16–28.

11. Birdwhistell, Ray L. "Background to Kinesics," *Etc.*, 1955, 13, 10–18.

12. Broadbent, D. E. *Perception and Communication*. New York: Pergamon. 1958.

13. Broadbeck, May. "Models, Meaning, and Theories," in L. Gross, ed., *Symposium on Sociological Theory*. Evanston: Row, Peterson, 1959. pp. 373–403.

14. Bross, I. D. J. "Models," in J. H. Campbell and H. W. Hepler, eds., *Dimensions in Communication*. Belmont, Calif.: Wadsworth, 1965, pp. 10–26.

15. Carpenter, E. and M. McLuhan, eds. *Explorations in Communication*. Boston: Beacon Press, 1960.

16. Dahling, R. L. "Shannon's Information Theory: The Spread of an Idea," in *Studies of Innovation and of Communication to the Public*. Stanford University Press, 1962, pp. 119–139.

17. Dale, E. *Audio Visual Methods in Teaching*. New York: The Dryden Press, 1954.

18. DeFleur, M. L. *Theories of Mass Communication*. New York: David McKay Co., 1966.

19. Deutsch, K. W. "On Communication Models in the Social Sciences," *Public Opinion Quarterly*, Vol. 16, 1952, 361.

20. Doob, Leonard W. "Exploring Eidetic Imagery Among the Kamba of Central Kenya," *Journal of Social Psychology*, 1955, 67, 3–22.

21. Festinger, L., *et al. Social Pressure in Informal Groups*. New York: Harper, 1950.

22. Festinger, L. *A Theory of Cognitive Dissonance*. Evanston: Row, Peterson, 1957.

23. Gerbner, G. "The Interaction Model: Perception and Communication," in *Research, Principles, and Practices in Visual Communication*. Washington, D.C.: National Education Association, 1960, pp. 4–15.

24. Gibson, James J. "A Theory of Pictorial Perception," *Audio-Visual Communication Review*, 1954, 2, 3–23.

25. _____. *The Perception of the Visual World*. Boston: Houghton Mifflin, 1950.

26. Greenberg, B. S. and E. B. Parker, eds. *The Kennedy Assassination and the American Public*. Stanford University Press, 1965.

27. Gross, N., W. S. Mason, and A. W. McEachern. *Explorations in Role Analysis: Studies of the School Superintendency Role*. New York: Wiley, 1958.

28. Guetzkow, H. and H. A. Simon. "The Impact of Certain Communication Nets upon Organization and Performance in Task Oriented Groups," in A. G. Smith, ed., *Communication and Culture*. New York: Holt, Rinehart & Winston, 1966, pp. 244–253.

29. Hall, Edward T. *The Hidden Dimension*. Garden City, New York: Doubleday, 1966.

30. _____. *The Silent Language*. Garden City, New York: Doubleday, 1959. (New York: Premier, 1961.)

31. Hayakawa, S. I. *Language in Thought and Action*. New York: Harcourt, Brace & World, 1949.

32. Heider, F. *The Psychology of Interpersonal Relations*. New York: Wiley, 1958.

33. Hovland, C. I., I. L. Janis, and H. H. Kelley. *Communication and Persuasion: Psychological Studies of Opinion Change*. New Haven: Yale University Press, 1953.

34. Hovland, C. I. *Personality and Persuasibility*. New Haven, Yale University Press, 1959.

35. Innis, H. *The Bias of Communication*. Toronto University Press, 1951.

36. Jackson, J. "Structural Characteristics of Norms," *The Dynamics of Instructional Groups*, 59th Yearbook of the National Society for the Study of Education, Part II. University of Chicago Press, 1960, pp. 136–163.

37. Johnson, W. *People in Quandries*. New York: Harper, 1946.

38. Katz, E. and P. F. Lazarfeld. *Personal Influence*. Glencoe, Ill., The Free Press, 1956.

39. Kelly, G. *The Psychology of Personal Constructs*. New York: W. W. Norton, 1955.

40. Kelman, H. C. "Processes of Opinion Change," *Public Opinion Quarterly*, XXV (Spring, 1961), 67.

41. Klapper, J. *The Effects of Mass Communication*. Glencoe, Ill.: The Free Press, 1960.

42. Korzybski, A. *Science and Sanity: An Introduction to non-Aristotelian Systems and General Semantics*. Science Press, 1941.

43. Lasswell, H. D. "The Structure and Function of Communication in Society," in L. Bryson, ed., *The Communication of Ideas*. Institute for Religious and Social Studies, 1948, p. 37.

44. Leavitt, H. J. "Some Effects of Certain Communication Patterns on Group Performance," in A. G. Smith, ed., *Communication and Culture*. New York: Holt, Rinehart & Winston, 1966, pp. 222–243.

45. Lewin, K., "Group Decision and Social Change," in E. E. Maccoby, T. M. Newcomb, and E. L. Hartley, eds., *Readings in Social Psychology*. New York: Holt, Rinehart & Winston, 1958, pp. 197–211.

46. Lowenfeld, Viktor. *Creative and Mental Growth*. New York: Macmillan, 1952.

47. Martin, M. W., Jr. "The Measurement of Value of Scientific Information," in B. V. Dean, ed., *Operations Research in Research and Development*. New York: Wiley, 1963, pp. 97–123.

48. McLuhan, M. *Understanding Media*. New York: McGraw-Hill, 1966.

49. Merton, R. K., L. Broom, and L. S. Cottrell. *Sociology Today*. New York: Basic Books, 1959.

50. Miller, G. A. "The Magical Number Seven, Plus or Minus Two: Some Limits on Our Capacity for Processing Information," *Psychological Review*, 1956, 63, 81–97.

51. Miller, G. R. *Speech Communication: a Behavioral Approach*, New York: Bobbs-Merrill, 1966.

52. Morris, Charles. *Signs, Language and Behavior*. Englewood Cliffs, N.J.: Prentice-Hall, 1946.

53. Newcomb, T. M. "An Approach to the Study of Communicative Acts," *Psychology Review*. 1953, 60, 393–404.

54. Ogden, C. K. and I. A. Richards. *The Meaning of Meaning*. New York: Harcourt, Brace & World, 1956.

55. Osgood, C. E. and T. A. Sebeok. *Psycholinguistics*. Bloomington: Indiana University Press, 1965.

56. Osgood, Charles, George J. Suci, and Percy Tannenbaum. *The Measurement of Meaning*. Urbana: University of Illinois Press, 1957.

57. Preston, I. "Inconsistency: a Persuasive Device," in J. H. Campbell and H. W. Hepler, eds., *Dimensions in Communication*. Belmont, Calif.: Wadsworth, 1965, pp. 95–102.

58. Rogers, E. M. *Diffusion of Innovations*. New York: Free Press, 1962.

59. Rokeach, M. *The Open and Closed Mind*. New York: Basic Books, 1960.

60. Rommetviet, R. *Social Norms and Roles*. Minneapolis: University of Minnesota Press, 1955.

61. Rudner, R. S. *Philosophy of Social Science*. Englewood Cliffs, N.J.: Prentice-Hall, 1966.

62. Ruesch, Jurgen and Weldon Kees. *Nonverbal Communication: Notes on Visual Perception of Human Relations*. Berkeley: University of California Press, 1956.

63. Surbin, T. R. "Role Theory," in G. Lindzey, ed., *Handbook of Social Psychology*, Vol. I. Reading, Mass.: Addison Wesley, 1954, pp. 223–258.

64. Schramm, W. *The Process and Effects of Mass Communication*, Urbana: University of Illinois Press, 1954.

65. Shannon, C. E. and W. Weaver. *The Mathematical Theory of Communication*, Urbana: University of Illinois Press, 1963.

66. Sherif, M. "Group Influence upon the Formation of Norms and Attitudes," in E. E. Maccoby, T. M. Newcomb, and E. L. Hartley, eds., *Readings in Social Psychology*. New York: Holt, 1947, pp. 219–232.

67. Simon, H. A. and A. Newell. "Models: Their Uses and Limitations," in E. P. Hollander and R. G. Hunt, eds., *Current Perspectives in Social Psychology*. New York: Oxford University Press, 1963, pp. 79–90.

68. Taylor, W. L. "Close Procedure: A New Tool for Measuring Readibility," *Journalism Quarterly*, 1953, 30, 415–433.

69. Thibaut, J. W. and H. H. Kelley. *The Social Psychology of Groups*. New York: Wiley, 1959.

70. Troldahl, V. C. "A Field Test of a Modified 'Two-step Flow of Communication' Model," *Public Opinion Quarterly*, 1967, 30, 609–623.

71. Vernon, M. D. *Experiments in Visual Perception*, Baltimore: Penguin Books, 1966.

72. Weintraub, D. J. and E. L. Walker, *Perception*. Belmont, Calif.: Wadsworth, 1966.

73. Westley, B. H. and M. S. MacLean. "A Conceptual Model for Communications Research," *Journalism Quarterly*, 1957, pp. 31–38.

CHAPTER FOUR

Learning and Communication

Robert M. Gagné

Education may be looked upon in a total sense as a process of imparting new and increasingly complex capabilities to the student. In this
sense, education is itself a process of communication, which can be
analyzed into a number of subordinate functions to be carried out by
designers of instructional materials and equipment, teachers, and others.
When viewed in this way, it is evident that there are several important
channels of communication that are in need of study and improvement.
For example, some years ago a panel of psychologists (National Research Council, Advisory Board on Education, 1958) identified the following channels as important to the educational process, and deserving
of increased research efforts: (1) the channel from curriculum-maker to
pupil; (2) the channel from psychologist to educator; (3) the channel

from educator to adult public; and (4) the channel from counselor to counselee.

The varieties of communication that enter into the process of education, globally conceived, continue to be of fundamental importance to any more narrowly defined component of the educational system. Recent developments, for example, have seen a heavy concentration of effort on curriculum, in mathematics, science, social studies, English, and many other areas. It is apparent that consideration of the outcomes of these efforts, and their effects on the total sysem, raises questions about educational objectives which properly involve the channel of communication between educators and the adult public. The design of curricula represents only one channel of communication, but the objectives which are sought inevitably interact with other channels when the system of education is viewed as a totality (cf. Gagné, 1965a).

It will be useful to bear in mind these interacting components of the total educational system, as attention is focused in this chapter on those varieties of communication that are involved in the specific function of *instruction*.

COMMUNICATION AND ITS ROLE IN INSTRUCTION

The typical model of school instruction appears to embody communication as an obvious and prominent component. This is the model in which a teacher stands at the front of a room containing thirty students and conducts various kinds of verbal communication with them. The teacher may tell things to students, orally, or write them on a chalkboard; he may elicit communications from the students in the form of oral or written answers to questions; or he may invite students to formulate more extensive communications to other members of the class in the form of oral or written reports. When conceived in this manner, instruction may seem to be simply a kind of directed and structured conversation. It is tempting, even, to consider the possibility that instruction is simply equivalent to communication.

Further reflection will show, however, that this model of instruction is far too simple for analytic purposes. Students learn much in situations that do not involve conversations with the teacher—they learn from observing events, natural or contrived; they learn from reading books, examining pictures, and watching pictures that move; and they learn from their own self-generated mental operations.

There is much interest nowadays in computer-assisted instruction. Here, too, however, those who are engaged in serious research with this new tool recognize that the conception of a computer as a means of storing and locating information to be presented constitutes only the simplest part of what must be accomplished (cf. Suppes, 1966). Programs and routines of various degrees of complexity must be designed to engage the human learner in activities that require him to accomplish many kinds of codings and transformations of the materials displayed. And these transformations, in turn, create needs for even greater varieties of units of information to be communicated.

It seems clear, therefore, that one cannot simply equate communication with the process of instruction. Communication in its broadest sense of an event involving apprehension of a situation may be said to be an inevitable part of instruction, but by no means the whole. Thorndike (cf. Joncich, 1962, p. 74) pointed out that a common error of the scholar, inexperienced in teaching, was to expect students to know what they were told. "Telling," he said, "is not teaching."

Accordingly, a consideration of what communication has to do with instruction must properly begin with a description of the process of instruction itself. Particularly, one must consider what happens to the student, or learner, during the events of instruction.

INSTRUCTION AND THE LEARNER

The purpose of the process of instruction is to bring about a change in the capabilities (knowledges, skills, attitudes, and other dispositions) of the human learner. At some particular point in time, it may be determined that the student is not capable of executing some class of performances, let us say, adding sets of two-digit numbers. Activities that are called instruction are then undertaken with the aim of making it possible for the student to change his starting capabilities, including his inability to add two-digit numbers, to a new set of capabilities that includes this latter one, as indicated by his performance when given a sample of such numbers to add. The change that takes place as a result of the instruction is referred to as learning. Although he may frequently play other roles, the student is functioning as a *learner* while in the instruction situation. When he learns, his capabilities at time x are changed to a new set of capabilities at time $x + 1$.

What Is Learned?

To conceive of learning as a change in human capabilities is a first step in understanding the process of instruction. Such a view accomplishes two major clarifications. First, it puts the emphasis for instruction

where it must be—on the student. However elaborate or compli-
cated the process of instruction may turn out to be, or may be designed
to be, its outcomes must be referenced to the changes that take place
in the student. Whether instruction involves a teacher, a textbook, a
class, a motion picture, a television set, or whatever, its ultimate function is to bring about a change in the student. As will be seen later, the
kinds of communications that form a part of instruction must also be
judged in relation to changes in the capabilities of students.

A second kind of elucidation arising from this view of learning is
that the outcome of instruction pertains to its emphasis on an inferred
internal state, or capability. Sometimes, it is said that learning is a
change in "student responses" or "student performance." While this
manner of referring to the outcomes of learning may be convenient as
a shorthand, it cannot be correct in any strict sense. A number of kinds
of events may affect student performance at any given moment, but it
is the underlying capability that is changed by learning. To be sure,
observations of performance are what convince the instructor that a
change in capability has taken place. The difference between two performances in the same student is the observation employed to make the
inference about a change in capability: at one time the student does
not add two-digit numbers, and at another time he does. But the aim
of the instruction is to bring about the change in capability, and the
observations made on performance must be carefully designed so that
this inference can be made with confidence.

The specific capabilities that are newly formed by learning can be
described and classified in several different ways. Adding numbers,
for instance, can be categorized as part of a larger set of capabilities in
"whole number operations," which is part of a still larger set sometimes
referred to as "arithmetic," which, in turn, forms a part of "mathematics." Forming correctly structured English sentences may be classified as a capability belonging to the larger class of "grammar," or of
"language arts." Accordingly, one can, if he wishes, design a technology
of instruction that is broken down into such subject-matter categories,
as in "mathematics instruction," "English instruction," "science instruction," and so on. But it is evident from common usage that there must
be a set of instructional categories that cuts across subject-matters.
Thus, one thinks of instruction designed to establish knowledge of
facts, whether these be facts of natural science, history, or mathematics. Similarly, it is not uncommon to find consideration given to the
learning of concepts, whether language concepts or science concepts;
or to problem solving, whether in mathematics or social studies. Phrases
of this sort imply that designers of instruction, and teachers, commonly

think of categories of human capability as organized along dimensions which are independent of subject-matter. There seem to be different kinds of learning, each of which requires, in certain respects, a different kind of instruction.

The view that categories of acquired capabilities may be distinguished in terms of the way they are observed or measured (that is, the kinds of performances to which they lead), as well as in terms of the kinds of change they imply, has been previously described (Gagné, 1965a, 1967). It is of particular relevance here because these categories of learning set the bounds of what can be accomplished by instruction, including the communications which form a part of instruction. In brief form, much of what is learned in school may be described in the following categories:

1. *S-R Connections.* These are simple unitary motor acts that are usually acquired very early in the child's life, but some of which may be learned during school years. Making a mark on a piece of paper is an example; as is pronouncing the letter "l." For the most part, early school instruction simply assumes such capabilities as these.

2. *Discriminations.* Often, several simple connections must be learned so that different responses are made to different parts of the stimuli impinging on the learner. The performance to be observed is that of *distinguishing* colors, brightnesses, shapes, sizes, sounds, or various other portions of the environment. For example, the child must learn that the printed letter *d* is associated with the sound "duh," and also that printed letter *b* is associated with the sound "buh." He must not only acquire the two individual connections, he should not get them mixed up. Acquiring multiple discriminations is a matter of learning the capability of making a number of differential responses to an equivalent number of different stimulus categories.

3. *Motor chains.* Integrated motor activities such as tying shoelaces, printing letters, describing circles with a compass, focusing a microscope, and many others, are frequently learned in school. A motor chain may be described as the capability of carrying out a sequence of movements leading to a specifiable class of result in the environment of the learner. Printing a letter, drawing a circle, opening a lock, pronouncing a previously unfamiliar foreign word, are all examples of motor chains.

4. *Verbal chains.* A good many verbal sequences are learned in school, and appear to underlie the learning of more complex verbal and intellectual skills. The young child learns to say the names of the numerals one to ten in order, and he may also learn the alphabet as a

sequence. In addition, he acquires many common phrases, such as "boy and girl," "back and forth," "yes I will," and many others. Even later, verbal chains such as "one point four one four" may be a small but useful capability learned in mathematics. Considerably longer verbal chains, such as verses of songs or poetry, may also be learned as a part of school instruction. As a capability, a verbal chain is reflected in the performance of reinstating a sequence of verbal entities (usually words) which in its totality represents a specifiable outcome (the alphabet, a particular phrase or stanza).

5. *Concepts.* The most basic kinds of concepts appear to be capabilities of classifying objects (chair, table); events (expanding, contracting); or spatial and temporary relations up, down, before, after) into categories. What is notable about such classes is that the physical appearance of their members may vary tremendously (a table, for example, may be large or small, high or low, three-legged or four-legged, and so on), yet the concept makes possible an identical response to them. Many fundamental concepts appear to be acquired by direct interaction of the learner with members of the class of objects or events concerned, and without the use of language. Other more abstract concepts (like "uncle," or "symmetry") are apparently most readily learned by means of language which itself refers to simpler concepts. In other words, they are learned by definition (cf. Gagné 1965b, 1966a).

A large proportion of school learning is concerned with concepts. Learning to use language requires the student to acquire many concepts beginning with those of letter and word functions. Mathematics depends upon the learning of concepts pertaining to numbers and number operations. Science and social science are replete with new technical terms for a student to master, each of which is a concept. There are concepts of art and music, as well as concepts relating to bodily movement and physical development. One has only to attempt to acquire new knowledge by reading in an unfamiliar field to recognize at once the necessity for learning the concepts of that field before further learning can transpire.

6. *Principles.* Another large class of learner capabilities reflected in school learning consists of principles or rules. Generally speaking, principles are combinations of concepts. They may be represented by such simple sentences as "Water pours," or by such complex ones as "When a body is in equilibrium, the sum of the movements of force about an axis of rotation is equal to zero." It needs to be emphasized that a principle is an idea, or perhaps a set of ideas, but is not the verbal statement of the idea. The latter merely *represents* the principle. Ob-

viously, a verbal statement may be learned as a verbal chain, but this capability is different from the capability usually meant by "knowing a principle."

A great deal of systematic knowledge acquired in the school situation consists of principles. As the psycholinguists have frequently pointed out, the learning of principles governing the use of language begins in early childhood (cf. Brown and Fraser, 1963). The child does not undertake the learning of the principles of syntax deliberately, but learn them he does, as can easily be proved by his performance in using them to communicate. Many kinds of principles are acquired in much the same way during the ordinary lifetime of the individual, while many others are learned as a result of formally planned instruction in the school.

Principles are frequently arrived at by the individual himself, in a largely self-instructional manner, as a result of a kind of performance called *problem solving*. In this activity, the individual learner "discovers" a relationship among concepts or principles which leads to the acquisition of a "higher-order principle" (cf. Gagné, 1966b).

7. *Strategies*. Another kind of capability, which may be considered a variety of principle in its essential nature, is called a strategy, and is emphasized in the work of Bruner (1961), among others. A strategy is a principle governing choices of the individual's own actions. Thus, an individual may acquire a strategy of solving algebra problems, or a strategy of persuading his parents, or a strategy of investing his money. This kind of higher-order principle is likely to be a highly generalizable capability (or so it is thought by many writers), and therefore to pervade a great many different aspects of his intellectual life. Behaving "creatively" may perhaps best be viewed as a matter of performing in accordance with certain previously learned strategies. Many strategies are acquired in connection with formal schooling, while others are learned outside of school.

Instructional Implications of What Is Learned

There are, then, six or seven *different* classes of capabilities that are acquired by the human learner during the course of his lifetime. Not only do these differ in indicating the variety of things an individual can do, they differ also in terms of the *conditions required for their learning* (Gagné, 1965a). The conditions for learning any single type of capability vary in respect to both the internal conditions of the learner (the state of his nervous system, including memorial traces), and the external conditions surrounding him and impinging upon him. These

external conditions as a whole constitute instruction and, accordingly,
they are centrally involved in the question of how communication is
related to learning.

It is easy to choose extreme examples to demonstrate that the conditions for learning one type of capability differ markedly from those
required in the learning of another type. The learning of a motor skill
like batting a baseball, for example, is markedly little influenced by
verbal communications on "how to do it," whereas it is strongly affected
by a regime of practice with knowledge of results. In contrast, the basic
rules of the game of baseball, although they could be incidentally acquired during long periods of practice and watching, are most readily
and rapidly learned by being verbally communicated. The sharp contrast provided by these particular instances of learning is not an excep-
tional one. Rather, it is a familiar illustration of the general rule that
learning different capabilities requires different conditions. The external
components of these different sets of learning conditions are what must
be identified in exploring the role of communication in learning.

COMPONENTS OF INSTRUCTION

The external conditions of learning may be said to embody the various kinds of communication made to the learner during the period of
instruction. In this context, communication is meant in quite a broad
sense. It often takes the form of verbal statements delivered to the
learner in a language with which he is familiar. Frequently, communication assumes the form of printed or written statements in the familiar
language. It may be noted that either of these forms may be mediated
by a teacher (speaking or writing on a blackboard), or alternatively, by
a device (a tape recorder or printed book). Pictures constitute another
major category of communication available to the learner. These may
be still or moving; and there are many ways to present them (slides,
film, television). A somewhat specialized form of communication is
comprised of nonlinguistic symbols, a form particularly relevant to the
learning of such subjects as mathematics, science, and music. Other
types of communication, including gestures and visual art, have even
more highly restricted and specialized uses as part of instruction.

The important question to be answered about communication in relation to learning does not concern the medium that is used for communicating, but rather, what functions the communication serves. The
various conditions required for different forms of learning partake of
communication in various ways. At any given moment during a period

of instruction, the communication to the learner is fulfilling a function different from that of any other moment. It is necessary, therefore, to address the question of what these various functions might be.

In the broad sense employed in this chapter, communication enters into every variety of learning described in the previous section. It would be possible to describe the specific functions of communication in the learning of S-R connections, multiple discriminations, motor and verbal chains. However, since such a large part of educationally relevant learning comprises concepts and principles (including strategies), the discussion which follows will give primary emphasis to these kinds of learning.

It is possible to analyze the instructional event into a number of component stages, occurring in an approximate time sequence. The functions of communication may most readily be described for each of these stages separately. First, communication to the learner may have the function of *gaining and controlling his attention*. Next, the *stimuli for learning* are to be presented. At some point early in instruction, the learner needs to be *informed of the required performance* he will be expected to exhibit after learning. Some sort of communication must be made to stimulate the learner in *recalling previously learned capabilities*. Now the stage is set for the essential act of learning, but in achieving this, one must often make provision for communication which accomplishes the *guidance of learning*. Once the new capability has been initially attained, communication may *provide feedback* or confirmation of the learning. Finally, if the newly learned entity is to be broadly useful, provision must be made to *promote the transfer of learning*. The following paragraphs briefly describe how each of these parts of the instructional process may be influenced by communication.

Gaining and Controlling Attention

The idea that the learner must attend to relevant stimuli in the learning environment comes from an accumulation of instructional experience (James, 1958, pp. 77-86) as well as from modern evidence about the functioning of the brain (Berlyne, 1965; Lindsley, 1957). Whatever stimulus objects are to form a part of the learning event, whether they be actual objects, pictures, symbols, or words, they must have an initial *registration* effect in order for learning to occur. Essentially this means that they must be perceived, or coded, in some way that makes it possible for them to mediate the neural events necessary for learning. As a simple example, a word such as *flower*, when occurring in a printed communication, must in the usual instance of learning be registered as the referenced concept "flower," and not as merely a printed word.

The young and undisciplined learner must acquire a whole set of habits of attention in order to begin the process of learning. Original stimuli for the arousal of attention, which function also in the establishment of these basic attentional habits, are known to be such things as intense stimuli (loud sounds or bright flashes, for example); repeated stimuli, rapidly changing stimulation (movement or other forms of change); or objects which are associated with certain basic needs such as hunger and sex. As is well known, these same stimuli are widely employed as attention-gainers in advertising, in this case largely with mature and disciplined learners, whose attentional habits to certain products have become extinguished because these stimuli are encountered so frequently in the absence of need. Under these circumstances, the basic attention-getters are used again and again in great variety to re-establish the desired attentional habits for intervals long enough for the advertisement, or a portion of it, to be perceived and its "message" to be learned.

For these two classes of learners (those whose attentional habits are not yet established, and those whose attention has been extinguished), communication must take a particular form in order to arouse attention. It needs to be loud, varied, repeated, and perhaps associated with prepotent drives. For the young child, the state of arousal which leads to the establishment of attentional habits may take the form of relatively intense visual or auditory stimulation, supplied by a teacher or parent, or rapid movement and change as contained, for example, in a motion picture or television presentation. Actually, this kind of attention-getting communication may take many forms, too numerous to catalog here. In any case, the intention of such communication is to establish habits of attention which are eventually to be controlled by much less intense stimuli. Accordingly, when this purpose is being pursued, the intensiveness of the stimuli needs to be progressively reduced, in order that attention will be more readily controlled for purposes of subsequent learning.

For the student who has acquired basic attentional habits related to the kind of stimuli normally encountered in school, there is, of course, no need to resort to communications having this markedly intensive character. Similarly, the disciplined adult learner whose need for learning is unambiguous, presents no requirement for communication of the intensive sort. Attention can readily be aroused in such learners by brief verbal directions such as "Now notice . . . ," or "Look at the diagram . . . ," or by symbols (arrows, etc.), or signals (beeps, etc.) which sometimes serve the same function in such media as motion pictures or recorded presentations. Under these circumstances, the maintenance of attention can generally be insured so long as the relation of the material to his wants or purposes is evident to the learner. Making this relationship clear to the learner is, to be sure, an important function of communication, which will be further discussed in a later section.

Presenting the Stimuli for Learning

An important component of the external conditions for learning consists in the stimuli or stimulus objects toward which the behavior, once acquired, is to be directed. In some instances, the use of physical objects as stimuli is quite essential, as is the case when motor skills are being learned. One would not expect to learn how to adjust a microscope without actually including the microscope as a part of the learning situation, and the same is true for driving an automobile, tying a shoelace, playing tennis, and many other varieties of motor skill. There are also instances of learning in which the use of physical objects, while not essential, may be highly desirable. For this reason, many of the concepts of physics are best learned in the physics laboratory, and of biology in the biology laboratory. Basic concepts may turn out to be inadequate if they are learned without direct practice involving the class of objects to which they refer (cf. Gagné, 1965b).

Ordinarily, one does not think of the learner's interaction with relevant physical objects as falling into the category of communication. Yet, conditions of learning that include physical objects are on a continuum with those that include pictures or demonstrations, and the latter may usually be classed as instances of communication. Provided the learner has acquired suitable attentional habits, as well as requisite picture-observing habits, the activity of observing demonstrations or pictures of demonstrations may be a highly effective substitute for reactions to real objects. For example, a well-designed demonstration (live or in motion pictures) of Archimedes' principle, or of the concept of a lever, may be quite as effective a condition of learning as requiring the student to manipulate objects directly, provided the student has had certain other kinds of prerequisite experiences.

An important function of communication, then, may be to substitute for reality in representing concrete stimulus objects or events of the sort that are the direct objects of the behavior being learned. This function of presenting the stimulus, it may be noted, is only a single step in the set of external events that is necessary to bring about learning. Yet, the existence of communication media which can represent and provide a substitute for the real thing enormously extends the range of possibilities for learning. Many concepts of earth strata and rock formation can be learned via the communication of pictures; architectural features that characterize buildings in remote parts of the earth can be identified and classified by means of pictures. It would be of little use to attempt to multiply these few examples to emphasize a generalization that obviously applies to virtually every field of study. Learning is extended to great limits by the use of pictures as media of communication even when one considers these as performing the restricted function of presenting stimuli.

Similar considerations apply to moving pictures, quite irrespective of the system used to display them (movies, television, etc.). Moving pictures are important means for communicating stimuli that embody motion, as in the case of the operation of engines, the movement of water, or the behavior of animals. As is well known, they can also marvelously extend the range of possible events to be communicated, as in the speeded-up display of plant growth, the motion of planets, or the representation of historical events.

The function of presenting the stimulus is also performed by communication which is verbal, using words and sentences. This is probably the most widely used method. The learner is presented with a sentence describing cell division, rather than with a picture or with the actual cells. The conditions of family life in colonial days are described rather than being pictured, and of course cannot be observed directly. The concept of potential energy is defined in sentences and equations, rather than being demonstrated or pictured. The verbal means of communicating the stimulus for learning is relatively easy to use, and has virtually no limits at all with respect to what kinds of stimuli can be displayed.

It may be noted that there are many media by means of which verbal communications may be presented. The human being in the person of an instructor or teacher comes first to mind, and in this case the representation of the stimulus is usually presented orally to the student in a direct, face-to-face manner. The same kind of stimulus presentation, virtually undiminished in effectiveness so far as this restricted function is concerned, may be carried out by speech recordings. In printed or written form, an even wider variety of media may provide the learner with symbolic representations of the stimulus. These include the teacher's writing, printed pages of books or papers, and various forms of filmed or electronic displays of words and sentences.

The sophisticated learner has little difficulty in learning concepts and principles, in any content field, under learning conditions that include verbal representations of stimuli. But the inexperienced learner may have serious difficulty. This is because the experienced learner is well aware that words are *merely* representations of reality; that it is the referents of the words which are the true stimuli, not the words themselves. The inexperienced learner may not have acquired this basic strategy, and therefore may fall into the trap of learning mere words or word-sequences. The capability he acquires becomes that of a verbal chain, rather than a principle. He learns to give an answer to a verbal question, and is not able to respond correctly when confronted with reality. This is surely one important reason why pictures have advantages over words as representations of stimuli; they are less likely to lead the unsophisticated learner astray. This fact should probably not be used, however, as an argument against attempting to teach the unskilled learner to acquire the capability of responding properly to verbal presentations in learning.

Informing the Learner of the Required Performance

Another function performed by communication within a learning situation is informing the learner of what he will be able to do once he has learned. If a student is to learn a motor chain for printing an E, he is first shown a printed E. If he is to learn the concept of *cell nucleus*, he is first shown examples of the class of objects which are called cell nuclei.

It appears that the procedure of giving the learner information about the expected performance (which he will be able to do after learning) may not be followed consistently in typical school learning. To the extent that this is so, a probably important function of communication is being neglected.

Suppose the learner is confronted with a passage in a textbook reading as follows: "The kinetic energy of a body moving with speed v can be determined by calculating the work done in accelerating the body from rest to speed v. Since work, $W = Fs$, we can show by Newton's second law, $F = ma$, that $W = mas$, or $W = \frac{1}{2}mv^2$. That is, the work done in accelerating the body is equal to the change in its kinetic energy, or $E_k = \frac{1}{2}mv^2$." It is evident that this communication, by itself, does not inform the learner of what he is expected to learn. Several different requirements are possible, including: (1) stating that work done in accelerating a body is or is not equal to the change in its kinetic energy; (2) calculating the change in kinetic energy of a body, given the mass and velocity associated with the change; (3) demonstrating that the change in kinetic energy of a body is equal to the work done on the body.

In view of the fact that each of these possibilities requires the learning of a somewhat different set of principles, it is not difficult to understand the need for telling the learner which of the performances, or what combinations of them, he is expected to acquire. In practice, this kind of communication may have been given to the student at the beginning of a course, or in the early pages of a textbook, so that it does not have to be repeated in connection with each new stimulus presentation. Too frequently, however, this kind of information is not systematically included as a part of the learning situation.

Recalling Previously Learned Capabilities

Arousing attention, presenting the relevant stimuli, and informing the learner about his expected performance, are all early events in the process of instruction. But there is still another communication function which may sometimes precede these in time. This is the stimulation of recall of capabilities that have been previously learned, and which are essential components of the new learning about to occur. Learning a concept, for example, requires the recall of discriminations which differentiate positive and negative instances of the class of objects conceptualized: learning the concept of a rectangle involves recall of the discrimination of inequality of lengths of sides. Similarly, learning a principle takes place under conditions in which the learner recalls previously learned concepts or simpler principles. Before the learning occurs, communication may be necessary to arouse the recall of these previously learned entities.

Suppose the young child is learning about number qualities, specifically, that he is expected to learn that the quantity called eight is formed when a single member is added to the quantity (or set), seven. (Note that the kind of learning being described here is not merely that of acquiring the verbal chain "seven and one is eight.") To learn this principle, he must be able to recall four major things he has previously learned: (a) the quantity seven; (b) the single unit or member; (c) the operation of "add to"; and (d) the verbal response "eight." These things seem rather trivial to us as adults, but it must be remembered that this is a kindergarten child. The teacher may use communication to stimulate recall, by means of an orally presented sequence such as the following: "Here we have a set of objects whose number is seven. You remember what seven is? Suppose we add a member to this set. What do we do when we add? How do we add a single member to this set?" This part of the instructing is almost entirely concerned with the recall of relevant concepts that have previously been learned by the students. All of this precedes the statement which, together with the displayed objects, constitutes the stimulus presentation itself: "When we do this, we have a new set, which is called *eight.*"

Obviously, any of several media of communication may be used to perform this function of stimulating recall. In the example given, the oral communication of a teacher is combined with the display of a group of small objects. But it appears that these tasks could be done with the use of a recorded message or a sound motion picture.

Guidance of Learning

At some point in an instructional sequence, communication may be employed to guide learning. Typically, verbal statements or questions are presented which determine the direction of the learner's internal intellectual processes, although there are occasions when pictures or symbols may perform this function equally well or better. The effect of such communication is to permit the learner to arrive at the new principle without wasting his time considering possibilities which are wrong in extreme degree (cf. Gagné and Brown, 1961).

The function of guidance is perhaps most strikingly illustrated under conditions in which the learner is expected to arrive at a new principle by problem solving. For example, in one of Katona's (1940) studies the learners were asked to learn to perform a card trick. The correct performance of the trick results in alternate red and black cards being placed in order on the table, when successive cards from the top of the deck are dealt alternately to the table and to the bottom of the deck. The principle being learned is one which makes possible the arranging of the deck so that this result will be achieved. In this study, a blackboard demonstration was employed to guide the learning. During the demonstration, the known and unknown cards were displayed on the board in a sequence, the unknown ones being represented by question marks. Instructions were given which led the learners to examine each of these questions in a systematic order, until they discovered for themselves the principle involved in arranging the cards. The experiments showed that subjects instructed in this way retained the capability of performing the card trick, and variations of it, much better than did subjects who memorized the order of the cards.

The amount of guidance provided by instructions can obviously be varied within a wide range. When little is given, instruction is said to emphasize discovery (Gagné, 1966b). At the other end of the spectrum, the principle to be learned may be stated verbally, thus providing a maximum amount of guidance. Such a method of didactic instruction is one which is often used (most textbooks are written that way), and is usually one of the most rapid methods of learning for the experienced learner. Methods with intermediate amounts of learning guidance, called guided discovery, have been shown in some studies to yield better retention of learned principles (Wittrock, 1966).

Providing Feedback

The learner often needs a kind of communication that provides him with feedback, or confirmation that he has managed to acquire the new capability. If he is acquiring the concept of *gas* as a state of matter, he may need to be told the correctness of his identification of the bubbles arising out of a boiling liquid as a gas. If he is learning a principle relating potential energy to mass and velocity, he may need to be told the correctness of his identification of the amount of potential energy possessed by a specific body in a specific situation. Feedback has the effect of preventing the retention of incorrectly learned acts. More importantly, in the view of many students of the learning process, it provides reinforcement, and thus tends to perpetuate what is learned.

Although there are undoubtedly instances in which pictorial media could be used to some advantage for purposes of providing feedback, this communication function is typically conducted by verbal means, either printed or oral. One of the most important varieties of feedback communication is that which occurs during instructional periods that are dynamic in the sense that the feedback is graded and selected according to the degree or quality of correctness of the student's response. Interchanges between the individual student and the teacher are likely to have this characteristic, and such a quality of instruction is often aimed for in the seminar or free-discussion group. In dynamic instruction of this sort, the student's attempts at problem solving can be subjected to many gradations of feedback, and in this manner his newly conceived ideas can be refined and sharpened in a highly selective and individual manner. It seems unlikely that the personal interaction involved in this form of instruction can ever be fully supplanted by any combination of mechanical communication media. Most experienced teachers are highly cognizant of the peculiar value of this form of instruction. Such an evaluation, however, need not blind one to the fact that there is a great deal of necessary instruction which does not need to be of the dynamic sort.

Promoting Transfer of Learning

A final function of communication to be described is the promotion of transfer of learning from the immediate instructional situation to new tasks of learning both inside and outside of the school situation. Learned capabilities are useful to the individual to the extent that they can be generalized in their application to subsequent learning or to the performance of a variety of practical tasks.

In serving this function, communication takes the form of providing a variety of examples, or a variety of opportunities for application of newly acquired knowledge. A principle such as that of proportional representation in legislative bodies, for instance, may need to be demonstrated by the student in a number of specific examples pertaining to nations, states, and local governments, in order to insure its generalizability to subsequent learning or to the activites of a citizen. Most often, such additional instances are provided by verbal descriptions made by a teacher or textbook. Again, other media can perhaps be of value, but hardly of unique importance in the presentation of this kind of instruction.

It appears that oratory communications are of little value in "instruction for transfer." The student may be made aware of the necessity for generalizing his newly learned capabilities, but is unable to do so simply as a result of urging. General communications of the sort "Keep this in mind always," or "Be careful" have never been demonstrated to be effective in generating transfer to new situations. Practice in application to a variety of specific examples appears at least to constitute a long step in the proper direction.

Summary of Communication Functions

The preceding analysis is designed to make the major point that the relation of communication to the accomplishment of learning is by no means a single-faceted affair. *Communication has a number of different functions in the instructional situation.* The range from the attention-arousing function which occurs immediately preceding the actual learning event to the promotion of transfer which follows the event by a shorter or longer period of time.

Following this function-by-function analysis, it will perhaps be useful to attempt a synthesis of an entire instructional sequence, in order to show how the particular kinds of communication fit together in some reasonable manner. The instructional sequence shown in Table 1 elaborates on a shorter example, previously employed, regarding the principle relating work to kinetic energy. With some rearrangement of the verbally presented material, it has been possible to illustrate all of the separate functions of communication previously discussed.

TABLE 1

Functions of Communication in an Instructional
Sequence on a Principle Relating
Kinetic Energy and Work

Function	*Communication*
Controlling attention	Look at the formula below.
Informing the learner of required performance	Since work is a change in energy, the question is how work can be expressed in terms of kinetic energy, as follows: $E_k = 1/2\, MV^2$
Recalling previously learned capabilities	Remember that the kinetic energy of a body moving with speed V can be found by calculating the *work* done in accelerating the body from rest to speed V. Remember that work $(W) = F_s$.
Guidance of learning	How can an expression containing the variables F and s be related to one containing F and V?
Recalling previously learned capabilities	By Newton's second law, $F = ma$
Presenting the stimulus	$W = F_s$ $W = mas$ $W = 1/2\, MV^2$
Providing feedback	Thus, work is related to kinetic energy, or $E_k = 1/2\, MV^2$
Promoting transfer of learning	What is the work done in accelerating a body from a state of rest to a speed of 128 cm/sec?

It may be noted that a considerable portion of the total communication in this example is concerned with preparation for the learning act (controlling attention, recalling previously learned principles) and that a fairly substantial amount pertains to events subsequent to the learning itself (feedback, promotion of transfer). This leaves a relatively small portion of the total message to deal with presentation of the essential stimulus and the guidance of learning. Insofar as this division of function is concerned, this is probably a quite typical instance.

Certain kinds of communication of the sort identified in the table might be omitted for the experienced learner. For example, it might not be necessary to gain attention in such an obvious fashion. Direct reminders of what has been learned previously might not have to be given. In addition, guidance of learning might be omitted or at least reduced to the barest hint. The table suggests merely that these kinds of communication are necessary for *some* learners. When they are used, each is performing a different function in the instructional situation.

MEDIA OF COMMUNICATION

Some implications of this analysis of the functions of communication for learning may now be drawn. Of particular significance, perhaps, are the conclusions suggested regarding the important problem of choosing communication media for instruction.

Matching Media and Instructional Purposes

For a number of years, investigators of the uses and effectiveness of communication media in instruction have pursued certain research questions vigorously (cf. Hoban and VanOrmer, 1950; May and Lumsdaine, 1958). One of these has been the question: Which medium, or combination of media, is best for teaching mathematics? or chemistry? or history? It is well known that these investigations have generally not yielded consistent findings. Sometimes motion pictures have been found to be advantageous as compared, say, to a lecture, and sometimes not. Sometimes recorded speech has been found to be effective for learning, as compared with a live teacher, and sometimes not. The answers obtained do not seem to be any more consistent with one kind of subject matter than with another.

The implication of the present analysis is clearly that dependable answers to the question of matching particular subject matter with particular media are unlikely to be obtained except in highly specialized instances. There are two reasons for this. The first is that a number of functions of communications in learning might be equally well performed by *any* medium. For example, it is difficult to think of a reason why stimulus presentation which requires verbal statement could be performed with differential effectiveness by a teacher's written statement on a blackboard, by a printed statement in a textbook, or by a printed statement projected on a television screen. Similarly, on what basis could one suppose an advantage for the oral reminder of a teacher, versus the pictorial reminder of a projected film sequence, in stimulating recall of previously learned concepts?

The second reason why matching subject-matter and media seems an infeasible task resides in the fact that a medium well adapted for one communication function may be ill-adapted for a second and different function within the same instructional sequence. For example, in a lesson concerned with mechanical advantage, pictures may be well suited for the function of recalling to the learner previously learned concepts concerning the length of lever arms, but quite ineffective in presenting the stimulus and guiding learning for the principle $F_1 \times d_1 = F_2 \times d_2$. Thus, any advantage which accrues in learning from the performance of the first function pictorially may well be cancelled by a disadvantage of using pictures to perform the second function.

Highly similar considerations would seem to apply to the related attempt to seek an answer to the question of matching media and learners (cf. Lumsdaine and May, 1965). Generally speaking, the idea that "some people learn better from pictures" has by no means received any marked amount of confirmation from studies carried out over a period of years. Again, the possibility suggested by the present analysis is that while some communication *functions* may be better performed by particular media for particular kinds of learners, other functions within a single instructional sequence may not be. For example, a highly verbal learner may be able to translate a picture into a verbal statement of the stimulus situation quite readily, whereas an individual of low verbal ability may not. Quite the reverse may be true, however, if the function to be performed by the picture is the recall of previously learned concepts. Thus, a consistent answer to the question of who learns best from pictures, where learning refers to a total sequence of instruction, may be unreasonable to expect.

Analysis of Functions for Media

The suggested route to the continued search for a match between communication media and effective learning is through a process of analysis of the sort previously described. In making such an analysis, several steps are necessary, which may be described as follows:

First, it is essential to determine what kind of capability is to be learned. Is it a verbal chain? a motor chain? a concept? a principle? a strategy? The characteristics of these learned entities have been briefly describd in an earlier section, and more fully elsewhere (Gagné, 1965).

Second, the requirements that each type of learning imposes on the process of instruction need to be described. Concept learning, for example, requires the recall of a different type of previously acquired capability than does principle learning. Practice means something quite different in verbal chain learning and in concept learning. A more extensive treatment of these points may be found in Gagné (1967).

Third, the functions which can or should be performed by communication within the instructional situation must be differentiated, in the manner previously described, and exemplified in Table 1. An extensive discussion of this procedure and its relation to the choice of media is contained in a report by Briggs, Campeau, Gagné, and May (1966).

Fourth, an instructional sequence incorporating these communication functions may be designed, identifying the medium or media which are best suited to perform each of these functions.

Finally, if a choice of a single medium is to be made, or a combination of media, this may be done by selecting the ones which can serve as vehicles for the various communication functions without having conflicting effects on the instruction to be undertaken (cf. Briggs, Campeau, Gagné, and May, pp. 50-60).

The most general statement of the point of view presented here is that selection of media for instruction is a matter which has no single rationale, and can expect to have none, insofar as a match between medium and subject matter is concerned, or for that matter between medium and individual ability of the student. The basis of such matching needs to be sought in an elaboration and empirical testing of classes of communication functions, several or all of which are involved in every unitary instructional sequence, regardless of subject matter. On the basis of an analysis of such functions, decisions can be made regarding the medium or combination of media most likely to accomplish the total purpose of instruction.

REFERENCES

Berlyne, D. E. *Structure and Direction in Thinking*. New York: Wiley, 1965.

Briggs, L. J., P. L. Campeau, R. M. Gagné, and M. A. May, *Instructional Media: A Procedure for the Design of Multi-Media Instruction, a Critical Review of Research and Suggestions for Future Research*. Palo Alto: American Institutes for Research, 1965.

Brown, R. and C. Fraser. The acquisition of syntax, in C. N. Cofer and B. S. Musgrave, eds., *Verbal Behavior and Learning*. New York: McGraw-Hill, 1963, pp. 158–196.

Bruner, J. S. The act of discovery. *Harvard Educational Review*, 1961, 31, 21–32.

Gagné, R. M. *The Conditions of Learning*. New York: Holt, Rinehart & Winston, 1965. (a)

————. The learning of concepts. *School Review*, 1965, 73, 187–196. (b)

————. The learning of principles, in H. Klausmeier, ed., *Conceptual Learning*. New York: Academic Press, 1966, pp. 81–95. (a)

————. Varieties of learning and the concept of discovery, in E. Keislar and L. M. Shulman, eds., *Learning by Discovery*. Chicago: Rand McNally, 1966. (b)

————. Instruction and the conditions of learning, in L. Siegel, ed., *Contemporary Theories of Instruction*. San Francisco: Springer, 1967.

Gagné, R. M. and L. T. Brown. Some factors in the programming of conceptual learning. *Journal of Experimental Psychology*, 1961, 62, 313–321.

Hoban, C. F., Jr. and E. B. Van Ormer. *Instructional Film Research 1918-1950*. Port Washington, New York: U. S. Naval Training Device Center, 1950 (Tech. Rep. SDC 269-7-19).

James, W. *Talks to Teachers*. New York: Norton, 1958.

Joncich, G. M. *Psychology and the Science of Education. Selected Writings of Edward L. Thorndike*. New York: Teachers College, Columbia University, 1962.

Katona, G. *Organizing and Memorizing*. New York: Columbia University Press, 1940.

Lindsley, D. B. Psychophysiology and motivation, in M. R. Jones, ed., *Nebraska Symposium on Motivation, 1957*. Lincoln: University of Nebraska Press, 1957, pp. 44–105.

Lumsdaine, A. A. and M. A. May. Mass communication and educational media. *Annual Review of Psychology*, 1965, 16, 475–534.

May, M. A. and A. A. Lumsdaine. *Learning from Films*. New Haven: Yale University Press, 1958.

National Research Council, Advisory Board on Education. *Psychological Research in Education*. Washington, D. C.: the Council, 1958 (Publication 643).

Suppes, P. Plug-in instruction. *Saturday Review*, July 23, 1966, 25–30.

Wittrock, M. The learning by discovery hypothesis, in E. Keislar and L. M. Shulman, eds., *Learning by Discovery*. Chicago: Rand McNally, 1966.

CHAPTER FIVE

Educational Philosophies and Communications

A. W. VanderMeer

Our purpose here is to explore some of the implications of educational philosophy as they might relate to educational communications. This, of course, assumes that there *are* implications, and it would perhaps be advisable to begin by pointing out what the implications are *not*. It is not assumed that educational philosophy is to be applied *to* educational communications to the enhancement of either philosophy or communications. To imply this would be to make the same mistake that is so often made when considering the implications of the newer and currently popular field of psychology; namely, that there are rules and principles that can be derived from psychology and applied to communication processes so that the process will work more effectively. If there are such rules and principles, they are indeed few and far too fallible to apply with assurance of uniform success across the tremendous spectrum and complexity of differences encountered in the real-life, day-to-day conduct of educational tasks. Rather, the implications of psychology and philosophy for eductional communications derive from their methods. The teacher can benefit by judicious borrowing from the methods of these disciplines as he makes his many decisions in conducting his professional enterprises. He must, of course, view his problems and decisions through the eyes of the artist, as well as though those of the sociologist, the psychologist, and the philosopher.

Henry Johnstone, in his excellent book, *Philosophy and Argument*[1], has pointed out a distinction between science and philosophy which is particularly pertinent. Vastly oversimplified, it is that philosophy depends on rational criticism, internal logic, and consistency, whereas science depends on empirical proof and verifiability of predictions. One comes very quickly to the realization that science raises far more questions than it answers. In fact, an exceedingly larger proportion of the decisions that must be made in controlling any communications act must, if they are made on the basis of established scientific principles, go so far beyond the data available as to make the process seem ludicrous. Yet, this is not to imply that only when all else fails should the communications worker rely on philosophy. Rather, it underscores the utility of philosophy as a starting point—as, in fact, the alternative to wild extrapolation from scientific data or to mindless improvisation based on incoherent impulses.

Perhaps, the choice delineated in the preceding paragraph is too harsh. What does one do when he is confronted with a welter of opposing possibilities as to how to shoot a scene in a motion picture? or which camera position to use at a particular point in a television show? or what sequence of pictures to use in a filmstrip? or any of the myriad larger or smaller problems he faces? Clearly, since he cannot always *or even usually* call up a scientific principle to test the answer, he relies on his general ability as a communicator. And what is the source of this common-sense ability? It is a combination of intelligence and artistry based on an accumulation of ideas and convictions derived from his training and experience as a communicator. These ideas and convictions are shared, to a greater or lesser extent, with his colleagues; perhaps the extent to which they diverge is a measure of his creativity, if not of his naïveté.

---

[1] Henry Johnstone, *Philosophy and Argument* (University Park: Pennsylvania State University Press, 1959).

Could it be said that all teachers use philosophy whether they realize it or not? Probably so, if logic, consistency, and rigorous thinking are the hallmarks of philosophy. There are other necessary conditions, however. Have the basic assumptions, on which the solution of the communication problem depends, been subjected to critical examination? Is there an unproved but essential element at the heart of one or more of the assumptions? This is vital, since assumptions are often remarkably unobtrusive and elusive. It may often be the case that the best among many ill-supported solutions depends upon a number of assumptions that are difficult or impossible to validate; and it is necessary to identify these assumptions and make them explicit. In a like manner, the educational communicator must be precise and consistent in his definition and use of basic terminology and concepts— a task made more difficult by the fact that he works in a field where words fail. (The failure of words is a major justification for pictorial communication.)

One final word on the relative uses of science and philosophy for the educational communication worker. It could be said that the study of philosophy; social sciences basic to communication such as sociology, psychology, and speech; and the study of educational communications themselves, can logically be thought of as a hierarchy of disciplines. The continuum starts with philosophy which is concerned with ultimate or final causes or solutions, whereas sociology, psychology, and those elsewhere on the continuum are concerned with proximate or efficient causes and predictions relative to practice. At the same time that philosophy that has greater generalizability and, some would say, intrinsic worth, communication as a field of study has greater practical and instrumental value in achieving the aims of mankind.

It is assumed that, for the most part, the teacher performs his professional functions in concert with other people concerned with education rather than in isolation. He may be part of a group effort to prepare the communication media for some instructional or educational purpose, in which case he will find it to his advantage to be able to conceptualize the philosophical position and methods of his colleagues. To be able to do so, and to be able to modify his own actions, proposals, and solutions accordingly, is to be able to work most effectively as a professional. No less importance may be attached to the uses of philosophy and philosophic method in situations where the media specialist assists others in the selection of media appropriate for particular purposes with particular groups of learners. Here, he functions, in essence, as a critic among critics of media, and it behooves him to have a clear understanding of the philosophic bases from which his colleagues are operating as they reject one medium or approach and accept alternative media and approaches.

Philosophy of education is concerned primarily with three questions: the nature of existence or being; the nature of knowledge or truth; and the question of value. The individual's beliefs in these three domains, whether the beliefs be verbalized or conceptualized, or whether they be tacit or assumed, ought to determine or at least influence his conceptions of education and the way in which he approaches and solves educational communication problems. The equivocation in the preceding sentence recognizes the unpleasant fact that in all too many cases the educator's actions and those of the communication specialist are consistent with a philosophical position that he would (and often does) roundly condemn and reject when he hears it stated. Be this as it may, the questions of being, knowledge, and value have a deep and overriding significance for everyone involved in education.

CONCEPTS OF COMMUNICATION AND REALITY

A basic question of reality is whether there is any reality at all apart from the physical senses of mankind. Do things exist in and of themselves, or do they exist only in relation to a human being who senses them and perhaps learns from them? If things exist in and of themselves in fixed and inalterable patterns, then it would be entirely appropriate for educators to express the aims of education in terms of enduring verities, and it would be equally appropriate for the educational media produced to assist the learner to learn about these verities and to recognize their immutable character.

A somewhat more pervasive notion is that the relations between things may change the very nature of the things themselves. If such is the case, a change in the relationships that exist among things cannot fail to rob reality of its independent character. If, on the other hand, changes in relationships among things are viewed as external to the things themselves, then the elements of the world and the universe can more easily be viewed as independent and unchanging. In this conception of reality, individuals may be conceived of as the basic elements of all social phenomena.

The relevance of these opposing views to education and, therefore, to educational communication is related to, among other things, the content of education and, therefore, the content of communicaion. If reality exists beyond the power of modification due to changed interrelationships, then there must be facts, customs, and information that should somehow be taught or communicated. The problem, once these realities are acknowledged, is simply how they may be identified and communicated. The criterion of validity of the content of a given communication will have to be the extent of its conformity to reality. If, on the other hand, the nature of reality depends on interrelations among its various aspects (and the learner must, of course, be included among these aspects), then the validity of the content of education will depend, in large part, on the nature of the learners and their reaction to it. The referent for the educational communicator here is either reality itself or the perception of reality on the part of the receivers of the communication.

The sense of the preceding paragraph is set at a given point in time. But time goes on, and things change. Or do they? Is it that we are only now beginning to see more clearly the true nature of things—a nature that has been in existence throughout time and has only been awaiting our discovery? Or is it that things really have changed as our perception of them—our relationships to them—have changed? The fact of change is obvious. It can be seen in the seasons, the growth of living things and, over the eons, in the evolution of species. But it can be argued that all of these changes occur in accordance with cycles which are, themselves, stable. Education and learning presuppose change. If change requires new concepts of the nature of things, then education and communication media must be directed toward the exploitation of change. The processes of change and growth are, themselves, the goals, and nothing is more important than additional growth. The media specialist in such a system will not look forward to producing the epic; he will know that there are no epics in the universal sense. There are only epics that individuals produce, and these are epics only to themselves.

More generally stated, the opposing views of the nature of reality thus far expounded may mean this: Those who hold the view that change itself proves that the nature of reality depends on the knowledge of humans must also believe that novelty and change are genuine. The value of a given communications medium is measured to a large extent by the degree to which it impels the learner toward creative activity of some kind. The products of this creativity are viewed as reality itself and, therefore, as having inherent, primary value. They are not viewed as discoveries or reasonable facsimiles of pre-existing reality, but rather as essential parts of the real world. On the contrary, those who hold that reality *does* exist, and has existed unchanged throughout eternity, may confront their learners with challenges to solve problems, but they do so with the solution already in mind. The process whereby the right solutions are found is important because reality is not necessarily revealed to the inept or the unperceiving, but the *right* solution is waiting, always ready to be discovered.

THE NATURE OF LEARNERS AND COMMUNICATION

While the preceding paragraphs have obliquely referred to the nature of the human beings who are the receivers of the professional products of the educational communication worker, they have been more fully directed at questions relative to the nature of the world in which we live and communicate with one another. It might appear that in paying special attention to the nature of human beings we are departing from the philosophical field and encroaching on that of psychology of education. To a certain extent this is true, for, although there are no points of conflict here, it is intended that philosophers should go beyond the scientific description of the nature of mankind. All too frequently, educational psychologists appear to take the view that if a force or characteristic cannot be measured it must not be real. Such concepts as the soul, the will, and the mind should not be sacrificed simply because they are not neatly measurable (or measurable at all).

What is it to be human? One point of view is that there is an entity in human nature which, while it has the capability of learning and of relating itself to the environment in the time and space in which it finds itself, nevertheless remains relatively constant and unchanging. In this view, although the human being is constantly buffeted by changes of all sorts, being possessed of a constant entity in itself, it is free to make choices among these changes relative to a predetermined and immutable good. The opposing point of view denies the constancy of the nature of the human being; rather, it holds that man is by nature but one component in a field of forces which is forever shifting and changing. As the field changes, so must the nature of human existence change, and, as a result, the constancy that can be attributed to human nature is proportional to, or rather a function of, the totality of the ever-changing environment.

A concomitant of the first view is the notion that the human being can be thought of as consisting of two separate and distinct parts: the mind and the body. Mental processes are paramount in this case because it is they that control activity. Therefore, the focal point of educational activities is the mind, and the educational or communications worker's major concern with the body is that it not interfere with the mind. Obviously, this view is hospitable to the possibility that mind and body may work at cross purposes. This is neatly avoided by the opposing theory which holds that mind and body are one rather than a duality. In this view, everything can ultimately be reduced to a concept of mind. The structure of the mind can be determined by analyzing it in terms of its elements. The entirety is the sum of the parts and their interconnections; therefore, learning consists in assembling the parts in proper sequence and in proper relationships among each other. Obviously, this view would be encouraging to those who are interested in advancing programed learning, be it linear or branching, although this philosophical point of view is far from sufficient grounds for a complete justification of programed learning.

THE NATURE OF KNOWLEDGE—
THE CONTENT OF COMMUNICATION

Points of view concerning the nature of knowledge have obvious implications for defining the curriculum which, in turn, have major implications for the materials and systems of educational communications. One basic question is whether the subject matter in the curriculum *is* knowledge which is independent of the "processing" of the learner as he works, or whether it becomes knowledge as it is used by the learner in solving problems or engaging in learning activities. If the former represents the truth of the matter, then a curriculum that is relatively stable can be set up in advance, and the major questions have to do with the ordering of knowledge. Such a procedure would be inconsistent with the view of subject matter as data and information to be transformed into knowledge by the learner, through use. In this case, the problem or the inquiry is basic, and problems and interests are so heavily dependent upon the course of events and on the vagaries of chance that it is folly to specify far in advance what the curriculum should be. Perhaps this is a slight overstatement, since the relativist view would permit drawing up a list of areas of learning which, from past experience, could be considered as strong possibilities for inclusion. (The adversary of the realist point of view who nevertheless desires the security of predetermined scope and sequence in the curriculum can "cheat" a little by arranging the environment so that certain problems *will* come up and certain interests will emerge.) Beyond these general probability areas and those areas which can be "managed" into the environment, the day-to-day content of the curriculum will be determined by what problems come up. Subject matter will be selected which bears on these problems, and it will be learned as it is adapted to the solutions of the unique problems at hand.

In reality, there are three major viewpoints regarding knowledge. One is that one cannot ever know reality except in terms of one's sensory and mental reactions to it. Knowledge is found in the consistency of one's *constructs* of reality. This is the point of view illustrated in the second part of the previous paragraph. It holds that what is true is theoretically different for each person. The wise man seeks consistency between his ideas and those of others, and he is perhaps comforted when he finds it; but in the final analysis, reality and truth are what he, and he alone, sees.

An alternative and opposed point of view is that reality is "knowable" and, although it may be "seen through a mirror, darkly" at a given point in time, human intelligence is ultimately capable of knowing reality. Truth may be defined as correspondence between the knowable and the known. (The former is immutable; the latter capable of error or incompleteness.) The curriculum ought to be based upon and selected from what is known.

Dewey's pragmatism largely ignores the two opposing views just stated; they are considered to be irrelevant. Knowledge is a byproduct of successful adaptations to the environment. More precisely, knowledge is generated by problem solving and adaptation to (reconstruction of) the environment. It is indeed in the curriculum, but not as an end in itself, rather as a sort of data bank upon which the learner can draw for future inquiry.

PHILOSOPHY AND EDUCATIONAL OBJECTIVES

In the previous section, it was pointed out that, in one philosophical viewpoint, the problem of curriculum making consists of the ordering of the known. As a matter of fact, of no less importance to teachers are questions of value, which are central in all matters of education and are dealt with in all systems of philosophy.

Major philosophic theories concerning values—what is good or worthwhile—can be divided into two fairly clear-cut points of view. The first of these holds that values are intrinsic. Whether an entity is valuable does not depend upon the use to which it is put, but rather is related to the entity itself. This is not to say that some things may not be valuable because they are instrumental in achieving or maintaining other values; rather it is to say that when intrinsic and instrumental values appear, the former take precedence. The nature of man is basic, and the objectives of education properly relate to the fulfillment of man's intrinsic and enduring potentialities. Self-realization is the highest aim, and all other objectives of education ultimately take their direction and their validity from it.

An alternative view regards values subjectively rather than objectively. This view ascribes value to personal feelings *about* value; that is, that is valuable which is *believed* to be valuable. When entities appear to have values in competition with each other, that value is accepted that best promotes the purpose currently at hand. Therefore, there are no *intrinsically* enduring values because purposes change as times and conditions change. The aims or objectives of education cannot be set up for any significant period in advance, and there cannot be established a hierarchy of aims which will be equally valid for all times and for all occasions. While education and the advancement of education itself may be an ultimate aim or value, the immediate objectives of education are constantly emerging from the learning situation and from life.

Obviously, the latter view gives sanction to a form of teaching in which improvisation plays a central role. Such plans as are made in advance must be of an ad hoc nature, and, as such, subject to the availability of such resources as may be at hand for their fulfillment. This is because, if value depends on use and interest, learners can be expected really to study only that in which they are interested or that which they perceive as leading to results that they find intrinsically attractive. These desires and perceptions are influenced by social factors, of course; otherwise, complete chaos would result.

On the other hand, the conception of values as intrinsic and objective can be used to give sanction to the inclusion of and maintenance of subjects in the curriculum at considerable cost in motivation. An ultimate resort to force may be required, or, less distasteful but no less worthy, to a shift in focus from the motive to learn to the motive to achieve extrinsic rewards such as prizes or the approval of teachers or parents.

Clearly, the kind of instructional materials prepared to be consistent with the first view would, paradoxically, be relatively devoid of such motivational gimmicks as protagonists, story lines, etc., because they would be used in situations where the learner was self-motivated. The learner uses materials only as instruments or data to achieve ends that he himself desires to achieve.

In the latter case, materials of instruction would appropriately include a powerful dose of motivational content. The kernel of truth that constitutes the intrinsic value may be better, so it had better be sugar-coated!

By the same token, the view that holds values and aims to be objective and immutable includes a logical hierarchy into which the various kinds of values can be placed. Lowest in the hierarchy are those values that arise from the mindless satisfaction of desires and appetites. Next are those values rationally chosen for the results that they have achieved throughout the past and those that they may be predicted to achieve in the future. The highest values are those that do not depend upon results which themselves are considered good at any given time and place; these are intrinsic values, and their higher place is justified in terms of their stability, durability, inclusivity, and creativity.

Implicit in the hierarchy of values just elucidated is the notion that that is best which is least materialistic. The more the value is concerned with form, the greater the value. By extension, the more abstract; i.e., independent of matter, the greater the value. There is perceived a connection between somatic faculties and matter on the one hand, and between rational faculties and form or abstraction on the other. This consideration explains much about the academic pecking order— philosophy, logic, mathematics, physics, and so forth down to applied art, shop, and vocational subjects. It also explains the derogation of the pictorial and graphic and the exaltation of the verbal and linguistic. The principle of proceeding, in communication and education, from the concrete to the abstract is, however, entirely consistent with this philosophy, and it is this and the temporal deficiencies of verbal and symbolic language that forms one primary justification for audio-visual materials.

SOME APPLICATIONS: THE CURRICULUM

Two main streams of philosophical thought can be discerned in what has been presented up to this point. The first has been summarized by Wild in terms of three theses[2] of *realist* philosophy:

The Metaphysical Thesis. The universe is made up of real, substantial entities, existing in themselves and ordered to one another by extramental relations. These entities and relations really exist whether they are known or not. To be is not the same as to be known. We

---

[2] John Wild, "Education and Human Society: A Realistic View." *Modern Philosophies and Education.* Fifty-Fourth NSEE Yearbook, Part A, 1955, pp. 17–18.

ourselves and other entities actually exist, independent of our opinions and desires. This may be called the thesis of independence.

The Epistemological Thesis. These real entities and relations can be known, in part, by the human mind as they are in themselves. Experience shows us that all cognition is intentional or rational in character. Every concept is *of* something; every judgment *about* something. The realist holds that this is a peculiar relation by which the knowing act becomes united with, in a nonmaterial sense, or directly identified with, something really existent. The mind does not become physically one with its object. To know an explosion is not to explode. Nevertheless, cognition is not merely a matter of containing states within one's self. To have gray cells inside the cortex is not to know this fact. To know something is to become *rationally* identified with an existent entity as it is. This is the thesis of direct realism.

The Ethical Thesis. Such knowledge, especially that which deals with human nature, can provide us with immutable and trustworthy principles for the guidance of individual and social action. All men share certain common traits which determine vague tendencies in every child. These tendencies must be realized together in an orderly way if human life is to be really fulfilled. In subhuman entities, such tendencies are determinate, inflexible, and realized automatically with the sole support of external natural agencies.

In man, this is not the case. He has not been endowed with an exhaustive array of inflexible instincts which automatically propel him to the proper acts. Instead, he has been given very flexible tendencies together with the power of cognition by which he may rationally understand his needs and freely determine his conduct in accordance therewith. The invariable, universal pattern of action, individual as well as social, required for the completion of human nature is called *the moral law* or *natural law*. By self-observation, every individual has some minimal knowledge of it. By disciplined study of human nature and the events of history, the knowledge may be increased and clarified. Such knowledge is the only trustworthy guide for human action.

The opposing point of view which Butler[3] calls the *idealist* philosophy is summarized in his interesting book, *Four Philosophies and Their Practice in Education and Religion.*

The Idealist Metaphysics. The self is the prime reality of individual experience. Ultimate reality *is* a self. Ultimate reality may be one self,

---

[3] J. D. Butler, *Four Philosophies and Their Practice in Education and Religion* (New York: Harper and Brothers, 1957), pp. 191–201.

a community of selves, or a Universal Self within whom are many individual selves.

Idealist Epistemology. Idealism holds that the qualities we perceive in the world are rooted in existence. Either we have direct experience of the self; i.e., that it is a self-evident fact, or the existence of the self is a necessary inference. Selfhood being what it is, and the surrounding world being to well tuned to the experience of self, it is believed by idealists that reality is a Self. Since nothing can be conceived to exist without being in relation to other things, reality is a logically unified, total system—a Universal Mind.

Idealist Ethics. The values human beings enjoy and desire fundamentally are rooted in existence. The values of human life are what they are largely because there are individual persons to possess and enjoy them. One important way in which individual persons can realize value is by actively relating parts and wholes.

The curriculum of the common school is conceived of as being a function of aims or objectives, subject matter related to the achievement of these objectives, the materials and methods whereby the subject matter may be mediated with relation to the learner, the characteristics of the learners themselves (broadly speaking), and the concepts and principles that govern learning. Clearly, how one views each of these factors, and the relative importance one attaches to each, is at least partly (some would say mainly) determined by one's philosophical position. And the media specialist is required to work in an implicit or explicit framework of philosophical positions whether he is in a position to plan, produce, and control the utilization of media according to his own philosophical predispositions or whether, as is more likely the case, he is required to plan and produce communication media and influence their utilization more or less "on order" according to the philosophical predispositions of others—school authorities, individual teachers, etc.

Aims and Objectives

The realist position is that aims are fixed and relatively immutable. The idealist holds that aims should be flexible and subject to continual modification. The idealist believes that aims should emerge from individual and group experience; the realist considers such a source to be temporary and vacillating, and prefers the security of external aims which come from outside and above experience. Regarding the relationship of aims to other considerations in curriculum making, the realist gives first and highest place to aims. State the aims, then find the means of achieving them. The idealist would shuttle back and forth between aims and the other factors related in curriculum build-ing because he would consider it impossible to establish aims intelli-gently unless the means of and constraints on achieving them are taken into consideration.

A closely related question is that of the authority to establish aims. The realist would be disposed to establish a hierarchy of authority. The communications specialist would likely find himself placed in the upper reaches of such a hierarchy, but distinctly below the top. The idealist would tend to give nearly equal voice in goal setting to stu-dents, teachers, and administrators. Idealists tend to emphasize the importance of children's present interests and capacities, and are there-fore threatened by ultimate aims, however well stated and well justi-fied, because such aims are likely to be remote in time and to lack psychological intimacy. Such remoteness would make them seem un-real and unattractive to children; such aims would be largely devoid of motivating power. Better it is, goes the idealist point of view, to accept the more wavering and less valid aims that take into account the in-terests and capacities of children on the grounds that these will be accepted by the children and will consequently be more likely to result in growth. Present growth, the position goes on, is the best guarantee of future growth.

If the teacher or communications specialist looks wistfully at the realist position, it is understandable. He might prefer the stability of well-defined aims that are presumed to be relatively constant over time. Planning will be greatly simplified and operations can be more clearly routinized. His place in the planning structure is definite and assured. If, on the other hand, he views planning as the most exciting part of his work—if he thrives on encounters with the unexpected and enjoys im-provization more than preplanned execution—he will be far happier if his colleagues are idealists. In this latter case, he will find himself on numerous committees, usually as a resource person interacting with supervisors, teachers, and students. He will find himself covering familiar territory time and time again as different groups identify for themselves the proximate aims of education and seek to devise some of the means to achieve them. He will have to learn to live with the fact that what the individuals and groups decide about aims may be "old stuff" to some, but brand new to others. He will have to share in the enthusiasm of their "discoveries" and to avoid stealing these dis-coveries from them by telling them too much too soon. And he will have to be willing to let them make mistakes.

The teacher or communications specialist who objects to a work en-vironment dominated by realist philosophy, it may appear, trades the tyranny of an established hierarchy with commensurate divisions of authority for the tyranny of the democratic process. Paradoxically, some may consider it the greater freedom to be permitted to work within a clearly established and well-defined set of external aims or goals than to be required continually to construct and reconstruct aims and goals in response to every real or perceived change in the human condition. Witness the school child who asked his teacher plaintively, "Do we have to do what we want to again today?"

Subject Matter or Content

Obviously, the teacher or anyone connected with instructional communications cannot plan media in isolation from message or content; therefore, it behooves him to understand the ground rules that are invoked in determining what content goes into the curriculum and what stays out.

It should be no surprise that conceptions of what the curriculum should be can be related to the philosophical positions previously described. Taking the surface view, one could say that the process of education has two basic ingredients: something to be learned and someone to learn it. But this is the surface view. Is there really a discontinuity here between the learner and what is to be learned? or is it more logical to presume an essential continuity between the learner and the curriculum?

What has been called the realist philosophical position accepts the dualism posited in the preceding paragraph. The learner is viewed as the particular, the changeable, the temporal, while the curriculum is viewed as the general, the universal, the stable, the timeless. The learner is, therefore, in the final analysis, adapted to the curriculum, not the other way around. To be sure, what is known about the characteristics of learners plays a part in determining the sequence of the curriculum, but so also does the inherent logic of subject matter.

The alternative to this view of the curriculum could be termed *"learner centered."* This view rejects the notion of a curriculum "imposed from outside" in favor of one in which the content of the curriculum is the content of the experience of the race—which differs in degree rather than in kind from the experience of the child. As Brubacher puts it:

> The child's experience and his studies in school are but the initial and terminal aspects of a single reality or process—education, life. The one flows into the other, is continuous with it. It is one of the functions of method to discover the steps which intervene between the child's present experiences and their richer maturity in the social heritage. The curriculum is the social stuff out of which the self

realizes itself. To think of these two as opposed to each other would produce the unnatural result of putting the nature and destiny of the child at war with each other.[4]

There may have been a time, perhaps even in the memory of the older generation, when, by diligent effort sustained throughout the childhood years, adolescence, and early adulthood, one could hope to master at least the rudiments of all of the major disciplines. If this happy state did once pertain, it is now long gone. The so-called knowledge explosion grinds out new information at such a prodigious rate that true scholars complain of the difficulties of "keeping up with" their narrow specialty *within* their academic discipline or professional field. The advocates of the learner-centered curriculum may have the solution to the dilemma of what portions of this expotentially expanding volume of information should be included in the curriculum. They take their cues from child experience. Each new problem or situation calls for a selection of subject matter from a variety of fields. These data are checked as relevant or irrelevant, and the problem is solved. To the extent that today's problem or experience has features or aspects in common with tomorrow's, there will be something to transfer and to apply; but the new problem is expected to have new features and these new features will demand a new synthesis of data from various fields and will result in a new integration of knowledge.

This solution to the curriculum problem has two major weaknesses. First, it calls for a kind of broad and flexible planning that is prepared for a wide variety of contingencies. The progress of the child or group must inevitably be chancy if not downright idiosyncratic. The technique of planning only in terms of large units of work that require a long time to finish in reality begs the question, for if the curriculum is really an extension of the child's experience, the teacher must be ever-ready to drop everything and seize upon a contingent opportunity in the interests of exploiting its learning potential. Such a curriculum is likely to appear fragmentary, discontinuous, and unrelated. It lends itself to repetition and to overlap over the span of time. Experience begets experience, and teacher-pupil planning can all too easily result in children working on a unit on the Indians of the Southwest again and again—a development that may or may not bring the invigorating breeze of fresh challenges to their minds and spirits.

A second weakness of the learner-centered curriculum is that it is extraordinarily susceptible to corruption by the inept or the lazy

_____

[4] John S. Brubacher, *Modern Philosophies of Education* (New York: McGraw-Hill Book Company, Inc., 1950), p. 225.

teacher. If goals are subjective, who is there to challenge the goals that the class has ostensibly set for itself? If Miss Jones' fifth-grade seems to find its experience leading it to a compelling interest in Latin America, just as did each of its predecessors down the dusty corridors of twenty-seven years of time, who is there to say that the fact that Miss Jones has had the materials and organization for such a unit pretty well in hand for the past twenty-seven years has had any influence?

The alternative notion of the curriculum, of course, calls for an ordered sequence of content selected for its inherent worth. Selected by whom? By those who have the authority? or by those to whom authority is delegated? This could be the local curriculum committee, the state department of education, the Committee on Undergraduate Programs in Mathematics, or the American Society of Biological Science. The selections in such cases are likely to give only passing attention to the learner's viewpoint. The obvious difficulty is that learning may become sterile and so removed from real life that the enduring values attributed to the subject matter may not only be lost but actually replaced by anti-values and rejection.

The problem of the overcrowded curriculum which has been exacerbated by the knowledge explosion can, in this view of curriculum making, be ameliorated if not actually solved by invoking the slogan often trumpeted by communications specialists; namely, "more learning in less time." While it is clear that improved means and techniques of educational communication can indeed pack more into the curriculum, it is entirely possible that there are finite limits to communications efficiency, and, worse yet, that the efforts of the communications experts may result in teaching more effectively much of that which should not have been taught at all. In such a case, the errors of the now generally discredited survey courses are perpetuated. An approach that is clearly more promising and, at the same time, is consistent with realist philosophy is that of focusing on the structure of disciplines and on their methods. Thus, a problem may be viewed by the learner successively through the eyes of an economist, a geographer, an historian, and a social psychologist. Presumably, the result is that he attains, in part, the immutable essences of these disciplines.

The methods of the communications specialist differ in terms of the philosophical viewpoints that dominate the process of building and implementing the curriculum in his educational environment. Clearly, the learner-centered curriculum does not easily tolerate neat schedules of film use and single or double screenings of television programs. To consider April's schedule in October is laughable. Rich resources of materials within easy reach of the learner are required. This means classroom and building libraries, equipment in every room, and free access to both by teachers and students. Textbooks give way to individualized learning materials unless the books can be adapted to those ends. Production of materials is likewise decentralized. Teachers and students make their own learning materials—full of flaws and imperfections, but nevertheless, *their own*. Rarely is it worthwhile to expend sizeable sums for "slick" productions or for filmed series, regardless of how well made and how closely integrated. Television is used more as a medium for children to learn how to use knowledge and less as a source of organized knowledge. The children engage in such activities as broadcasting their own version of the news—whatever the content.

The communications worker in a system dominated by realist philosophy is more concerned with the right material in the right place at the right time, with the latter factor being considerably more negotiable than the first two. He emphasizes quality of materials and media, confident that the investment will prove worthwhile. He is greatly concerned with field-testing materials because he can predict that the film or textbook that produces the best results in the test situation will be applied in reasonably similar situations over time and thus vindicate its selection. He views television principally as a device whereby excellent teaching and learning experience can be economically distributed. If he establishes building or room libraries, it is largely for reasons of economy; it is cheaper to have them near the scene of use than to transport them. Local production is viewed as a means whereby the supply of commercial material can be supplemented by those peculiarly adapted to bringing the immutable values of some sections of the curriculum to this particular school group in response to its individual needs.

Methods of Teaching

The communications specialist is likely to be concerned with method in a way which is intimately related to his concern with the curriculum, viewed as content. He will have to advise on the production, selection, and use of materials differently, depending upon the school situation in which he finds himself; the differences in these situations spring from the dominating philosophy of the school.

It is consistent with the realist view that aims are objective, external, and immutable—and that the curriculum consists of content which has inherent value and is to be learned, hopefully, with interest, but in any case, to be learned—that the method of teaching that prevails be characterized by benevolent authoritarianism. More accurately, perhaps, it should be said that an emphasis is placed on adult authority, not because of any desire to usurp the learner's freedom, but rather to establish it as an end, rather than as a means, of education. Efforts *will* be made to interest the learner, to motivate him to learn, to adapt method and, to some extent, content, to the relevant characteristics of individual learners, to pace instruction within the capabilities of learners, and so on. Ultimately, however, the children must learn, and the effective teacher adapts his methods so that this valuable insight is gained by all. Those who are unreachable by other means may be punished or, as a last resort, removed from the learning situation.

The learner-centered curriculum and the monistic theory of educational value calls for a different approach to method. In this view, the curriculum is stated in terms of child nature, and method is determined by conceptions of learner activity. Problems arising from the experience of the learner or learners establish the structure of "lessons." Beginning with problems perceived by the learners, the method of instruction is, in reality, the method of inquiry. The teacher encourages learners to seek answers to their own problems. He is tolerant of trial-and-error activities and interferes with student activities with reluctance, and only then to protect the learner from the more unfortunate consequences of his problem-solving activities. Since the problems *belong* to the learners, motivation and interest can be assumed. "Interest will be the parent of effort, which in turn will be disciplined by the inherent difficulties of the problem."[5] Punishment is therefore rare or non-existent. When it occurs, it is administered only for its educative value.

The communications specialist working in the situation governed by realist philosophy will find that the most appropriate materials are those that are well adapted to group use. They are largely didactic in nature and approach. If they do not include devices for motivating the learner, it is because the teacher conceives this as reducing his position of authority. The internal structure of the materials conforms to logical sequence based upon the structure of the subject matter being presented. "Discovery materials" are included, but they are in a somewhat separate category of use from the primarily conceptual material. By the same token, materials primarily for the development and reinforcement of attitudes are frankly emotional, ranging from the performances of great artists in music, drama, and literature, to contrived narratives designed to instill attitudes conducive to safety, health, and morality.

By contrast, the communications specialist working in a learner-

---

[5] Brubacher, *op. cit.,* p. 275.

centered school environment must provide materials that lend themselves well to individual and small-group use. They are generally fragmentary in nature. Film clips, picture sets, realia, trade books, and the like are emphasized. While materials presenting outstanding performances of great artists are available, they are used primarily for individual enjoyment and individual analysis and study. There are relatively few "well-organized" and structured longer presentations, and it is commonplace to use only selected parts of those that are furnished. Attitudinal materials do not appear as a separate category since attitudinal learning is conceived of as an integral part of learning concepts, attitudes, and methods of inquiry.

REFERENCES

Broady, Harry. *Building a Philosophy of Education.* Englewood Cliffs, N. J.: Prentice-Hall, 1954.

Brubacher, John. *Modern Philosophies of Education.* New York: McGraw-Hill, 1950.

Johnstone, Henry. *Philosophy and Argument.* University Park: Pennsylvania State University Press, 1959.

Modern Philosophies and Education. National Society for the Study of Education, 54th Yearbook, Part I. University of Chicago Press, 1955.

Education for the Professions. National Society for the Study of Education, 61st Yearbook. University of Chicago Press, 1962.

CHAPTER SIX

A Learning-Systems Concept as Applied to Courses in Education and Training

Donald K. Stewart

INTRODUCTION

The term "system" has many applications and is often used to refer to such things as a telephone system, payroll system, transportation system, school system, etc. During and after World War II, researchers developed a special meaning for the term "system" which concerned man-machine relationships such that as a particular machine was designed, developed, and completed, the necessary training of personnel to operate and work with the particular machine was designed, developed, and completed simultaneously. A critical part in this "system" was the specification of the operational objectives or purposes of the machine, of the man or men working with the machine, and their interrelationships. It was not until after the advent of programed instruction that this system concept could be applied to education with a meaning similar to that just described. Programed instruction introduced the need for specifying educational objectives and the techniques for making general and ambiguous objectives more specific. Although education has been concerned with stating educational objectives for decades, these objectives were not specific and measurable. As a result, educators stated objectives, described educational activities, and then designed tests almost as three separate functions with little if any correlation between them.

In adapting the system concept to education, several differences must be noted. In industry, the end product or goal is a machine of some kind with trained people to operate and work with the machine; consequently, this system is often referred to as a man-machine system. In education, the end product, or goal, is learning; consequently, this system is referred to as a learning system. Machines are the major emphasis throughout the man-machine system, whereas in a learning-systems concept, the importance of machines is dependent upon their contribution to the learning process. Although the man-machine system and the learning system differ in several respects, there are also similarities. In industry, quality control is built into the man-machine system to increase the effectiveness and efficiency of the developmental processes. Likewise, in education, quality control can be built into the learning system to increase its effectiveness and efficiency. In both the man-machine system and the learning system, all activities should be based on verifiable or measurable specific objectives, not on guesses, opinions, or other nebulous or ambiguous statements.

Why should educators consider the use of a learning-systems concept? What is wrong with the present educational system which has been used as an example for the whole world to follow? In order to answer such questions, let us look at our present educational system.

THE EXISTING EDUCATIONAL SYSTEM

Society expects educational institutions to carry out at least the following three functions:

1. prepare students in such a way that they will have an even happier and more successful life than their parents;

2. be sure that the experiences necessary for each student to achieve the first function happens by choice—not by chance;

3. develop each child to the maximum of his capabilities.

These three functions are stated in various ways in most educational institution charters or constitutions. They sound good, but their implied goals are often not achieved because those goals implied by the first function have never been specified precisely enough to allow absolute measurement. In fact, very few teachers have ever specified, in measurable terms, the terminal objectives which are the desired student behaviors at the end of a course. Various state departments of public instruction have tried to define the content of each course at each grade level in the form of guidelines for the teachers. Most of these guidelines describe activities for the teacher or for the students. Objectives that are listed are so general that the interpretation of any one objective is actually up to the individual teacher.

If teachers do not know specifically what the terminal objectives of their courses are, then how can students be tested for achievement that has not been defined? Consider the following questions:

1. Can you make a test that would *fail all of the students* in your class? (yes or no)

2. Can you make a test that would *pass all of the students* in your class? (yes or no)

If you answered "yes" to both questions, then consider this question: If you can make up a test that could pass all of your students and you can also make up one that could fail all of your students, where do you find that magic something to help you select test items that will pass those who should pass and fail those who should fail? This magic something does not exist, so most teachers grade according to some kind of curve (normal or skewed) which indicates more about how a student learned in comparison to his classmates than in comparison to the objectives of the course. When grading "by the curve," a failing student in a class of smart students could be an "A" student in a class of not-so-smart students without any difference in the amount learned by the student.

If a teacher knows precisely what the student is supposed to learn, and tests are designed to measure the achievement of the specific content, then a student's grade should reflect his progress towards the course goals.

In a situation where the teacher is a "presenter of content," and the schools concentrate on moving students through the system *regardless* of learning, the system fosters "cumulative ignorance" (the cumulative effect of non-learning that inhibits subsequent learning). Cumulative ignorance is responsible for a majority of dropouts and discipline problems. Consider the following anomalies:

(a) Almost every tenth-grade teacher will agree that any given class of tenth-grade students will contain students with reading levels from fourth or fifth grade up to college level. Knowing this fact, teachers will give these students tenth-grade reading level materials in literature, history, geometry, biology, etc., and when some of the students are unable to comprehend what they are reading, they are failed.

(b) Students who go through the "fail one year, pass the next" cycle several times usually find themselves in a situation where they couldn't learn if they wanted to because they don't have the prerequisite knowledge and/or skills.

(c) If a "C" grade in addition and subtraction means that a student didn't learn everything he was supposed to know about addition and subtraction, then chances are that this student will get a "C" or a "D" in multiplication and division, a "D" or an "F" in decimals and fractions, and an "F" in algebra, if the student elects to take it. Most educators would say that some students just are not capable of doing mathematics. Could the "F" in algebra be a result of "cumulative ignorance" rather than lack of innate ability?

THE LEARNING-SYSTEMS CONCEPT

To many professional educators, the notion of a systems approach, which has been borrowed from engineering and industry, may seem harsh and ominous in its implications for the management of instructional processes. But instructional planning in modern educational institutions cannot be conducted on a piecemeal basis without some effort toward a rational and efficient deployment of human and technical resources. Consequently, the use of the systems concept is intellectually and practically inescapable.

For the purposes of this chapter, a "Learning-Systems Concept" will be defined as follows:

(a) The requirements or objectives of the system will control the design of the system.

(b) The system will maximize learning effectiveness through procedures such that all, or almost all, of the stated objectives of the system are achieved; i.e., 90 per cent of the students will learn 90 per cent of the material.

(c) The system will maximize learning efficiency by adapting the system to the learner rather than making the learner fit the system.

(d) The design and procedures of the system will reflect the educational philosophy consistant with the requirements of the system and society.

Learning can occur under almost any set of circumstances; in fact, a great deal of learning takes place without the assistance of formal instruction. Experience itself is learning. The contribution of formal instruction is to assure that the student's learning experiences will occur by choice and not by chance.

A learning-systems concept, when applied to educational or training courses, offers an opportunity to develop or redesign courses that will be significantly more effective and efficient in relation to the learning tasks and goals of students.

It is necessary to begin with two objectives that exist irrespective of course content. They are:

1. to utilize more fully available educational resources and enriched teaching techniques;

2. to develop course patterns so that students can pursue their education or training as much as possible at their own pace, on their own schedule, and at a convenient site.

The first objective is particularly important in a society where both knowledge and the population are expanding at an ever-increasing rate. Educators must investigate ways of making our educational process more efficient and effective. Changes must be made in existing educational patterns.

The first objective is based on the following assumptions:

• Education's primary purpose is to facilitate learning by establishing an appropriate environment conducive to learning.

• In any program, it is necessary to find out where the student is on the ladder of learning and to proceed from that point without gaps or unnecessary overlap.

• Programs must be revised if it is found that learning has not taken place. Revisions should be made after an examination of the learner, method, media, and environment.

- If the learning objectives of a particular course could be definitely stated, and if all of the learners could achieve these objectives, they would all receive an "A" or some equivalent symbol indicating 90-100 per cent achievement.

- Some learning objectives cannot be defined specifically, but can be described as a result of other specific observable and measurable behaviors.

- Grades based on undefinable objectives and temperament of the grader do not contribute to an effective and efficient educational system and should not be included as a course requirement for grading procedures.

The second objective of the learning-systems concept, as stated previously, is to develop course patterns so that students can pursue their education or training as much as possible at their own pace, on their own schedule, and at a convenient site. This objective is important because students taking educational or training courses are "individuals" with different abilities, interests, past experiences, and environmental limitations. Most educators subscribe to this concept of individuality, yet in our schools they continue to insist on uniformity in performance within scheduled slots of time and at specific locations only.

The second objective is based on these assumptions:

- As educators, we want *to help* as many students through high school and college as possible.

- Many capable ex-students would like to continue their education or training if they could proceed at their own pace. A higher percentage of students could graduate from high school, and from college, if education could be geared to individual needs.

- "Cumulative knowledge," which is best defined as a situation where a student learns 90 per cent of each unit before he can proceed to the next unit, can be self-motivating and rewarding.

- Teachers can utilize the time released from presenting information, to "individualize" and make meaningful the learning experiences of the student.

The learning-systems concept should be considered from two points of view: the development, testing, and revising of the software system which actually helps the student learn; and the design and development of the hardware system which will store, transmit, and present the software.

LEARNING-SYSTEMS APPROACH TO THE DEVELOPMENT OF SOFTWARE

What is the student's greatest problem in a learning situation? All too often, students have to play a guessing game with teachers concerning the content of the course to be learned. If the students guess wrong, it is reflected in their grades. Most teachers probably believe that they have pointed out the learning objectives of their courses, but if the students do not understand, then there is a problem in communication and in perception as well. Of course, communication, in a sense, is teaching; and perception, learning.

In the process of communication, there are four levels of communication which can occur.

1. *Independent*

   This is a level of communication carried on by everyone in the form of self-communication (thinking to oneself).

2. *Physical Interdependence* .

   This is a type of communication in which the communicator just needs a "warm body" to talk to. Illustrations of this level of communication were typified in recent television commercials in which a man talks to his wife about his business and the wife talks about a new soap. Although both talk, neither one listens to the other.

3. *One-way*

   This is a type of communication which predominates the present educational system and is typified by the one-way lecture presentations or by most other instructional materials including books. Over the years, this one-way form of communication in education has been portrayed in cartoons by a teacher pouring knowledge from a pitcher into a student's head. With one-way communication, there is no way to know to what degree the student is attending to the message and learning, or even whether or not the student is capable of attending to the message and learning from it.

4. *Two-way*

This is a type of communication that is typified by the tutorial approach to teaching and recent instructional approaches such as programed learning and computer-assisted instruction.

Although all four of these levels of communication exist in education, learning which is a result of the association or interaction between teachers, of the association or interaction between teachers and students, or between instructional materials and students (fourth level), is the most effective and efficient. The major problem consists in the development of materials to be used at the third level which, through appropriate developmental techniques, takes on characteristics of the fourth level.

A brief review of David Berlo's communication model will be of value in laying the foundation for a learning-systems approach to the development of instructional materials. Berlo's S-M-C-R model[1] breaks the communication process into the characteristics of four parts: the Source, the Message, the Channel, and the Receiver.

Source	*Message*	*Channel*	*Receiver*
Communication Skills	Code	Seeing	Communication Skills
Knowledge	Content	Hearing	Knowledge
Attitudes	Structure	Touching	Attitudes
Social	Elements	Tasting	Social
Cultural	Treatment	Smelling	Cultural

FIGURE 6-1.   S-M-C-R *Communication Model*

Three points should be kept in mind.

1. The most important feature of Berlo's model is that the characteristics of the Source and the Receiver are identical.
2. One of the most important assumptions of the learning-systems concept is that educators "*want* to help students progress through our educational institutions." This does not mean just to give the students good grades, it means to *help* the student learn what is appropriate and necessary.

---

[1] See Chap. 3, pp. 65–67 for a further discussion of Berlo's model by Randall Harrison.

3. In the communication process, the Receiver or learner can mentally "turn off or tune out" the Source at any time much easier and faster than closing a book, hanging up the telephone, or changing a television channel.

In order to help the student learn, we must design messages that will motivate the learner to keep his communication channels open to teachers' messages. For example, if the *Source* uses one language but the *Receiver* uses a different language, communication is impeded. In many schools, teachers using a sophisticated form of classroom English are teaching culturally disadvantaged students who speak and understand an entirely different form of English. The teacher must change the message to fit the students' needs. In other words, *instructional messages need to be learner-oriented*.

In presenting information, we often make the assumption that the students perceive the information in the same manner and with the same meaning that we do. This is especially true in regard to verbal information. For some reason, many of us are under the impression that words have meanings. Words *do not* have meanings. People give meanings to the symbols we refer to as words, and because each of us has had a unique combination of experiences, these meanings may be highly personal or they may be almost coincident with the meanings held by other people.

Visual perception has a great deal to do with learning. It is of value, therefore, to consider the validity of what we see. In Fig. 2, does the line *AB* appear to be equal to the line *BC*? Measure them and you will see that they are equal.

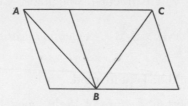

FIGURE 6-2

Figure 6-3 is disturbing to many people. The amount of disturbance appears to be in relation to prior exposure to art, mechanical drawing, etc. Young children are not as bothered as are adults. In fact, some young children see nothing wrong with the picture. If you cover up one side or the other, the figure looks all right. It is the middle section that is distracting because prior experiences preclude a rationalization of

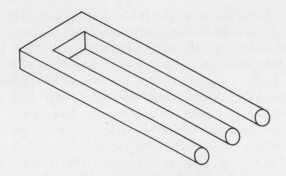

FIGURE 6-3

the two extensions becoming three. The interpretation of information sent to the brain from the different senses are mediated by past experiences; consequently, perceptions of this information may vary from person to person. Therefore, if we are truly concerned that students perceive a specific message and have a meaning for that message that is coincident or at least similar to our own meaning, we must be willing to vary the mode of presentation until this condition occurs.

Do you see the face of Christ in Fig. 6-4? Few people can see it right

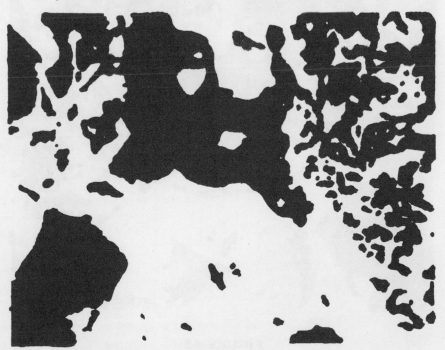

FIGURE 6-4

away. Some see the face only after hours of study and some never see it at all. In education, the learner is often expected to "see" a visual concept, or a situation with the same perspicacity as the teacher. If he fails to see this "something," he may not learn material that is important to his future progress. In the learning-systems concept, if the learner does not see what he should see, the stimulus is changed.

If you did not see Christ's face in Fig. 6-4, look now at Fig. 6-5. In this figure, some lines and shadows have been added to give more detail and, therefore, more visual cues to the viewer.

In Fig. 6-6, even more detail has been added to make it easier for the viewer to "see" the face. Even so, it may be necessary to study the illustration for a moment. Once you see the face in Fig. 6-6, look again at Fig. 6-4. Perhaps now the face will be visible in the first illustration.

Usually, by increasing the visual clues, learning can take place, whereas initially, many would fail to achieve the objective (in this case a recognition objective).

Because of the restrictions of the printed medium, it is difficult to present actual examples concerning the problems of perception through

FIGURE 6-5

FIGURE 6-6

our other four senses, but without too much trouble, examples of mis-perception in hearing, tasting, touching, and smelling can be demonstrated. An understanding of the communication process and how perception affects the fidelity of communication is vital to a successful use of a learning-systems approach to the development of instructional materials.

Development of a Course

The development of a course utilizing a learning-systems concept includes the same steps that are followed when preparing materials for programed instruction. A program consists of a sequence of carefully constructed items leading the student to mastery of a subject through self-study.

The change from programed instruction to the learning-systems concept is a matter of a greater degree of sophistication. The name change is necessary because "learning systems" is more descriptive of the process involved and because the stereotype already established by those familiar with the term "programed instruction" limits the mode of presentation to some kind of verbal format presented in a textbook form or by a teaching machine. People who are unfamiliar with the term often confuse it with computer technology. Extra steps are necessary, however, in order to apply a systems concept to the process.

Course development involves two major stages: (1) the behavioral analysis of the course content which is the preconstruction stage; and (2) the synthesis of learner behaviors which is the construction stage. Learner behaviors are anything that a student does purposely in response to an appropriate stimulus and which results in observable and measurable activities; e.g., writing, speaking, performing, etc.

In the first stage, the task is to specify learner behaviors and learning objectives so that the nature of the behavior can be discovered, past learning can be measured, behaviors to be modified can be identified, and objectives can be communicated.

The development of a typical course during this first stage follows a sequence designed to analyze and delimit the course content.

1. The first step in the analysis is the specification of the terminal behaviors (i.e., those behaviors which the course instructor wishes the learner to exhibit upon completion of a course). After each terminal behavior (objective) is stated, the following three questions should be asked:
   (a) Why should the student learn this behavior?
   (b) What is the student supposed to do with the behavior once he has attained it?
   (c) How long should the student retain the behavior after once attaining it?
   Answers to the first two questions could affect the inclusion of the objective in the course content and answers to the third question could affect the design of the instruction materials.

2. The construction of a post-test is the next step and will enable the observer to determine whether or not the terminal behaviors can be exhibited by the learner. Usually, a slight change in the wording of the specified behavior will result in the test item for this behavior.

3. The third step is the specification of the assumed entry behaviors of representative learners (i.e., those behaviors pertinent to the course content that are exhibited by prospective learners of the course—see Fig. 6-7) and the relevant characteristics of these learners (e.g., I.Q. level, educational background, etc.—see S-M-C-R Model).

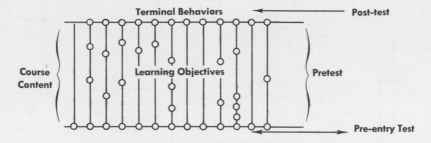

FIGURE 6-7. *Behavioral Analysis Outline*

4. The fourth step is the construction of a pre-entry test that will enable the observer to determine whether or not the assumed entry behaviors can actually be exhibited by representative learners who would take the course.

5. The fifth step is the specification of learning objectives of the course content which will be achieved through learning experiences and convert the learner's entry behaviors into terminal behaviors.

6. The sixth step is the construction of a pretest that will enable the observer to determine which of the learning objectives of the course content, if any, have been learned previously by representative learners.

7. The last step of the analysis is a preliminary tryout of the pre-entry test, pretest, and post-test on a sample of students that are representative of the intended learners for the course.

The tryout of the three tests is to verify the existence of assumed entry behaviors, the lack of terminal behaviors, and the lack of knowledge concerning the learning objctives which constitute the course content. Ideally, the learners would score 100 per cent on the pre-entry test and zero on the pretest and post-test. This would indicate that the entry assumptions made by the course instructor were correct (see Fig. 6-8).

The tryout test scores will usually vary from the ideal. If the pre-entry test scores are less than 100 per cent, it is an indication that the course instructor's assumptions regarding student entry behaviors were overstated (see Fig. 6-9).

If one were to write programed materials without testing for the existing entry behaviors of the intended audience, one would probably find many errors during the tryout of the complete program. Most writ-

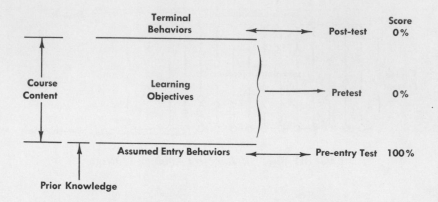

FIGURE 6-8. *Ideal Assumed Entry Behaviors*

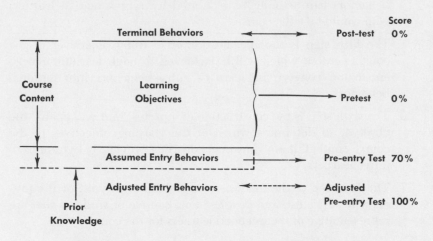

FIGURE 6-9. *Assumed Entry Behaviors—Too High*

ers would tend to expand the program by making the steps smaller and by overcueing the required responses to make up for the missing entry behaviors. Very seldom will a program developed under these circumstances be successful; a high percentage of the dropouts will result because the steps will be too small and students working through the program will consider it very dull and an insult to their intelligence.

If the pre-entry test scores were 100 per cent, the pretest scores greater than zero, it is an indication that the course instructor's assumptions regarding student entry behaviors were understated (see Fig. 6-10).

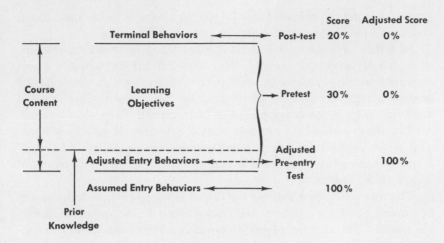

FIGURE 6-10.   *Assumed Entry Behaviors—Too Low*

Programed materials developed without testing for existing entry behaviors might enable learners to reach the terminal behaviors, but there is a built-in boredom factor which will inhibit positive growth of motivation as learning takes place during the program.

Programs of this type are exemplified by situations where learners are able to score high on the post-test without going through the program. A review of the literature on research concerning programed instruction reveals that many programs fall into this category. Almost every research article, where the pretest data are given, indicates that students knew from 30 per cent to 75 per cent of the content of the program before even going through the program. Generally, if the program is written before the students are tested, the excess frames stay in. It is not surprising that many students make the statement about programed instruction being boring and repetitious.

Often, when the intended audience is heterogeneous, students will be found in all three levels; above, below, and right at the assumed entry behaviors. Such data indicate the need for branching, and the same data can be used to locate and construct the appropriate branches.

This discussion has some rather obvious implications for the use of pre-entry tests and pretests in the classroom. If tests of this kind are not used, and subjective intuitive measures or traditional course limits are relied upon, the students' fund of cumulative ignorance may grow because the material presented may be too far above or below them. Such a situation fosters low grades and/or potential dropouts.

In either of these two situations, overstated or understated entry assumptions, it is important to go back over the first six steps of the pre-construction stage and make appropriate adjustments in the behavior analysis statements and the accompanying tests before going into the synthesis stage of the development of instructional materials.

The most successful programs start the learner from where he is. This gives support to a very important learning principle: *Paths of learning proceed most effectively and efficiently when going from the known to the unknown.*

The analysis stage concerns the use of this principle in locating the beginning point for a course, but not necessarily the sequence during the course. The need for a specific sequence varies from subject to subject and from unit to unit within a given subject. The achievement of some learning objectives is more dependent upon prior learning than the achievement of other objectives. In determining sequence, the developers should remember that the best sequence is ultimately the one that results in the greatest progress for the learner. As a starting point, the sequence could follow tradition or an experienced instructor's best guess. To develop a sequence that will proceed from the known to the unknown, a matrix method can be used. This method becomes cumbersome with a large number of objectives (over 50). Therefore, it may be useful to perform the matrix method using units or groups of objectives when a great number of objectives are involved.

THE MATRIX METHOD FOR SEQUENCING

List the learning objectives (represented by numbers) across the top of a matrix and duplicate the list of numbers down the left hand side of the matrix (see Fig. 6-11).

Identify any and all relationships between the learning objectives by placing an (X) in the square representing the intersection between the objectives represented by columns and the objectives represented by rows. (See Fig. 6-12. The diagonal from the upper left-hand corner represents the intersection of the column and row designated by the same object number.)

Rearrange the vertical columns and the corresponding horizontal rows (some objective numbers; i.e., column 6 and row 6) in such a manner that the (X)'s on the matrix, indicating relationships between learning objectives, are brought closer and closer into an elliptical pattern

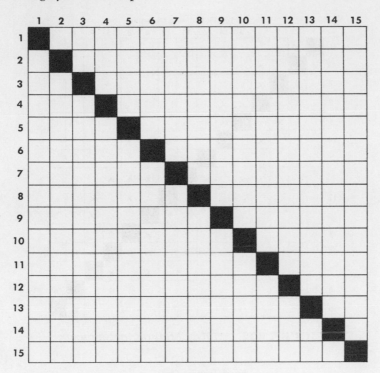

FIGURE 6-11. *Matrix Method for Sequence*

with the matrix diagonal as the major axis (see Fig. 6-13).[2] The ultimate goal of this step is to fill all the spaces adjacent to the diagonal with (X)'s. This would result in a particular sequence of objectives in which each objective would have some relationship with the previous objective and also with the subsequent objective or "the path of learning could proceed from the known objective to the unknown objective." The extra (X)'s not along the diagonal indicate relationships which can be used in testing, review, or for presenting content from a different point of view.

The second stage, the synthesis of learner behaviors, can start after all of the objectives have been defined, tests constructed and tried out on representative students, and objectives sequenced. The synthesis of the course content should not be started until all necessary adjustments

---

[2] If the formation of the (X)'s around the diagonal take on the appearance of two or more ellipses, this would indicate the possibility that the content can be divided into two or more units in which sequence is not important.

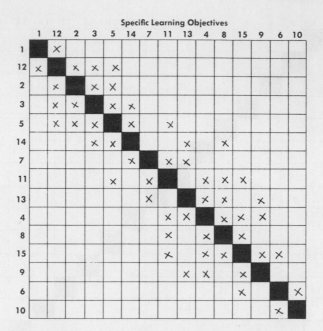

FIGURE 6-12. *Matrix Method for Sequence*

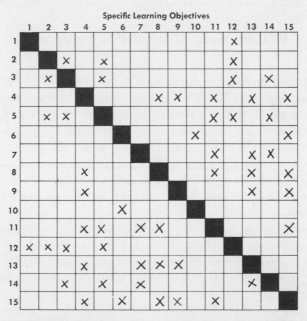

FIGURE 6-13. *Matrix Method for Sequence*

indicated by the results of the tryout of the tests have been made in the terminal- and entry-behavior lists and in the learning-objective list.

The first step in the synthesis or course-construction stage is the examination of the adjusted learning objectives to determine the most efficient and effective media and methods to be used in presenting the material associated with each objective (see Fig. 6-14), keeping in mind why that particular objective or terminal behavior is desired, what the learner is expected to do with this behavior, what budget is available, what the feasibility is of the media and method, how portable the course materials have to be, etc.

The second step of the construction or synthesis stage is the construction and preparation of the materials necessary to help the learner attain the learning objectives and terminal behaviors of the course, keeping in mind these four principles:

1. The content of the course is presented to the learner in small, single-concept steps or units that are appropriate to the learner's abilities; e.g., reading level, educational level, age, etc.

TERMINAL
LEVEL

Group

Demonstration

Trip

ETV

Face-to-Face

Film

P.I.

Audio

Models

ENTRY
LEVEL

FIGURE 6-14

2. For each step or unit, the learner is covertly or overtly involved, depending upon the behavioral requirement of that step.

3. In steps or units where the system requests specific responses, immediate confirmation of the correct responses is *usually* available.

4. The course materials are self-paced to meet individual differences. This may necessitate a certain amount of branching[3] from the main system to accommodate differences in the needs for the terminal behaviors of the course, the differences in learner abilities, or differences in entry behaviors (see Figs. 6-15 and 6-16).

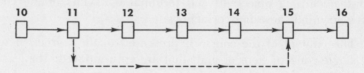

FIGURE 6-15.   *Modified Linear*

The form in Fig. 6-15 allows check points from time to time, such that if a student answers frame 11 correctly he may be able to skip further redundancy by being advanced to frame 15. Another version of this form will send the student back to frame 11 for further review if he answers wrong on frame 15. In one case, redundancy is avoided, while in the second version, redundancy is increased.

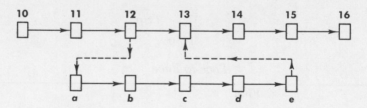

FIGURE 6-16.   *Linear with Subroutines*

Figure 6-16 illustrates another form that can be used in two ways. For the advanced and interested student, this form may allow him to

[3] "Branching" refers to a technique of designing self-paced instructional materials with interlaced alternate pathways so that each student is guided along a pathway that is appropriate for him.

pick up additional information relevant to the topic but not necessary for the terminal behaviors—an embellishment. For the slow student who was unable to answer frame 12 correctly, a variation of the previous frames may be used to present the particular topic or point from another viewpoint; i.e., frames *a* through *e* will be essentially the same as frames 8 through 11.

For the student without some specific entry behaviors necessary to continue on with frame 13, the branch (*a* to *e*) could be used to teach the student the necessary material. In this instance, frame 12 acts as a testing frame or "gate keeper" to be sure the learner is capable of continuing the course successfully.

The third step is the assembly of course materials and examination of them for clarity, continuity, and subject-matter validity.

The fourth step, and one of the more important steps of the course development, consists of trying out the course materials on representative learners and revision of the materials based on learner comments and errors. This "tryout-and-revision" process is repeated enough times so that 90 per cent of the learners are able to exhibit 90 per cent of the terminal behaviors.

This last step is very important in the development of a course where materials are "learner-oriented" rather than "instructor-oriented," and will enable students to master the material to the appropriate level.

In testing out the units or total courses, the *developer* has to be especially aware of individual differences. The following learning variables should be kept in mind as being contributing factors to individual differences:

(a) rate of learning;

(b) amount to be learned;

(c) mode of learning;

(d) interpersonal relationships in learning;

(e) motivation to learn.

The fact that students *learn at different rates* is probably accepted by most teachers. The problem is, that while most teachers agree that students learn at different rates, their teaching behaviors in the classrooms are based on techniques that require all students to learn at the same rate. If the students in a learning situation do not learn at the same rate, both techniques and materials must be changed.

The *amount to be learned* varies from student to student. The

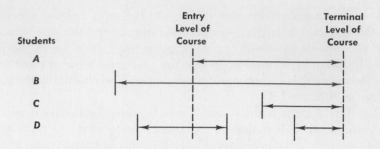

FIGURE 6-17. *Amount to be Learned*

amount to be learned can be identified through the use of pre-entry tests, pretests,[4] and post-tests (see Fig. 6-17).

For example, student *A* has the right entry behaviors for the course and doesn't know any part of the course. Student *B* needs some remedial work before he can start the course. Whether or not student *B* takes his remedial work prior to the course or concurrently with the course depends upon the subject matter, the student, and the dependency of the course on the student's knowledge of prerequisite material. Student *C* knows most of the course and in most instances would be wasting his time if he were to go back through material he already knows. Student *D* is more typical of most of the students today. Even though he knows a considerable part of the material, he also needs a certain amount of remedial study. Some kind of branching is indicated in dealing with students like *C* and *D*.

Mode of learning is also an important learning variable. One's assumptions about how students learn will usually determine the teaching methods used. For the purposes of this chapter, a presentation will be considered a "simulation" of the real-life situation when the same set of related objectives can be learned from various methods of presentation in a synthetic situation or learned by chance in a real-life situation.

A better understanding of the concept of simulation will be assured by beginning with a statement of the assumptions upon which this concept is based.

_____

[4] During the behavioral analysis stage, the pre-entry test (measuring what the student's experiences prior to the course were), and the pretest (measuring the student's knowledge of the course content), are kept as separate tests. After the course materials have been developed, tested, and revised, the pre-entry test and the pretest are combined into one unit and referred to generally as a pretest.

(a) There is such a thing as a "life environment."

(b) There is such a thing as an "academic environment."

(c) The purpose of the academic environment is to prepare the learner for the life environment.

(d) The value of exposure to the academic environment is measured by the learner's performance in the life environment as a consequence of behaviors that have been transferred and adapted from the academic environment.

In real life, the learner's performance usually consists of perceiving certain stimuli and responding to them appropriately. The learner's response generally is not made to one stimulus, but to patterns of stimuli. An objective of the academic environment is to present certain stimulus patterns that represent the appropriate specific experiences from which it is hoped the learner will be able to generalize when meeting real-life experiences. Transfer of learned responses from the academic environment to the stimulus patterns met in life is referred to as "stimulus generalization."

Because the evaluation of the academic environment is measured by the learner's performance in life as a result of "stimulus generalization," it is important that the stimulus patterns in the synthetic situations of the academic environment be such that:

(a) they establish in the learner certain responses;

(b) the responses transfer positively to the real-life or operational situation; and

(c) the responses constitute the desired and appropriate reaction to the real-life stimulus patterns.

When there is a demand for transfer of learning to superficially different situations, some modes of learning which emphasize response to *patterns of cues* will be more effective than others emphasizing responses to *specific cues*. Learning which directs response to the total configuration of the life environment will therefore enable the student to cope with wider varieties of real-life situations, including transfer from synthetic to life environments.

The process of setting up a synthetic situation which enables the learner to learn responses, which through "stimulus generalization" are desired and appropriate in a real-life situation, is called *simulation*.

As a process, simulation can be positive or negative. In the concrete-abstract continuum (Fig. 6-18), positive simulation refers to the

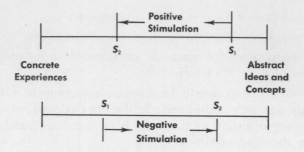

FIGURE 6-18.   *Concrete-Abstract Continuum*

condition wherein the synthetic situation (S_2) is *more concrete* than
the real life situation (S_1). Examples of positive simulation are the
three-dimensional models used in chemistry and mathematics as concrete demonstrations of abstract ideas or concepts. Negative simulation
refers to the condition wherein the synthetic situation (S_2) is less concrete than the real-life situation (S_1). Examples of negative simulation
are the simulated cars used in driver training, the simulated planes
used in air-crew training, and the scenery in theatrical plays.

Simulation is made up of two components: physical simulation—
the copying of that part of the real-life situation which is physically
involved in the desired responses or behaviors of the learner; and
psychological simulation—the copying of that part of the real-life
situation which is psychologically necessary to obtain the desired responses or behaviors of the learner. Psychological simulation can be
divided into three distinct types:

(a) the copying of that part of the physical environment of the
real-life situation that is *not* physically involved in the desired
responses of the learner but nevertheless does affect the learning of the desired responses. Examples of this are the use of
films with the driver-training simulators and the airplane
cabins in the air-crew training simulators;

(b) the substitution of symbolic stimuli for physical realism based
on stimulus generalization. Examples of this are the use of
stubby wings on the flight simulators and the use of a small
hood on the driver-training simulator to symbolize the real
thing;

(c) the use of symbolic stimuli (words and/or visuals) to retrieve
from the learner's memory information concerning past experiences that will help in the setting up of a synthetic situation.

> An example of this is the use of directions given prior to role-playing (a form of simulation); i.e., "You are the owner of a toy manufacturing business doing three million dollars worth of business a year. You have 100 employees, etc."

Given the task of simulating a real-life· situation, one may be tempted to produce a physical replica of the real-life situation, limited only by available budget and the state of the engineering art. There are kinds of behaviors and degrees of learning which may profit from a high degree of physical fidelity in the simulated environment, but other behaviors may be learned and may transfer quite adequately from synthetic situations having relatively little physical or functional realism.

Once it is recognized that there are degrees of both physical simulation and psychological simulation, practical decisions about the specifications for a synthetic environment will rest on economic and learning-objective compromises. From the standpoint of economy, the development of synthetic situations should rest on psychological simulation because as the degree of physical simulation increases, the physical environment (models, films, equipment, etc.) becomes more expensive to build and maintain. However, with low degrees of physical simulation, the student will be making verbal responses and will be transferring to the real-life situation little more than identificaton of specifics, and perhaps, certain ways and means of dealing with these specifics. This is adequate only if learning such specifics is the objec-tive.

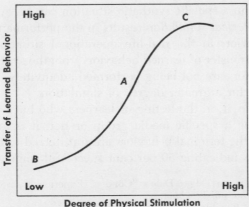

FIGURE 6-19. *Relationship between Degree of Physical Sim-ulation and Transfer of Learned Behavior*

Up to a point, increased increments of transfer of learned behaviors result from increased degrees of physical simulation (A section of transfer curve, Fig. 6-19). Human receptor channels, like other receivers, have limitations in sensitivity. For any stimulus input, there will be ranges of physical differences in the synthetic situation which will not be matched with behavioral differences (B and C sections of transfer curve, Fig. 6-19).

In setting up a synthetic situation, various intsructional media and varied methods and degrees of utilizations can be integrated providing flexibility in the desired simulation. It is important to remember that a particular synthetic situation (simulation) which involves a variety of instructional media should be designed in accordance with the predetermined learning objectives and not according to the characteristics of the instructional media. In other words, *fit the media to the objectives, not the objectives to the media.*

Figure 6-20 is, in a sense, a continuum ranging from abstract to concrete.[5] The placement of a specific medium in a specific tier is based on the general use of the medium; the number of senses involved; whether a synthetic situation is perceived directly (or indirectly through media); whether the synthetic situation is observed, heard, or both; and whether the perception involved is a synthetic situation or a verbal description of a synthetic situation. It is relatively easy to affect the placement of a specific medium by incorporating some new features or characteristics that would relate to the criteria used for deciding placement on the diagram; e.g., adding sound to filmstrips would move the combined media to the next tier below.

Simulation in a specific synthetic situation can be evaluated for its effectiveness. *Perfect simulation* results in the performance of specified terminal behaviors in the real-life operational situation as a consequence of the transfer of learned behaviors from the synthetic situation. If some behaviors are not being performed adequately, it is an indication of a need for a greater degree of simulation.

For example, if, in the testing of learners who have taken a course or unit utilizing a specific media group or tier, it is found that only 50 per cent of the terminal behaviors are transferred to the operational situation[6] (thus indicating 50 per cent successful simulation), then the

---

[5] Based in part on Edgar Dale's "Cone of Experience" as presented in his *Audio-Visual Methods in Teaching.*

[6] It might be possible in a given course developed in accordance with the systems approach to have 90 per cent of the learners learn 90 per cent of the content as measured by achievement of the *terminal behaviors of* the synthetic situation, but when presented with the *terminal behaviors in the operational situation,* the achievement is only 50 per cent. This result indicates a need for greater simulation in the synthetic situation.

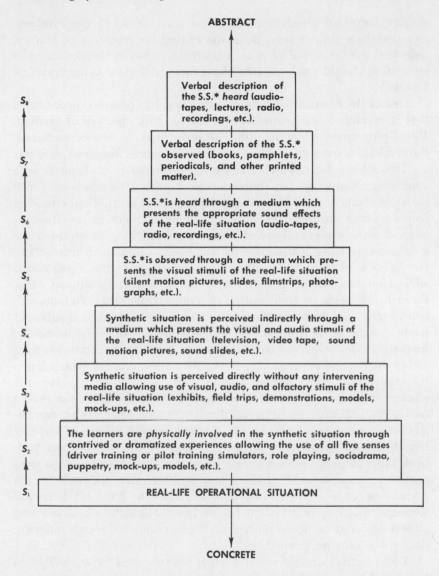

ABSTRACT

S_8 — Verbal description of the S.S.* *heard* (audio-tapes, lectures, radio, recordings, etc.).

S_7 — Verbal description of the S.S.* *observed* (books, pamphlets, periodicals, and other printed matter).

S_6 — S.S.* is *heard* through a medium which presents the appropriate sound effects of the real-life situation (audio-tapes, radio, recordings, etc.).

S_5 — S.S.* is *observed* through a medium which presents the visual stimuli of the real-life situation (silent motion pictures, slides, filmstrips, photographs, etc.).

S_4 — Synthetic situation is perceived indirectly through a medium which presents the visual and audio stimuli of the real-life situation (television, video tape, sound motion pictures, sound slides, etc.).

S_3 — Synthetic situation is perceived directly without any intervening media allowing use of visual, audio, and olfactory stimuli of the real-life situation (exhibits, field trips, demonstrations, models, mock-ups, etc.).

S_2 — The learners are *physically involved* in the synthetic situation through contrived or dramatized experiences allowing the use of all five senses (driver training or pilot training simulators, role playing, sociodrama, puppetry, mock-ups, models, etc.).

S_1 — REAL-LIFE OPERATIONAL SITUATION

CONCRETE

FIGURE 6-20. *Simulation through Use of Instructional Media (*Synthetic Situation)*

course materials should be restructured utilizing the media represented in the next lower tier or group—increasing the degree of simulation. The testing of learners who have taken the restructured course should indicate an increased transfer of learned behaviors as a result of a greater degree of simulation which has been set up in the synthetic situation. In a similar way, if, in the testing for retention of learned behaviors over a period of time, a decrease or loss is noted, increased simulation should be built into the course materials to increase retention.[7]

One of the reasons programed instruction has been so successful is that it combines active involvement along with the verbal content. When programed materials utilize records, films, or kits of materials, the resultant is even greater because the experiences are more concrete.

Throughout the research literature, the reader is confronted with conflicting comments; i.e., students were bored—students were captivated; students learned faster through programed instruction—students learned faster through television; students learned more—students learned less; students learned better by branching programed instruction—students learned better by linear programed instruction; etc. Because of their varied abilities, interests, and prior experiences, some students will learn better and faster in certain subject areas through one mode or combination of modes while other students will learn better and faster in the same subject areas through a different mode or combination of modes. The teacher should manipulate the learning environment for each student in order to facilitate learning rather than spend his time presenting the course content which limits the students to one mode of learning. This method necessitates the efficient utilization of a variety of media and materials for presenting course content: programed instructional materials, films, slides, demonstrations, face-to-face lectures, etc. It is not an efficient use of learning time to have a student go through an hour of the stereotyped, textbook form of programed material when the same learning objectives could be accomplished by having him read a regular textbook for ten minutes or view a five-minute demonstration; or have teachers and students in a lecture situation for an hour when the same learning objectives could be accomplished in fifteen minutes through independent study of a programed text.

The fourth learning variable, the *interpersonal relationships in learning*, has received increasing attention of late. Many people have

---

[7] As an indication of the need for greater simulation through more concrete learning experiences and less abstract verbalized learning experiences, suppose a random sample of graduating seniors in high schools were tested with the final examinations from a random sample of their freshman and sophomore courses? Chances are that a significant number of them would fail. If the behaviors that were not retained are not important, why try to teach them at all? If these behaviors are important, then something should be done to increase retention beyond the date of the final examination.

been aware of this variable for years, but little, if any effort has been made to classify it as a learning variable and to take it into account in the learning situation. For instance, in a programed instruction project, it was found that not all students like a partciular programed text; when given a choice of three programed texts covering approximately the same content, each student was able to choose a text that he liked and from which he could learn.

Why do we expect the learners to all like the same programed text, textbook, or even the same teacher? *If our ultimate goal is learning, then whatever will facilitate learning should be a part of the system.* If a student is not learning and a change in the textbook or a change in the teacher does result in learning, then why not do it?

The fifth learning variable, *motivation,* has been the topic of many conferences during the past two decades. For the purposes of this chapter, it is enough to say that, in general, educational institutions and educators are not paying enough attention to the need for motivation to stimulate learning. The concept of motivation is like the concept of individual differences; almost all educators will agree that what will motivate one child will not necessarily motivate another. Yet, in the classrooms, it is continually assumed that all children are motivated in the same manner with no individual differences.

These five learning variables are not taken into account largely because the teachers are too busy presenting the content of their courses. When a teacher is presenting the content of a course:

1. the student's rate of learning is determined by the teacher's rate of presenting;

2. the amount the student learns is limited by the amount the teacher presents;

3. the mode by which the student learns is determined by the mode the teacher decides to use to present the course;

4. the interpersonal relationship between the teacher and student is restricted to the teacher that is presenting;

5. if the teacher is presenting, the teacher does not have time to worry about individual motivation.

In the typical classroom situation, the teacher is the presenter of information, and is generally the focus of attention. Courses developed in accordance with a learning-systems approach replace the teacher as the presenter of information. Learning now becomes the focus of attention, and the teacher, who has been relieved of the time-consuming task of repeatedly presenting the same information, can concentrate on the task of *teaching*. The teacher becomes an educational diagnostician, a director, or a guide to meaningful learning experiences, adapting available materials and environment to the needs of the learner.

TESTING AND EVALUATION

Testing and evaluation are very important in the development of materials utilized in the learning-systems concept as well as for any significant improvement in learning.

In order to conserve time, energy, and money, one unit that represents a good sample of the skills and knowledge to be learned from the entire course should be selected and developed first. Once the media and instructional methods which will bring about the desired transfer of learning for the specific unit have been determined and tested, the development of the balance of the course may be carried out with a minimum of restructuring.

The most difficult job in testing and evaluation is to define what is to be tested and evaluated; consequently, meaningful testing and evaluation should be based upon specific objectives measuring achievement of course content. Tests developed from non-specific or non-definable learning objectives tend to show a very low correlation between the course content and the tests. Learning objectives may be classified as shown in Fig. 6-21.

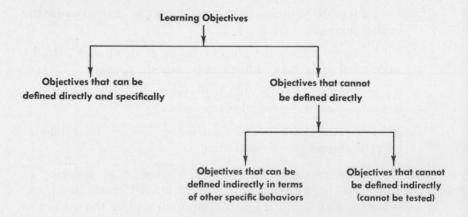

FIGURE 6-21. *Classification of Learning Objectives*

A test made from definable objectives (directly or indirectly) may serve three purposes, depending on the point of view, without changing the test form. It may serve as:

1. a *teaching test*, to help the learner become aware of what he has already learned and what he may have to review;

2. a *measurement test*, to determine what the learner knows at a given time. The learner can then be placed in a learning situa-

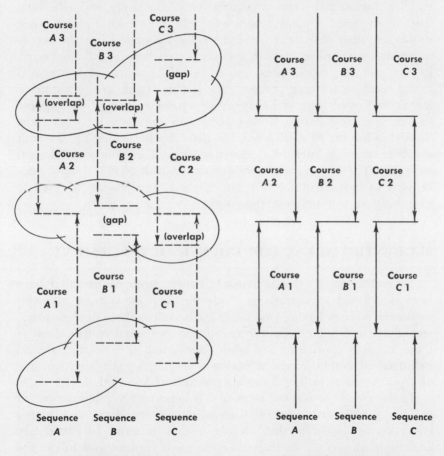

Traditional Patterns

Typified by obscure entry and terminal course behaviors permitting gaps and overlaps in a sequence of course

Learning System Patterns

Typified by defined entry and terminal course behaviors such that the terminal behaviors of one course are the same as the next course.

FIGURE 6-22. *Patterns of Course Sequences*

tion which will enable him to proceed without either an unnecessary review, or a gap in his knowledge in going from the known to the unknown (pre-entry tests, pretests, and placement tests);[8]

3. a *mastery test,* to determine if the learner has achieved mastery of the specified objectives of the course content (post-test).

It is useful to remember that the synthetic situation which has been validated by the transfer of appropriate learned behaviors to the real-life operational situation can be very effectively and efficiently used to evaluate student achievement. In almost all courses, some simulation other than at the verbal level is integrated into the course materials; e.g., films, models, artifacts, chalkboard, flannelboard, graphs, pictures, tapes, discs, and so on. If these materials are used in the teaching-learning process, why not use them in the testing of learning? Verbal tests of behaviors which were learned in response to more concrete forms of simulation may not only be testing the learned behaviors of the learner, but may also be testing the learner's ability to correctly interpret the instructor's verbalization of the desired behaviors. The same general considerations which go into the decisions of what to include in a course also go into the decisions of what to include in an evaluation of the course.

SUGGESTED AREAS FOR COURSE DEVELOPMENT

Several areas of education would benefit from courses that have been developed in accordance with the learning-systems concept: sequential courses having long-range goals such as those in elementary, secondary, and higher education; and non-sequential courses such as those found in continuing and adult education and in vocational- and industrial-education programs having short-range goals; e.g., learning of a psychomotor skill, gaining a finite unit of knowledge, etc.

In the area of sequential courses, it is important to point out one of the major differences between elementary, secondary, and higher education in regard to their developmental patterns. In elementary education, almost all students take the same content and follow the same pattern. In secondary education, almost all students follow one of four or five patterns. At the present time, the pattern which a student

---

[8] If a learning-systems approach were used for a total curriculum, the post-tests of one course would become the pretests of the next course. This approach would eliminate gaps and overlaps which characterize our present curriculum patterns (see Fig. 6-22).

might follow in secondary education is determined to a large extent by the amount of "cumulative ignorance" acquired by a student in elementary school. One can only estimate the effects of the approach to elementary education which would enable 90 per cent or more of the students to learn 90 per cent or more of the content.

1. The elementary curriculum would be completed by a high majority of students in a much shorter time.

2. Because of the decrease in learning time necessary to achieve the elementary curriculum, certain portions of the traditional secondary education curriculum would be transferred into the elementary curriculum.

3. Almost every student would enter and complete secondary education (only 71 per cent complete secondary education now).

Two approaches can be utilized in the development of instructional materials for sequential courses. One approach is the development of a subject from its introduction to some finite level; e.g., mathematics from kindergarten to twelfth grade. This is essentially a *vertical systems analysis and development*. The second approach is the simultaneous development of all the basic subjects from their introduction to some finite level; e.g., grades one through four, or kindergarten through eighth grade. This is basically a *horizontal systems analysis and development*.

It would be most efficient to apply the systems design at the elementary level before any of the other educational levels, because almost all students follow the some curriculum patterns and there is a need for interrelationships between basic subject areas. The horizontal systems analysis and development would be the best approach for a systems design at this level. It would allow the development of a continuous-progress type scale in each subject upon which a student's overall achievement profile could be recorded. The student, then, would experience a minimum of gaps and overlaps when transfering from school to school—or even from teacher to teacher. By varying the amount of time spent in each subject area in accordance with the student's needs, and by concentrating time and effort on the weak areas of the student's achievement profile, students should be able to complete eighth grade with a solid background and foundation in all subject areas.

Although the required courses in secondary education provide a core of course content which lends itself to a continuation of the horizontal systems analysis and development, several curriculum patterns in secondary education would benefit more from a vertical systems analysis and development. The area of mathematics provides one good example.

STAFF REQUIREMENTS TO DEVELOP A COURSE

Course development is a complex process. As a general estimate, 25-150 man-hours of labor are required to produce one hour of instructional materials for the average learner. This estimate can vary considerably depending on such factors as the degree of competence of those involved in regard to their particular specialty and the complexity of the subject matter.

In order to develop quality courses in accordance with the learning-systems concept, the services of a number of specialists may be needed.

1. Subject-matter experts or analysts are specialists who have taught the course content and are interested in learning-system orientation and behavioral analysis. Their job is to specify the entry and terminal behaviors and the mediating learning objectives necessary. They also act as subject-matter editors for accuracy of content of the final course materials.

2. Media specialists or examiners must be acquainted with the advantages and disadvantages of various instructional media. Their task is to determine collectively the media to be utilized in the presentation of each step or unit for maximum effectiveness and efficiency, and to initate the preparation of the necessary materials.

3. Subject-matter synthesists develop and synthesize the steps or units of the course on the basis of the behavioral analysis in the preconstruction stage. They are involved in the revision of those materials that have been tested with representative students.

4. Learning-system coordinators (behavioral technologists) must have a knowledge of a variety of media. In order to obtain the maximum benefits from utilizing the learning-systems approach in course development, their tasks are to conduct seminars; hold follow-up individual conferences; help define and analyze course content and accompanying tests as outlined in the preconstruction stage of the course development, and help in the validation of tests; make recommendations regarding the appropriate media for specified learning objectives; supervise the trial assembly of

course materials; and help in the testing and revision of the completed courses.

5. Production specialists from television, radio, graphics, film, computers, etc. produce materials designed to maximize learning most effectively and efficiently from the student's point of view.

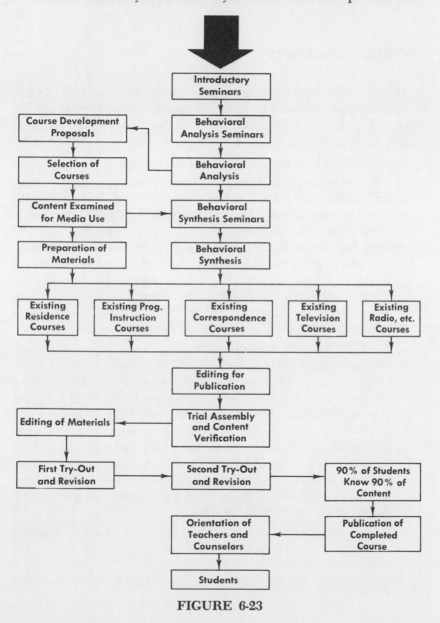

FIGURE 6-23

6. Publication editors edit the course materials prior to testing, after each revision, and prior to final publication for correct English, structure, continuity of format, etc.

Figure 6-23 indicates the sequence of events which might be followed in the implementation of a systems approach in education.

CLOSING COMMENTS

The use of the *total* learning-systems concept involves a lot of time, effort, and money. In order to facilitate educational innovation, several aspects of such an approach could easily be adapted into on-going courses as listed below.

1. Specify precisely the course objectives without using such vague and non-measurable terms as "understanding," "appreciation for," "familiarity with," "a knowledge of," etc. Robert Mager's book, on *instructional objectives*[9], has been helpful in the formulation of specific objectives. Just as it is possible to make test items out of specific objectives by a slight change of wording, it is also possible to make specific objectives out of test items. At the very least, specify the "critical objectives" of the course. "Critical objectives" are learning objectives which, if not achieved by the student, will inhibit or prevent learning in subsequent courses. Students should not be permitted to pass on to the next course without them.

2. Develop pretests which will clarify the student's standing in his class work, and indicate whether specific remedial work or advance placement is needed. A ready-made source of a pretest is a combination of a final examination from a prerequisite course or courses (just using the test items that are pertinent to the course for which you want the pretest) plus the first major test in the course itself (six- or nine-week examination). In this way, it is possible to measure whether the student has the necessary knowledge and skills to take the course and whether he already knows part of the course.

3. Look upon student errors as indications of possible learning problems. Most students try to answer test questions to the best

---

[9] Robert F. Mager, *Preparing Instructional Objectives* (Palo Alto, Calif.; Fearon Publishers, Inc., 1962).

of their ability. If a student's answers are incorrect, check into the learning situation. Maybe the objective was not taught right!

4. Make sure that tests are valid and actually measure the behaviors that represent the learning objectives of the course; test only behaviors which the student has had an opportunity to learn (no hidden objectives). For example, if a teacher wants a student to learn specific facts or to deal with facts in certain ways, a multiple-choice test may not identify whether or not the student has actually achieved these objectives. Multiple-choice tests usually measure ability to discriminate between answers (process of elimination) rather than demonstrate knowledge of a specific item or skill.

5. Keep in mind the five learning variables discussed earlier in this chapter concerning individual differences (see pp. 155-164).

In education, students come to teachers in order to learn. Generally, if the student does not learn by whatever method the teacher uses, he fails. The cumulative effect of failure cannot be measured in dollars and cents. Teachers have a moral responsibility to society to do everything in their power to help students learn to live.

SECTION 3.

THE PHYSICAL SYNTHESIS

A *School*, 1.	*Schola*, 1.
is a Shop in which	est Officina, in quâ
Young Wits are fashion'd	*Novelli Animi* formantur
to vertue, and it is	ad virtutem, &
distinguish'd into *Forms*.	distinguitur in *Classes*.
The *Master*, 2.	*Præceptor*, 2.
sitteth in a *Chair*, 3.	sedet in *Cathedra*, 3.
the *Scholars*, 4.	*Discipuli*, 4.
in *Forms*, 5.	in *Subselliis*, 5.
he teacheth, they learn.	ille docet, hi discunt.
Some things	Quædam
are writ down before them	præscribuntur illis
with *Chalk* on a *Table*, 6.	*Cretâ* in *Tabella*, 6.
Some sit	Quidam sedent
at a Table, and write, 7.	ad Mensam, & scribunt, 7.
he mendeth their Faults, 8.	ipse corrigit Mendas, 8.
Some stand and rehearse	Quidam stant, & reci-
things committed to	tant mandata
memory, 9.	memoriæ, 9.
Some talk together, 10.	Quidam confabulantur,
and behave themselves	10. ac gerunt se
wantonly and carelessly;	petulantes, & negligentes;

Introduction

Section 3 moves to the classroom level. The theory and philosophy of the preceding chapters serve as a backdrop to the frequently disorganized and generally unpredictable world of the classroom teacher.

A. Walden Ends begins his chapter by indicating that it is not possible to teach anyone anything. He does not imply, however, that all of teaching is a futile exercise. He believes that the challenge of teaching is to arrange an environment so that the learner or student can and will learn. Ends makes the point that teaching is not just telling, or presenting, but rather a complex matter which requires all the skills known about learning and communication The field of communication which he discusses is related to the communication models described in other chapters, but from the point of view of the classroom teacher and his students. When Ends discusses such matters as barriers to effective communication, he uses simple, straightforward words and terms which are, nevertheless, packed with considerable meaning and complexity of application.

June King McFee's chapter on "Visual Communication" continues Ends' discussion with an emphasis on communication problems which can be overcome by well-prepared visual symbols. McFee extracts from her special field of art and design the principles which a teacher should apply in designing visual materials for classroom use. She is very aware of the fact that such matters as culture and the background of the learner make great differences in the extent to which various kinds of symbols can be understood and interpreted. She suggests, however, certain rules of design which apply to a large class of learners and to many different kinds of content areas.

Anyone with classroom experience should be aware of the ideas presented in the chapter by Harry Wolcott, an educator and anthropologist. He identifies both ideal behavior and real behavior, and stresses the differences between them. He gives a great deal of attention to "concomitant" learnings, which are learnings other than the obvious and intended ones.

Wolcott discusses the problems of using media relevant to the classroom teacher under two major headings. The first includes problems of scope, accuracy, and relevance of the media. The participant-observer technique (which Wolcott says anthropologists favor) is employed. The participant-observers are prospective teachers who gathered ancedotal reports or "protocals."

Wolcott's second major heading deals with the place of media and some of the ways in which media produce stress for the classroom teacher. Mechanical problems, scheduling difficulties, and other similar matters often create situations in which some totally different things are taught than were planned.

Wolcott's chapter, then, examines the classroom from the bottom up as well as from the top down. He underscores what Ends and McFee describe as the complex world of the classroom teacher in which an understanding of communications is vitally needed.

CHAPTER SEVEN

Proficient Teaching: Communication in Process

A. Walden Ends

INTRODUCTION

A learned philosopher once wrote the following poignant description of the function, role, and responsibilities of a proficient teacher:

> No man can reveal to you ought but that which already lies half asleep in the dawning of your knowledge. The teacher who walks in the shadow of the temple, among his followers, gives not of his wisdom but rather of his faith and his lovingness. If he is indeed wise he does not bid you enter the house of his wisdom, but rather leads you to the threshold of your own mind.[1]

---

[1] Kahlil Gibran, *The Prophet* (New York: A. A. Knopf, 1959), p. 56.

Further, practice shows that it is not possible to *teach* anyone anything anyway! As the old saw explains, "You can lead a horse to water but you can't make him drink." So it is with children; you lead them through their lessons but you can't make them truly learn. Rather, the role of the teacher is more properly conceived as one which organizes and provides essential learning experiences for children. The process of learning does not occur until the learner interacts and becomes involved in the experiences which are provided.

Traditionally, teaching has been conceived as the act of imparting knowledge and selected skills; particularly those skills which our society has deemed necessary in order to achieve a fruitful life. It has also been traditional that the achievement of the teacher and the success of the students be assessed through determining each pupil's ability to answer selected queries posed by the teacher. However, this concept is not truly an adequate representation of the process of teaching and learning.

Teaching, when understood, implies a great deal more than the mere imparting of selected knowledge and skills; more than testing a student's ability to parrot back the facts and details of a lesson which has been presented. Fully understood, teaching implies content and a body of knowledge; it implies the activation and transfer of this knowledge from the unknown to one's storehouse of knowns; it implies relationships, associations, and discriminations which bring one area of knowledge into close harmony with other areas of knowledge. Further, teaching implies discovery, excitement, and the joy of experience. And, perhaps most important, teaching implies communication; the means of transmitting that which has been learned by one learner to another. Succinctly stated, "the whole art of teaching is only the art of awakening the natural curiosity of young minds for the purpose of satisfying it afterwards."[2]

Accordingly, and without question, it is the teacher who is the essential variable in the selection and presentation of the learning programs found within our schools.

> Meaningful and skillful teaching is not an accomplishment of a teacher who views his task with misgivings and cloudy objectives. Rather, meaningful and skillful teaching is reserved for those who comprehend the great responsibility of their profession and who, day by day, conscientiously seek to improve their own personal inadequacies.[3]

---

[2] Anatole France, quoted in G. Wagner, "What Schools are Doing," *Education,* Vol. 82, Nov., 1961, 188.

[3] E. Pack, "Precepts of Good Teaching," from the editor's preface, *Clearing House,* Vol. 36, Sept., 1961, 21.

Further, proficient teaching relies upon communication as its vehicle for dynamism. Without such forces and energy, it is indeed questionable whether or not the process of teaching would exist at all, as all modes of teaching require some form of communication in order to achieve the transmission of knowledge from one learner to another. Notwithstanding, even meaningful watching requires communication!

The concept of communication, as an inseparable element of teaching is neither new nor esoteric. It is a common element which is usually well known to any conscientious student of the teaching process. However, to know and to understand teaching theory does not insure one of the ability to put it into practice. Why?

Teaching is a highly complex process involving an interaction among a potentially unlimited number of elements in rapid sequence. The speed of this process if often so rapid that it would appear that teacher presentations and pupil interactions are simultaneous. Not every one can teach; *teaching takes talent*, and only a few are so gifted.

THE COMMUNICATION OF KNOWLEDGE

> Presenting information is an art; success depends on the teacher's insight into his pupils, his knowledge of the topic, and his use of a style suited to his personality. There is no single pattern or model to be followed. . . .[4]

The above statement rather ably identifies the qualifications necessary in order to achieve proficiency in teaching; except for one thing. It fails to take into account the means and devices available to the teacher in accomplishing his task.

For centuries, the only tool for the communication of knowledge and learning was verbalization. Men passed whatever they had learned from mouth to mouth in order that their future offspring and future generations might profit from their experiences. From these practices and procedures in instruction, we have inherited many legends and folk tales which advise and/or admonish the young toward certain selected modes of social standards or behaviors.

Generally speaking, it was not until the invention of printing that the verbal method of instruction was changed to any great extent.

The printing press provided, for the first time, an efficient means for reproducing and distributing man's knowledge in order that all

---

[4] L. J. Cronback, *Educational Psychology* (New York: Harcourt, Brace & World Inc., 1963), p. 397.

men might become educated. However, few people today look upon the invention of the printing press as the initial use of media in the process of instruction.

From this modest beginning, teaching aids and instructional media have opened the way to a more efficient system of communication between teacher and pupil than had ever been known in recorded history. Instead of telling pupils what they are to learn, as they do in less developed cultures, or having to have students respond in a read, write, and recite session, the modern teacher is now free to teach creatively in meeting the various instructional needs of his students.

How is this done? What is the process of teaching and instruction which meets the needs of the growing child? In what ways does the process of communication facilitate the process of learning?

There is much to be learned before the process of teaching and the process of learning can be fully understood. However, it can be quickly said that teaching does not occur in the absence of students. Teaching might best be thought of as the generator of interaction between the pupil and the learning experience.

Logical examination reveals that teaching is but one half of the reciprocal relationship between itself and the process of learning. As such, proficient teaching requires effective communication with the learner. "The more effective the communication process, the more effective learning is likely to be."[5]

Cassel has identified six independently organized phases of the process of teaching:

1. learner readiness;

2. pacing and individualizing;

3. goal-setting and goal-striving;

4. affectivity and learner aspiration;

5. transfer;

6. evaluation.

He states that "each of these phases is closely related to the other five phases, and all six of the phases are an integral part of effective learning when it occurs."[6]

---

[5] C. Collier, *et al.*, *Teaching in the Modern Elementary School* (New York: The Macmillan Company, 1967), p. 175.

[6] R. N. Cassel, "The Teaching Act and Learning Effectiveness," *Educational Forum*, Vol. 28, March, 1964, 303.

In order to achieve effective communication with the learner, the teacher must clearly understand and appreciate the importance of each of the phases. For example, readiness is not something that becomes a part of a child when he reaches school age, nor is it something which a teacher bestows upon a deserving pupil when he comes to school. Quite to the contrary, readiness is "the flame of knowledge that burns from within the learner, it cannot be imposed effectively by extrinsic manipulation."[7]

It has been said that "telling isn't teaching"; all meaningful learning comes from within as the learner interacts with his environment. The skillful teacher presents problems, experiences, and activities which will serve to fan the flame of knowledge into a blaze of intellectual accomplishment. But, be ye warned! This is no simple task. To achieve the fire of enthusiasm, the proficient teacher must establish an open line of communication between himself and the learner. This is the first and most necessary step in promoting achievement.

When the bonds of communication have been forged, it is then imperative that the teacher concern himself with the pacing and individualization of the learning experiences. To illustrate, all horses have the capacity to run; the Thoroughbred is best suited for racing whereas the Clydesdale is better suited for work-type activities. So it is with children. Some can mentally run as fast as the wind while others are more inclined to plod along, making good progress, but at a much slower rate of speed. It is only through effective communication that such individual differences can be ascertained.

The tasks of goal-setting and goal-striving can be independent activities, but, more often, group action is necessary. Were it not for the goals generated through social and intellectual interaction, man would probably have made little progress or improvement from his meager beginnings in the cave. In suggesting that goals are not necessarily self-originated, one must remember that man is a social creature as well as an intellectual being. From his various relationships and experiences, man creates and/or innovates changes in his surroundings and environment which appear to him as being more desirable than what he has. These goals are derived, most often, through communication with others.

The teacher serves the role of an expeditious agent, telescoping the periods of time required for achieving the goals; i.e., skills and abilities necessary for a fruitful life. Instead of having each child learn the same things at the same speed that children in preceding generations

---

[7] *Ibid.*

learned, the proficient teacher, via communication, is able to condense and compress selected learning experiences in order that children can learn more and learn faster than did the preceding generations. This task certainly is not for the incompetent or untalented.

Hopefully, a child will be able to apply what he learns in one area of study to the solution of problems which he encounters in other areas. This process is known as transfer. Some advocate that to achieve transfer of learning, a very formal, strictly intellectual curriculum must be presented, while others contend that learning which remains verbal and abstract; i.e., formal, only has negligible effect upon one's responses in real-life situations.

> The most imperative educational goal is to increase the pupils' ability to think, i.e., to replace trial and error or thoughtless response in a problematic situation with intellectual control of decisions. This outcome can be called many things—reasoning ability, intellectual power, mastery of the great disciplines, functional skill in problem solving—whatever the name, the aim is transfer.[8]

As with the other phases in this discussion, communication plays an integral part in providing the means necessary for transferring knowledge from one area to another. Further, it is not until the similarities and differences within a problem can be perceived that the learner can look back into his storehouse of experience and determine whether or not he has met a similar problem before. If he has, the alternatives to a solution may be at hand; if not, he then has to communicate his insufficiency in order to get assistance. "Transfer of a behavior pattern to a new situation is likely to occur whenever the person recognizes the new situation as similar to other situations for which the behavior has been appropriate."[9] To accomplish this, purposeful communication is vital and must occur within the learner himself as well as between the learner and his teacher. Primarily, transfer is accomplished when the learner engages in evaluation of a problem with which he is confronted.

Evaluation, the final phase presented by Cassel, is a process which is commonly not well understood. All too often, evaluation is conceived of only as a program for testing or a means of measuring accomplishment. This, however, is not an adequate concept of the process of evaluation. Simply defined, effective evaluation is best perceived as feedback to the learner regarding a particular event, situation, or experience which he can use to develop more adequate perceptions about

---

[8] Cronback, *op. cit.*, p. 314.
[9] *Ibid.*, pp. 318–319.

himself and his environment. Further, it should be understood that evaluation must serve two main purposes: (1) The purpose of assessment; and (2) the purpose of change, personal growth, and improvement. If growth toward greater personal adequacy is not the outcome of the process of evaluation, then time should not be wasted giving "lip-service" to this terminal element of the learning process.

A note of caution. Purposeful and effective learning, and thus the changing of behavior, can only be accomplished through purposeful and effective evaluation! Again, as in the preceding phases of learning, the most essential ingredient in the process of evaluation is communication. Without communication, little can be accomplished toward promoting change in pupil behavior and fostering a continuous experience for learning.

Thus far, we have examined the importance of communication in the process of education and, more specifically, the necessity of purposeful communication for affecting behavioral changes; i.e., learning, within the pupil. The next portion of this chapter will discuss selected patterns of communication and the affecting variables which are usually present to distort and/or prevent the learning message from being understood by the pupil.

THE COMMUNICATIONS PROCESS UNMASKED

Carefully examined, the process of communication requires the exchanging and translating of knowledge into information, ideas, or viewpoints in order that other people can develop common understandings and mutually agreeable commitments. Accordingly, the key to successful communication is the concept of *commonness*. In order for one to fully communicate with another, commonness—a channel for understanding—must be established.

Most communication between people is of the "two-way" variety Many hours are spent each day at home, at school, and at the office sharing ideas and conversing with others. This is not the case within most of our school classrooms today, however. More often than not, communication in the classroom is of the "one-way" variety, epitomized by the dissemination of information without the opportunity, on the part of the student, for discussion and verbal interchange.

In some situations, one-way communication can serve as an effective means of teaching; for example, for making known certain types of essential information in a brief period of time. However, in using one-way communication, the learner is usually not able to agree or disagree—his role is to accept that which is communicated to him. More cogently stated, in this mode of communication, the environment and circumstances surrounding the message to be learned are structured in such a way that the learner has only to pay attention and to heed the advice of the teacher. To illustrate this point, two examples of one-way communication are shown in Fig. 7-1.

Source — Message — Destination
Teacher — Lesson — Pupils

FIGURE 7-1

Obviously, it is possible for the teacher to convey the message, "Never run down the stairs," in many different ways. In the panel on the left, the teacher is pleasantly reminding the class that it is not safe to run down a stairway. On the other hand, in the panel on the right, the teacher is forcefully reinforcing the message. So it is in most of our verbal conversation. To change the emphasis upon the words within the sentence, or to change the manner in which the sentence is delivered, changes the meaning of the sentence.

A more graphic example of this phenomenon can be seen in the following sentence:

"I DID NOT SAY YOU STOLE THE RED BANDANA!"

By merely changing the emphasis which is placed upon any one of the words in the sentence, the entire meaning and context of the sentence can be altered. Emphasis upon the word "I" gives the sentence an entirely different context than does placing the emphasis upon the word "not."

To extrapolate a bit from the example above, it is not difficult to gain some understanding of the pitfall which confronts a good many of our contemporary teachers in regard to their use of communication in the classroom. All too often, out of supposed necessity or ignorance, teachers rely upon one-way communication to teach their lessons. And what of this method? What are the results? With few exceptions, they are usually not very successful or rewarding.

Telling is not teaching! Many of the subject areas studied in school do not lend themselves to the one-way pattern of communication. Any subject that requires discussion, interaction, and/or clarification is not appropriate for such a presentation. The study of ethical values within a cultural system, for example, is hardly an appropriate subject to approach via the technique of one-way communication. Values, in and of themselves, are relative in time, place, and culture, as well as in the understandings of the pupils studying them. Clearly, another means or design for communication is necessary.

In order to meet the requirements of an interactive discussion, two-way communication with "feedback" is required. Through the use of the feedback mechanism and the process of evaluation, a teacher can present an idea to a pupil and almost simultaneously determine whether or not it was properly understood. If it was, the teacher can then proceed to the next level of complexity. However, if the idea was not properly understood, the teacher can again present his idea to the pupil, perhaps with more explanation.

The student then can reinterpret the meaning of the idea and respond back to the teacher. If, upon this second examination of the idea, the learning is satisfactory, the teacher can proceed to the next step. However, if the student still fails to understand what it is the teacher is presenting, the idea, hopefully, can be presented in still another way in order that the student learn it.

In marked contrast to the process of two-way communication, a pattern of one-way communication is illustrated in Fig. 7-2. Note that there is no channel for feedback. Therefore, the efforts expended in explaining a concept (or in delivering a stern warning, as in the right-hand panel of Fig. 7-1) remain unassessed and, perhaps, unlearned by the pupil. It is only through two-way communication and the feedback mechanism that one can know whether or not the task has been accomplished.

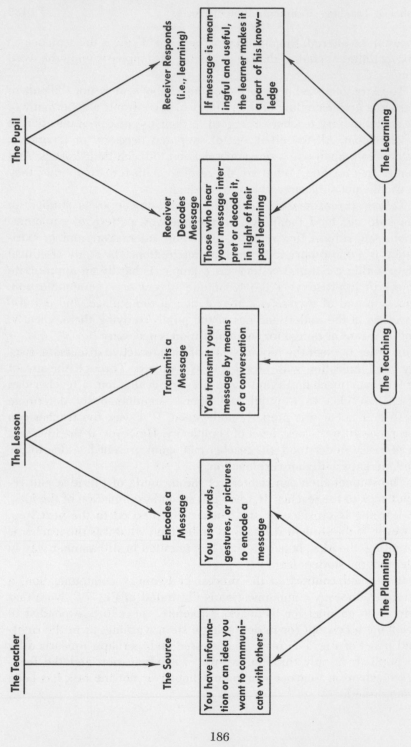

FIGURE 7-2

ELEMENTS WHICH INHIBIT
EFFECTIVE COMMUNICATION

Thus far, it would appear that all is required for effective communication in the classroom is an adequate measure of discussion and feedback. In theory this is true; but in practice there are numerous variables which affect the process of communication.

Wittich and Schuller have identified six elements which they suggest interfere with the process of affective communication. These variables, although not impossible to overcome individually, do pose increasingly difficult problems when combined within the communications process. In fact, the problems encountered in achieving effective communication seem to multiply geometrically in relation to the number of variables present.

Among those variables identified, two distinct groupings seem to be present. Group One includes those factors which are likely to have their origins outside the classroom, or are attributable to physical causes. Group Two includes those factors which are more closely associated with a teacher's behavior and his presentation of a lesson.[10]

Group One (External Variables)	*Group Two* (Internal Variables)
1. Disinterest	1. Referent Confusion
2. Daydreaming	2. Imperception
3. Physical Discomfort	3. Verbalism

In addition to these variables, there is a third group of factors which must be considered in studying the process of communication. Categorically, these are best perceived as *intervening variables* within the learning process, in that they affect the behavioral habits of teachers as well as pupils. However, the intervening variables are much more subtle than those of the first two groups, and are often mistaken or overlooked. Accordingly, the student of classroom communication patterns should train himself to become sensitive to them and to their consequences.

Group Three
(Intervening Variables)
1. Prejudice
2. Experience
3. Cognitive Knowledge

---

[10] W. A. Wittich and C. F. Schuller, *Audiovisual Materials: Their Nature and Use,* 3rd ed. (New York: Harper and Brothers, 1962), pp. 6–12.

More precisely, one is what one believes; one is what one has experienced; and one is what one knows. Figure 7-3 illustrates what is likely to happen to the flow of an instructional message as it filters through the selected variables in the communications process.

Certainly, all possible variables which might interfere with communication have not been considered. However, the nine variables which are presented represent the major elements affecting communication within the learning process and hence, will serve as focal points for the subsequent discussion.

The intervening variables are perhaps the most difficult of all the selected variables to control within the learning process. For the most part, they are the products of psychological conditioning, opportunity for learning, and/or one's ability to assimilate that to which he has been exposed. In order to control these factors, one must really alter the attitudinal and behavioral patterns of an individual before much progress can be made.

Of course, radically changing the personality structures of students is not within the limits of a teacher's capacities or responsibilities. However, the proficient teacher is always sensitive to the effects of the intervening variables and is ready to deal with them and the challenges they present in the best way he knows how.

In sharp contrast to the intervening variables, the external and internal variables possess factors which the teacher can readily control. Disinterest, for example, may have its source either in or outside the limits of the classroom, but it can usually be controlled through the application of a small measure of *vividness*. All too often, the lesson to which we expect a pupil to respond is slow moving, lacking in luster, frought with unnecessary repetition, lacking in the qualities of general interest, sometimes irrelevant to immediate needs, and worst of all, poorly taught. It is no wonder that students become disinterested and bored. It has always been a curious phenomenon that educators subject children to situations, conditions, and experiences that they would never apply when teaching adults. Certainly, children cannot be treated as miniature adults, but they can be treated as important individuals, possessing variable interests, needs, and abilities. Because students are a captive audience, this does not mean that they should be treated as such. A simple but skillful application of instructional media—motion pictures, 35-mm slides, specimens, recordings, television—may be all that is necessary in order to transform a dry, uninteresting discussion into a dynamic and vitally alive experience for the learner. All that is required is a measure of *vividness*.

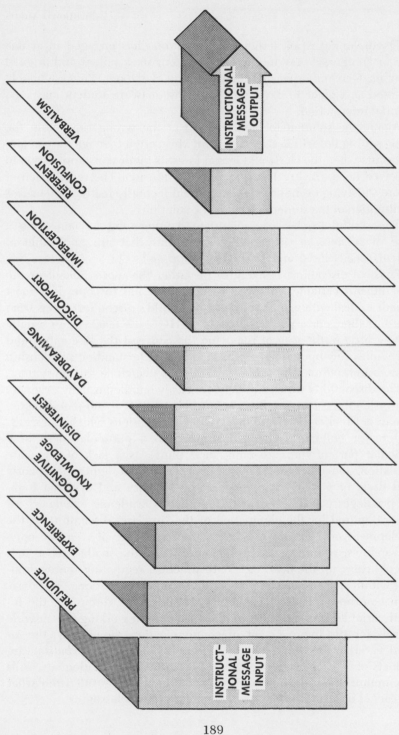

FIGURE 7-3. *Barriers in Effecting Communication*

Daydreaming is an activity that everyone has engaged in at one time or another; it may be the source of our most potent and original thoughts. Generally speaking, however, the classroom is not commonly accepted as a place to daydream since the unaware student may miss essential information.

Again, the solution to daydreaming at the wrong time or in the wrong setting lies within the classroom. More often than not, daydreaming occurs when the classroom lesson loses its vitality, its application to perceived needs, or breaks up in verbal confusion. The recollection of a more satisfying event or experience, held mentally ready, then usurps the attention of the student. What is the solution?

The skillful teacher can eliminate daydreaming by conveying a sense of *immediacy* through potent lessons that are applicable to students' needs and geared to their appropriate levels.

Physical discomfort is likely to be either the most difficult or the least difficult variable with which the teacher has to cope. It is most difficult to deal with when the source of a child's discomfort stems from a chronic illness or a physical handicap. Here, the teacher can usually do very little in the way of removing the cause of the discomfort and hence, must rely upon building a warm and understanding relationship between himself and the student in order to overcome this limitation.

The discomforts which can be more easily handled usually originate right inside the classroom. Because a teacher is active and mobile, often he may not feel or be aware of classroom conditions which cause discomfort for children. When constrained to a particular desk in a particular part of the classroom, such things as a lack of adequate ventilation, too much or too little heat, improper lighting, a poorly fitted desk, or a rigid policy concerning lavatory and drinking fountain privileges can interfere with a student's academic efficiency. All that is required for the elimination of the "in-class" discomforts is the development of a mental sensory-thermostat. When it is stuffy, open the windows; when it is too bright, pull down the shades; when it is too cold, turn up the heat, etc. With practice, regulating the environment within a classroom can practically become a conditioned response.

In contraposition to the external variables just discussed, the internal variables present quite another problem in working out suitable controls for the improvement of communication. Commonly, the internal variables, *referent confusion, imperception,* and *verbalism,* are products of a teacher's pedagogical style rather than inadequate skills in communication alone. These problems generally result from what the teacher does, or does not do, when he presents a lesson.

Referent confusion can be the result of hearing a new meaning applied to a word for which a prior (different) meaning has been established:

> . . . on crossing the state line into Vermont a geography teacher's son expressed great surprise at seeing forests of trees instead of the never-ending forests of chimneys which he had "learned" characterized heavily industrialized New England.[11]

Or it can be the result of hearing similar sounding words:

> A second-grader reported that she had ridden up and down on an alligator (escalator-elevator) on a field trip.[12]

Thus, it is possible for two people to hear the same presentation, yet for each to come away having an entirely different understanding of what was intended.

Imperception is the result of inaccurate observations which bring about inaccurate understandings. The terms "to see" and "to understand" are usually taken as synonyms. "To see is to believe" is a familiar expression which is based upon the assumption that what one sees, he understands.

The fallaciousness of this logic is easily shown through the presentation of an optical illusion or legerdemain. In addition, it is demonstrated in the mirage phenomenon which is common to most hot deserts and equatorial oceans. So it is with imperception; to see is not necessarily to understand.

Perhaps the best example of imperception is illustrated in the old parable of the blind men examining the elephant. The first blind man said, "I see, the elephant is very much like a tree"; he felt the trunk. The second blind man said, "I see, the elephant is very much like a wall"; he felt the elephant's side. The last blind man said, "Ah, the elephant is much like a rope"; for he had felt the tail. All three blind men were correct to a very limited degree. However, an elephant is not like a tree, or a wall, or a rope; in fact, it in no way resembles these entities. Imperception, thus, is the result of inaccurate perceptions based upon inaccurate or insufficient information. The result: misconception and confusion.

Verbalism, the final element to be discussed, is probably the most common variable which interferes with communication and the process

---

[11] *Ibid.,* p. 8.
[12] *Ibid.*

of learning. Simply defined, verbalism is the practice of using too many words, thus confusing the issue, or too much dependence upon words alone to get one's message across. As a prime example, Wittich and Schuller make the following comment:

> This point is well illustrated by one teacher's report: "During the first five or six weeks of school, pupils listen to me; they seem very interested in my descriptions. Then comes a curious change. As week follows week and more words follow more words, interest lags, and finally even I realize that it is time for a change, a change in the methods I use to get across the ideas I so urgently seek to teach.[13]

What happens? Why do words, the very ingredients of communication, inhibit the process for which they were created? Perhaps the answer can be found in reversing the familiar expression, "A picture is worth a thousand words." A thousand words are not always worth a picture! Sometimes only three hundred are enough, and anything more would serve only to confuse or be repetitive. The following poem very succinctly, yet fluently, describes the metamorphosis of a leaf with the coming of autumn:

To An Autumn Leaf

As if the gods of Nature
Know that you must die
So soon
They've changed your once green face
To rich ripe gold.
Your last attempt at gaiety
Has come
To give to all, who do behold
Your loveliness
A lasting memory before you die
So soon.[14]

A thousand words could be said regarding autumn and the turning of the leaves, but it is doubtful that any more words would render the statement more eloquent.

The effective use of words is an art and a skill. However, it would be insufficient to suggest that teachers talk too much or are not very skilled in communication, although, in many instances, this is true. As a counterpoint to the need for clarity and succinctness, L. J. Cronbach offers

---

[13] *Ibid.*, pp. 7–8.
[14] Leon E. Wright, ed., *Come Share With Us* (Philadelphia: Dorrance and Co., 1959), p. 30.

the following comment in support of a certain amount of repetition in teaching:

> The teacher should guard against the temptation to "cover ground" rapidly. This phrase itself reveals a false conception of teaching. Exposing the pupil to an idea is not teaching; the exposure must be thorough enough that he comprehends and retains the important part of the presentation. Information can always be presented more rapidly than it can be grasped; language is a highly distilled extract of the speaker's thought.
>
> . . . The pupil who misunderstands one part of the communication, either through inattention or because some word is unclear to him, can catch his error if the same thought is echoed in several sentences.[15]

Verbalism, then, can be an extreme. The redundancy of a repeated message does not help the learner to grasp an idea; rather, unnecessary repetition thwarts a learner's attempt to grasp the concept being presented. How much is enough, and how much is too much? Only experience can tell. Classes vary as do individual children; what is extreme for some may be entirely correct for others. Perhaps the best advice which could be offered here would be to *know* the material, have the essential points outlined, and stick to the point; i.e., avoid tangential remarks which may tend to detract attention or obfuscate the concepts which are being presented.

SUMMARY

Communication is the heart of teaching and its process the veins and arteries through which knowledge flows. Further, the concept of *classroom communication* implies a great deal more than merely achieving common understandings through verbal interaction. To really communicate with students, it is necessary that a teacher acknowledge and accept six essential ingredients in the process of teaching. The teacher must:

1. capture the interests and desires of his students;
2. select and present purposeful experiences which are within the intellectual abilities of his students;
3. choose problems of sufficient merit and value that they will evoke discussion and critical thinking on the part of his students;

---

[15] Cronbach, *op. cit.*, pp. 398–399.

4. present credible and acceptable experiences in order that his students can relate new experiences to earlier learnings;

5. reinforce learning in order that his students will remember what they have learned; and

6. promote socially constructive behaviors among his students.

Indeed, this is a large task—perhaps for some, an impossible task. Nonetheless, in order to achieve affective instruction, each one of these elements must be dealt with competently.

The simplest place to start in organizing for meaningful instruction is with the students. Certainly, proficient teachers are familiar with the following principle: *Begin where the students are; use their existing interests and learnings to broaden old concepts and to help in developing new ones.* Instructional programs which are planned and developed apart from the interests, desires, and needs of the students are most likely to end up in failure, or, at best be only minimally effective.

Instruction should be personalized by such qualities as genuine interest, warmth, understanding, empathy, and an alertness on the part of the teacher to non-verbalized, personal learning needs of the student. In this way, the teacher can transform an ordinary in-class activity into a very real and significant experience. Most important, whatever is taught must be credible and worthy of the attention of students. Time permits neither teachers nor students the luxury of aimless floundering in hopes of acquiring an education. Instruction must be well planned and well presented.

Accordingly, effective communication and instruction does not just happen! *It is planned.* Similarly, planning is not a haphazard activity either. Definite precepts are required and must be followed in order that confusion and the variables which spawn misunderstanding are eliminated or are reduced to an absolute minimum.

Traditionally, teaching has been perceived as a verbal experience between the learned and the learner. However, this conception and approach is severely limiting and a most inefficient method of instruction due to the many complex variables which interfere with the process of communication. To teach is to communicate; anything else is a deception! Meaningful communication is only achieved in the common ground of mutual understanding. In this attitude, affecting variables can be known and controlled, the instructional needs of students can be accurately perceived, and the presentation of vivifying experiences can be accomplished. Herein lies the challenge.

CHAPTER EIGHT

Visual Communication

June King McFee

Visual communications bombard civilized man most of his waking hours. Visual symbols that are neither literary nor scientific range from the symbolic meaning expressed in monumental architecture to children's drawings. The structures of visual symbols range from the simplest stereotypes of objects which have been abstracted from visual realism (highway signs, for example) to the symbolization of the complex culture of a people as expressed in national capitol buildings, monuments, and surrounding landscape.

In contemporary society, non-verbal visual symbols are used to transmit ideas; express qualities, feelings, and emotions; note varied rank, status, and social roles; and to persuade changes in behavior and decision-making. Advertising, package design, publishing layout, clothing and jewelry, furniture and household accessories, motels, drive-ins, amusement centers, housing, business buildings, main streets, and cities all communicate values and ideas depending upon the quality of the symbolism used. Mass media extend this communication multifold.

In education, we diagram, graph, and organize symbols to express relationships. We build two- and three-dimensional models to help students analyze complex problems. We use the newer mechanical and electronic instructional media to expose students to more varied visual experiences and learning processes than can be achieved through written and spoken symbols. Non-verbal symbolic communication plays a major role in interpersonal and intergroup communication, particularly since the development of the mass media. However, too few teachers or students are educated in how to use this communication to best advantage. In our traditions of education, most emphasis has been on learning through written languages and mathematical and scientific symbols.

Design is the grammar of the visual world. It is the ordering system that makes the symbol more or less readable. It helps the content come through to the viewer. If the symbols have no background referent for the viewer, they will have little meaning for him. For example, in written language, an elegantly designed poster in Greek will communicate an excellent design to someone who understands design but not Greek. For those who read Greek, the message will be enhanced by the design and made clearer by the arrangement and design of the letters. The same message in Greek, read by a Greek could be poorly designed and hard to read. Symbols and the quality of their visual arrangement are reciprocally related—they can enhance or deter the function of the other; thus, they are in large part interdependent.

Bohannon, an anthropologist analyzing art and communication, suggests that art is one of the modes of creating cultural images to improve subtle appreciation and increase communication. He says that part of the process of maturation for humans is learning to communicate what one perceives. Symbolizing from our experience with sensory reactions and things, we develop the images for social interaction, communication, and patterns of culture.[1]

By contrast, learning to read the symbols of our culture helps us to understand the culture. But the content and the form of the message must both be understood.

---

[1] Paul Bohannon, *Social Anthropology* (New York: Holt, Rinehart & Winston, 1963), pp. 33–34.

ASPECTS OF TRANSMISSION

Design has several aspects in message transmission. Out of individual or collective experience, symbols are invented to express the nature of experience. The symbols are expressed through visual design to project the meaning, and the meaning is responded to in terms of the readiness of the viewer. For example, a curving line with an arrow point at the top means curving road ahead to most drivers. The symbol illustrates the problem of driving on a curving road—it communicates a shared experience. But to people who don't drive, or have had experience in driving only in flat, open country, or have not seen such a sign, or have had very threatening experiences with such driving situations, the symbol will communicate somewhat different things. A visual symbolic message is not a direct transfer of one person's experience to another person, but is mediated through each step from the initial experience of the sender to the response of the receiver. The teacher in the classroom may assume that the same message, either verbally or visually symbolic, will be received in the same way by all of the students in the class. But even if the teacher and the pupils share the same background of experiences (which would be rare), other differences in readiness to respond will occur.

We are faced with the rather practical evidence that the elements of design, form, line, color, texture, and their "gestalt"—the overall interacting impacts they can be made to produce—affect people differently. Why is it that some combinations of the visual elements create images of chaos for some people, while for others, order, or excitement, or monotony? Why do some people find an arrangement pleasing, while other people find it repulsive? Some designs and art forms have symbolic meaning to some segments of society and have little or no meaning to others. Some retain their meaning for centuries, others only transitionally. Yet, even with all this diversity, there must be some common denominators that enable us to respond to art and craft forms of cultures whose value and attitudes vary widely from our own.

The structure in Fig. 8-1 is an attempt to identify a hierarchy of factors that are involved in individual responses to the visual environment, and, thus, to message design. It starts at the lowest common denominator of visual information handling which appears to be cross-cultural and evidences in some degree in all the arts of all periods. The next level is cultural—the perceptual conditioning and symbolic meaning that evolves within a given society in terms of its values and attitudes. Third are personality variables that, at least in Western culture, differentiate between individuals within the various sub-cultures in Western

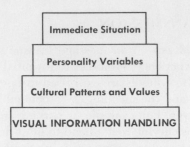

FIGURE 8-1

civilization, and, finally, the immediate situation in which an individual is responding. The message designer uses cultural symbols, appeals to personality, but basically he works at the level of visual information handling.

The message designer mediates between raw data—visual information before it has been organized by the viewer—by doing some of the organizing for him. To communicate to other people, the designer has to structure both the content, the "what is said" and the design, the "how it is said" so that there is a closer relationship beween the intended message and the one received by the particular audience for which he is designing. Since this chapter is concerned with making design more effective as an instrument for communication, the discusson will focus mainly on the questions: What is there about the design of the message that can help the message designer mediate more effectively between the sender and the receiver? What will such knowledge do to help the message designer get the information through in a better way than if the individual had responded to the experiences himself? How can experience be clarified through design? In other cases, How can message design create for the nonparticipant the essence of an experience he can have only vicariously? This last process is involved in much of education—learning about, prior to, or instead of the actual experience.

Research on these complex questions is meager. By operating rather broadly, the writer with background both in design and the psychology of perception will posit some perimeters of the behaviors involved, referring to applicable research where possible, and drawing upon experiences in teaching design when little research is available.

Visual perception itself is not a direct "image in the mind" of an outside stimulus. Rather, in very simplified terms, the visual-perception process involves a cognitive response to a sorting or ordering process from the "mosaic of retinal stimulation"[2] which is in turn, a reaction to the stimulating objects. Non-physical properties enter the sorting and cognition processes as well. These include past experience and prior learning. Gregory suggests that information from the other senses in past and present perceptual tasks are involved as well—"touch, taste, smell, hearing, and perhaps temperature or pain."[3] The author in her Perception-Delineation Theory includes success and failure, fear and anxiety as modifiers of the information-handling process.[4] Figure 8-2

FIGURE 8-2

symbolizes the simple process, but does not identify all the points where individual differences would operate.

The message designer may be able to design for a particular sub-culture of the society where identifiable traditions can be used to play upon the familiar. A teacher, knowing the cultural background and aptitude of his pupils can vary the symbolism and complexity level to their readiness. But all designers can use the common denominators of *visual information handling* to reach more of the population.

VISUAL INFORMATION HANDLING

At any given time, an individual responds cognitively with conscious awareness to only a small part of the visual information that is reflected on the retina of the eye. Look across the room—or whatever space you are in. To become aware of everything in your visual field, even if the room is very barren, takes considerable time. Most of us start our visual training by *identifying* things. Apparently, this is as far as many

---

[2] R. L. Gregory, *Eye and Brain: The Psychology of Seeing* (New York: Mc-Graw-Hill, 1966), pp. 7–8.

[3] *Ibid.*

[4] June K. McFee, *Preparation for Art* (Belmont, California: Wadsworth, 1961), pp. 147–151.

people go. If the room is a study, you would fairly soon be able to categorize books, maps, pictures, hanging coats, pens and pencils, drapes, rugs, chairs, etc. But, if you were to look for all the variations in color as changed by light and cast shadows, changes in forms in terms of their relation to your view, textures, lines, spaces, and planes—you could spend hours just looking at one view. Many people probably do not attend to the visual qualities unless specifically asked to do so.

In music and in all non-verbal sound, as well as in written and spoken language, systems of categorizing and systematizing information are necessary in order to conceptually handle the complexity. Apparently, man's capacity to differentiate between discrete things in single instances is much greater than his ability to handle them when he must respond to a great deal of information. In the latter case, he stereotypes and categorizes information, making it simple enough so that he can respond. In a study of color names, Chapanis estimates the number of color variations that the normal human can differentiate. By multiplying the recognizable 200 different hues by the 450 different steps between black and white and the degrees of saturation (strength of color) which range from 15 to 65, a figure close to 7,000,000 is achieved. For these differences, the National Bureau of Standards lists around 5000 color names, but in usage there is little or no standardization. On the basis of his study of color naming of subjects, he finds about 52 usable color names, which in common English is usually reduced to about 12 names.[5]

The message designer is a mediator, in this case with color, between the diversity to which man can physically respond and the ordinary name-categorizing of color.

The same is required with responses to objects. For example, if we have a box of conglomerate objects and are asked to tell someone what is in it, we have to put the contents in *order* to do so. If these are nuts, bolts, nails, pins, paperclips, and tacks, we have to sort them into some kind of order to identify and quantify them. We have a *use* classification already—fasteners. But this is often not definitive enough. We can order them by differences in fastening functions, or in terms of size, shape, or color. Color coding of manufactured parts is often used to denote a specific size of a given type of object that differentiates it from another similar object of different type and size. Color coding can be a quick recognition of differences, giving order to complexity.

Visual ordering in designed messages has to use visual ordering as

---

[5] Alphonse Chapanis, "Color Names for Color Space," *American Scientist*, Vol. 53, September, 1965, 327–346.

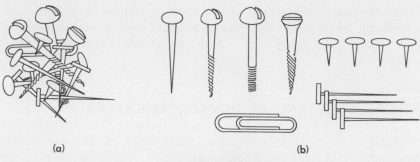

(a)   (b)

FIGURE 8-3

well as conceptual ordering or categorizing, unless all things in a concept category look alike visually. For example, in Fig. 8-3, the objects
pictured in part (a) are presented under the concept of fasteners but
are visually confusing. In part (b), they are not visually confusing because they are analyzed by size and shape. Visual ordering makes the
messages of content easier. Much of our responding is so fast that we
are unaware of the processing we do. One of the tasks of the message
designer is to make the sorting process easier; he selects and organizes
visual information so that it is easier for the viewer to assimilate.

The writer had been teaching design for some years before being
exposed to the theories of Gestalt psychology. The patterning in that
theory—proximity, similarity, and closure—began to make sense as to
why some designs "worked" and other "didn't." Experimentation with
teaching methods indicated that some people apparently used the organization of perceptual information at what the psychologist, Attneave,
calls a pre-cognitive level of awareness.[6] Students called this "intuition"
about what leads to a good pragnanz or sense of overall form. Some
students were consciously aware of perceptual organization and its
underlying functions in design, but were generally unable to achieve a
sense of design by "feeling." After becoming aware of the perceptual
dynamics of visual information handling, these non-intuitors became
aware of the elements of design. They could recognize the diversity of
impact upon themselves of the various combinations. They also seemed
to develop more "feeling" sensitivity to what was going on.

One of the most difficult problems for the intuitive designer is to
realize that other people do not respond as he does. The approach to
message design developed here is to help the intuitive designer under-

[6] F. Attneave, "Some Informational Aspects of Visual Perception," *Psychological
Review*, Vol. 61, 1954, 183–195.

stand the ranges of response among those for whom he designs, and to help the less intuitive designer understand some of the phenomena that appear to be going on in visual organization which underlie the design process.

VISUAL ORDERING AS DESIGN PRINCIPLES

Some of the Gestalt concepts continue to be useful even though explanations as to why they operate vary.

People need to make order, to group or pattern visual information so they may see objects. Figure 8-4[7] illustrates one's need to organize.

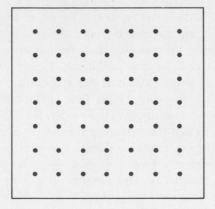

FIGURE 8-4

Each of the dots is the same in size, shape, and distance from the other dots. If you look at it awhile, you find yourself trying to make lines or squares, but the *images* do not last long because all the alternatives are equal, and your tendency to continually search for order keeps you busy reordering.

Grouping by the Principle of Similarity

Figure 8-5(a) is different from (b) because they involve different alternatives. In both, alternate rows of circles have open and solid centers. Figure (b) is the same as (a), but rotated 90 degrees. The circles are all equidistant so there are no "real" rows, but you see vertical lines in part (a) and horizontal lines in part (b) because you are sorting the

---

[7] Gregory, *op. cit.* (Used with permission of the publisher.)

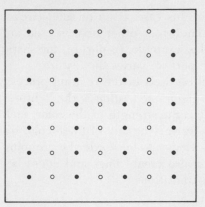

(a)   (b)

FIGURE 8-5

(a)   (b)

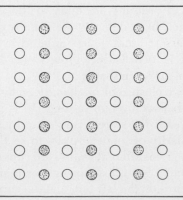

(c)

FIGURE 8-6

visual information into *similarities;* in this case, open or solid circles. This same principle operates if the circles, or other objects used are varied in any way. Figure 8-6 is another example. In part (a) the shape is varied, part (b) varies the size, and part (c) varies the texture.

Color, value and intensity can all be used in the relating process. *Color* is the hue, the red, blue, blue-green, etc.; *value* is the lightness or darkness of the color; and *intensity* is the strength of the color, such as the amount of pigment in a wash. By varying any of these color dimensions, the designer can direct the viewer to find order by grouping those things that are similar. He can also create lines and edges between groups of things by such simple transitions.

Grouping by Proximity

Another way the organizing system sorts information is by the response to the grouping presented by the design of the outside stimulus.

FIGURE 8-7

In Fig. 8-7, most people see three pairs of lines and an extra one on the right. Try to make yourself see three wide pairs with one on the left. This is very difficult to do. Proximity is a tool of the designer. If he wants things to be seen together, they need to be grouped together. If too much space is left between things, the viewer will try to find other ways of ordering.

All the systems of ordering are open to the viewer. The designer needs to analyze what he is doing to see if he is providing the choices he wants. He may assume that he has ordered by proximity; however, similarities of color in two distinct groups may be the stronger pull, or, perhaps, two similarities in shape.

In Fig. 8-8, the two clusters of small outlined figures are clearly separate, but a tension between group (a) and (b) is produced by the two *circles* which the organizing system is relating by similarity.

In Fig. 8-9, similarity of shape appears to be the strongest relationship even though the two different shapes are superimposed in one case. Proximity is functioning but not as strongly as is similarity. If one were to make the two figures on the left red, and the superimposed figures on

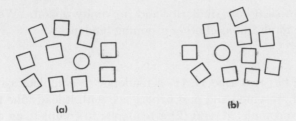

(a)   (b)

FIGURE 8-8

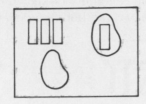

FIGURE 8-9

the right blue, using line alone to differentiate shape—then similarity of color and proximity would strongly outweigh similarity of shape.

Similarity and proximity can be used by the designer to solve difficult problems with very diverse objects. Differences in size, shape, and texture can be muted by grouping objects together or by ordering them by one common factor such as color. These principles also apply to designing messages in words or symbols.

In design, things do not exist as single entities but rather as *interacting factors* within the whole. Color, shape, texture, space, and lines have traditionally been used as the elements of design. Balanced, rhythm, and emphasis are considered key design principles.[8] Each of these has a basis in perceptual organizing. That which is balanced, creates rhythm, or stands out as emphasis depends on how both the designer and the viewer organize the visual information. In terms of organizing processes, the elements of design are not the color, the shape, or the texture; they are, rather, the ways these ingredients are used to create an ordered stimulus to which the organizing observer can respond. In other words, the designer plays upon the observer's tendencies to group things—the grouping tendencies become the principles of design.

---

[8] Ray and Sarah Faulhner, *Inside Today's Home* (New York: Holt, Rinehart & Winston, 1960), pp. 92–105.

We have seen how similarity and proximity operate. We will now explore the implications of other grouping tendencies.

Closure

Closure has two aspects: (1) a tendency to complete a form when part of it is presented and past experience with it leads one to respond as if it were completed; and (2) a tendency to complete an abstract or geometric form through the nature of the directions suggested by lines created by the forms.

Completion due to the continuity of known relational concepts can be shown in Fig. 8-10. In part (a), both symbol and mental closure give

(a)   **FIGURE 8-10**   (b)

us clues as to the whole. In part (b), we add a chin and other features to a face.

Completion also operates with abstract forms.[9] Figure 8-11 is an

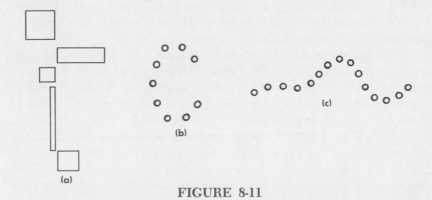

FIGURE 8-11

example. Part (a) is organized on a vertical line that is not drawn, but created by the relationship of the shapes. Parts (b) and (c) are made up of repetitions of the same shape, but their relationships to each other create different wholes.

---

[9] William Dember, *Psychology of Perception* (New York: Holt, Rinehart & Winston, 1960), pp. 166–167.

Good Continuation

"Good continuation" is defined as that arrangement of line separation of figure and ground, or symbol edge, that produces fewest interruptions or stopping points for the eye.[10] Figure 8-12, parts (a) and (b),

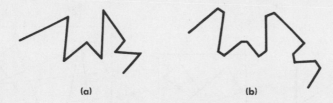

(a)   (b)

FIGURE 8-12

compares two continuations, one better than the other. In part (b), a short mediating line at all extreme angles produces a smoother effect; the eye is helped past the angles.

Figure 8-13, part (b), is the easiest to "read"; the same curvature is

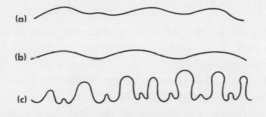

(a)

(b)

(c)

FIGURE 8-13

repeated. In part (a), there are four different wave sizes varying in width and height, and in part (c), size, height, width, and shape are all varied.

Averaging Processes

Attneave has demonstrated that one of the key visual sorting processes is taking an average of complexity[11]—another process of ordering so as to respond to the complex environment. When we see similar but diverse objects, we group them in terms of their likenesses, and we stereotype variations in shade and intensity in color into single colors. When we see textured surfaces, we tend to respond more to the average

---

[10] *Ibid.*, p. 167.
[11] Attneave, *op. cit.*

color or value the texture creates than to all the details of the texture over all the surface we are observing. This may be what operates in design when directional angles interact; we respond in terms of the average impact. In Fig. 8-14, part (a), the direction is singular and

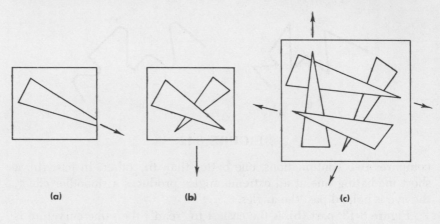

(a)   (b)   (c)

FIGURE 8-14

down right; in part (b), the left and right angles point in two directions down; and in part (c), a state of equilibrium is suggested because the angles counteract each other.

Part of this symbolism is our reaction to gravity. Ozenfant suggests that single lines at angles are less strong than verticals, as the force of gravity *we* experience we project to the lines;[12] the angle receiving more force to move to a horizontal position. As more and more people take off in jets and see rockets resist gravity, the symbol for falling may become the symbol for taking off.

Information Points

Contrasted with "good continuation" is the sorting of information by focusing on information points.[13] When subjects were asked to reproduce a form by using only ten dots, Attneave found they placed the dots at the points where the greatest changes took place in contour or angle. Salome found that fifth-grade children who were taught to utilize these key information points significantly improved their drawings over children who had the same drawing experience but not the perceptual

[12] Amédée Ozenfant, *Foundations of Modern Art* (New York: Dover Publications, Inc., 1956), pp. 259–261.
[13] Attneave, *op. cit.*

training.[14] Hochberg found that, to reproduce a form, the individual needed information most on the number of different angles and the number of different line segments of unequal length.[15] This would lead to the conclusion that change points are key factors in design.

One of the challenges to the designer is to produce enough good continuation to produce stability, but not so much that *no* averaging in scanning processes is needed. Too much stability would produce boredom and the viewer would look away. On the other hand, the designer should not create so much visual information that the viewer is lost in changes and detail. McWhinnie suggests that continuation is related to what designers call order and variety.[16] The scanning organism needs visual work to do, but not so much that it can't find order.

Figure and Ground

A final way of grouping to overcome complexity is to separate figure from ground. In this aspect of information handling, it is more difficult to separate what is a common denominator of perception from personality and learned values. We tend to look at forms and listen to sounds that have meaning to us. In most perceptual experiences, we attend to some things and not to others. This is one reason we get varied reports of happenings from honest people who looked at the same incident and perceived different things; what one brought into figure, another left in ground. This is part of the ordering process through which the individual finds meaning in his visual experience.

Part of attending is recognition of what is familiar; another part is attending to what is important or valued, or, conversely, what is feared or arouses anxiety-laden associations. Considerable research has been undertaken estimating the recognition threshold of words that arouse emotional responses as compared to mental words. There are identifiable figure over ground factors in the viewed objects that tend to make one figure, the other ground. Krech and Crutchfield indicate that what is figure tends to be better, more solid, to have clearer outlines; what is ground is less so.[17] Camouflage is based on this principle; with

---

[14] Richard Salome, "The Effects of Perceptual Training Upon the Two-Dimensional Drawings of Children," *Studies in Art Education*, Autumn, 1965, 7:2, 18–33.

[15] J. Hochberg, "The Psychophysics Form: Reversible Perspections of Spacial Objects," *American Journal of Psychology*, Vol. 73, 1960, 337–354.

[16] Harold McWhinnie, "A Review of Some Research on Aesthetic Measure and Perceptual Choice," *Studies in Art Education*, 6:2, Spring, 1965, 34–41.

[17] David Krech and Richard L. Crutchfield, *Elements of Psychology* (New York: Alfred A. Knopf, 1959), pp. 87–88.

false patterns, it diffuses the solidity, structure, and outline of the object which melts visually into the background.[18] Colors and value contrasts are stronger in figure than ground.

When the spaces between letters are used more strongly than the letters which are the figures, visual confusion or figure-ground reversal can result (see Fig. 8-15).

FIGURE 8-15

When the same line is used to separate two areas, one becomes figure and the other ground with different properties (see Fig. 8-16). The same line divides them. The arcs at the back are the same, but two distinct figures result depending upon which is figure and which is ground.

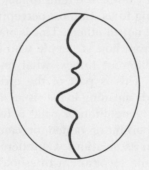

FIGURE 8-16

When the visual field is complex, the overall structure will tend to determine.[19] In other words, the strongest organization force will relate its elements as figure whether it be proximity, similarity, closure, or continuity.

---

[18] L. Postman, J. G. Brener, and E. McGinnis, "Personal Values as Selective Factors in Perception," *Journal of Abnormal and Social Psychology*, Vol. 65, 196–217.

[19] L. Postman and R. L. Crutchfield, "The Interaction of Need, Set, and Stimulus-Structure in a Cognitive Task," *American Journal of Psychology*, Vol. 65, 196–217.

Illusion effects that come with the interaction of ground on figure can be used by the designer to make things look longer or shorter, rounder, or flatter. The well known Mueller-Lyer illusion can make the same line shorter or longer (see Fig. 8-17). In part (a), the lines are the

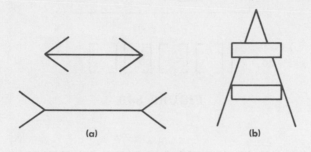

(a)   (b)

FIGURE 8-17

same length, and in part (b), the rectangles are the same size, but the ground lines in both figures give the illusion that one line or rectangle is longer than the other.

COMPETITION BETWEEN GROUPING PROCESSES

Only in a very simple stimulus is just one organizing process evoked. In most cases, similarity in some degree, proximity in some degree, closure, and figure-ground relationship are used in handling the visual information. In some cases, the systems compliment each other (see Fig. 8-18). Proximity of objects, similarity of objects as to size and

FIGURE 8-18

shape, and value reinforce the two groupings. In Fig. 8-19, part (a), the proximity is probably strongest, but the similarities of shape set up cross tensions. Proximity and closure counteract when lines suggesting closures are added to part (b).[20]

---

[20] Krech and Crutchfield, *op. cit.*, p. 93.

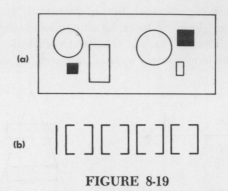

FIGURE 8-19

EXAMPLES OF PROBLEM SOLVING IN DESIGN

The following problem-solving examples show further ways the grouping principles interact. (See pp. 214-215 for Figs. 8-20—8-30.)

Using the concepts of proximity, the designer works from exact repetition in close proximity within a given field (Fig. 8-20) to the farthest reaches the perceiver can respond to and still see relationships. For example, the two forms in Fig. 8-21 are related because they are bounded within the same field, but they are different in shape, size, and color, and weak in proximity. We can increase the cohesiveness of the design by making both figures the same color or value (Fig. 8-22); by making them the same in size, which of course, increases the proximity; keeping the sizes different, but using the same shape (Fig. 8-23); or increasing the proximity within the bounding field, with enough space so that nothing else distracts or changes the interaction of the rectangle and circle (Fig. 8-24).

If we introduce another circle in reasonable proximity, then the likeness of the circles and the difference of the square sets up a new pattern (Fig. 8-25). Even though the left-hand circle is closer to the rectangle, it relates more to the other circle. This is the way the message designer creates suggestion of tension to his viewers—two systems working unequally in different ways.

Tension is also produced when forms are almost identical, but not quite; an overall flutter effect takes place (Fig. 8-26). Direct repetition is static; if the forms are all exactly alike, no movement takes place (Fig. 8-27). But if one rectangle is changed in value, size, or perspective, the organizer is stimulated to make a new organization and interest increases (Figs. 8-28, 8-29, and 8-30).

OPERATIONAL EXPLORATIONS IN
THE DIMENSIONS OF DESIGN

To help students become involved in problem solving in message design, the following tasks are suggested to explore the interaction of elements in the organizing processes.

1. Task: *Make order out of assorted unlike things.*
   Cut assorted sizes and shapes out of varied colored and textured papers.

   Similarity:
   Search for ways to organize in terms of *size*. Create groups according to similarities in *color*. Group with clearly identifiable similarities in *texture*. Group according to similarities in *shape*.

   Proximity:
   Without using similarity, group assorted things by *clustering* and *spacing*.

   Closure:
   Without using similarity, group assorted things using both *proximity* and *closure*.

2. Task: *Create order with variation.*
   Cut rectangular shaped pieces of colored paper. Keep the size, shape, and spacing the same—*vary the color*. Keep the color and shape the same—*vary the size and space*. Keep the shape the same—*vary size, color, and spacing*.

   In each case, analyze to see which of the perceptual organizing processes you are using: *Similarity* of size, space, shape, or color; *proximity* of sizes, spaces, shapes, colors; *continuity* by creation of line; *figure* and *ground* by creating some areas that come forward and others that recede.

3. Task: *Create a free form* so that:
   None of the parts are too large or too small to relate to the whole. None of the angles suggested are parallel to any other angles. None of the spaces created dominate the shape.

4. Task: *Using free forms, create color and variation.*
   Keep the size, shape and color the same—*vary the space*. Keep the color and shape the same—*vary the size and space* as necessary. Keep the size and spacing the same—*vary the color*.

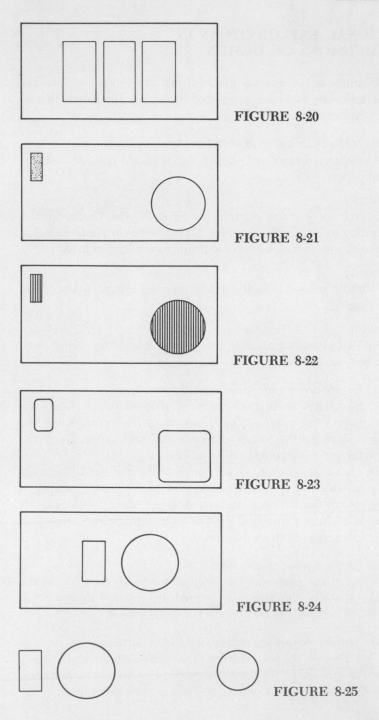

FIGURE 8-20

FIGURE 8-21

FIGURE 8-22

FIGURE 8-23

FIGURE 8-24

FIGURE 8-25

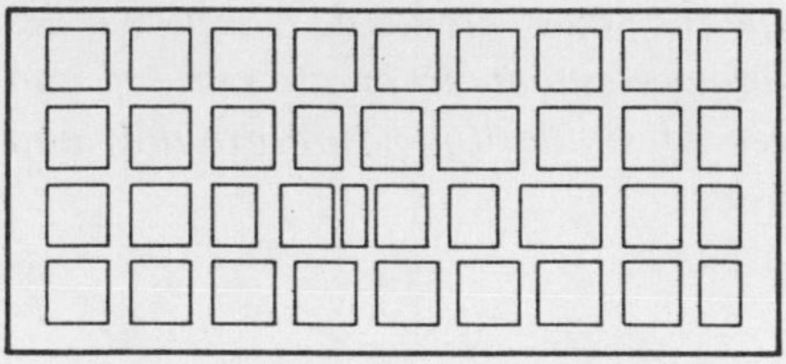

FIGURE 8-26

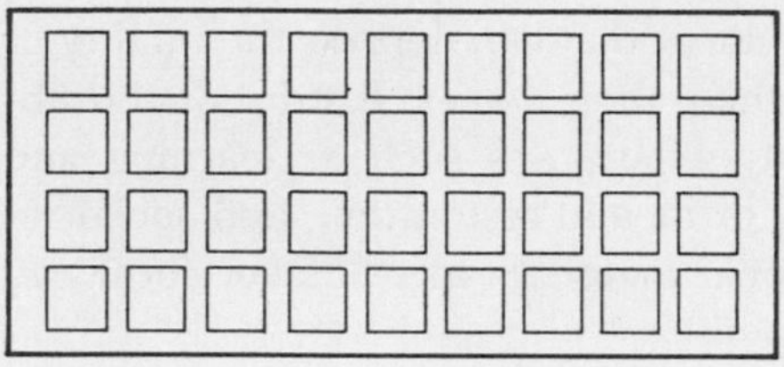

FIGURE 8-27

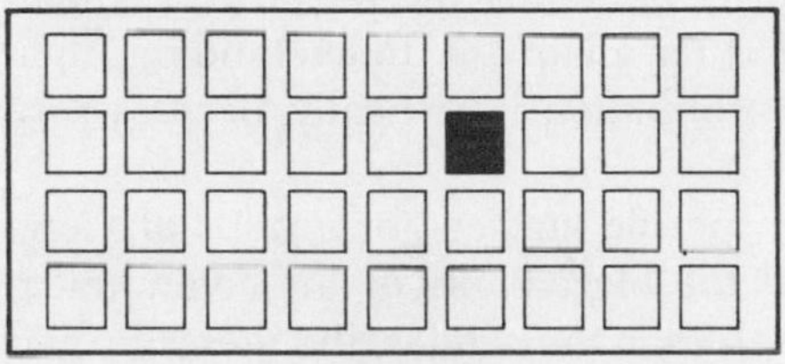

FIGURE 8-28

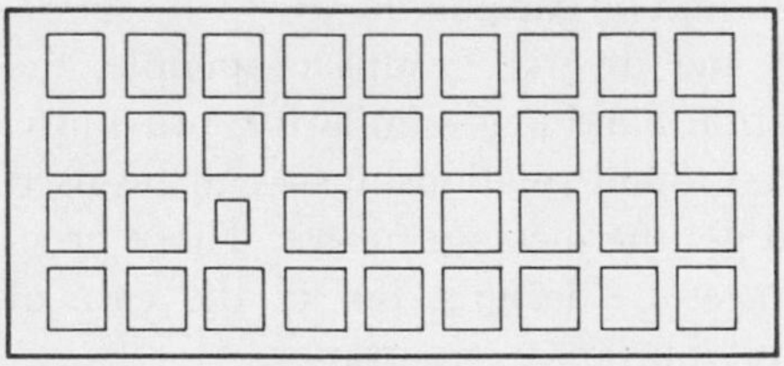

FIGURE 8-29

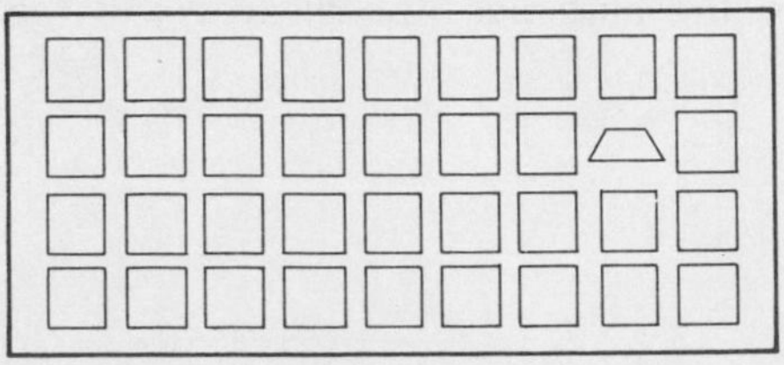

FIGURE 8-30

5. Task: *Keeping the basic shape the same, create as complex a de-sign as possible, varying all other elements to create variety, and using proximity, some degree of similarity, figure-ground, and continuity-closure to make order.*

SUMMARY

Too much order produces monotony. Rows of unmodified cement called "housing" creates an environment that can depress the quality of living of people who try to make these their homes. Institutional drabness can contribute to the defeat of purposes such as learning and creative problem solving, physical or mental restoration, and social rehabilitation. Monotonous educational materials in whatever form can slow the pace and intensity of response.

Overly complex visual stimuli can lead to confusion on the part of some viewers. Others will abstract from the environment or the message only what is familiar, or what is valued. If the purpose is educational and *all* the material is needed for adequate understanding, then the ordering and varying of the information is critically necessary to make learning possible.

To get the message through to specific viewers, or groups of viewers, the designer must understand the ingredients of his communication system. These include the variables in the sender, the message, and the viewer. Culture, background, and personality vary from person to person. Perceptual literacy ranges widely. Individual response to different kinds of viewing situations should be considered.

When the design is for large and diverse groups of people, the common denominators of information handling—similarity, proximity, closure and good form, and figure-ground relationships—can be used to direct the viewers attention and get the message across. These processes underlie all organizing of message designs, but in the case of messages to diverse groups, they are of primary importance.

Symbolic visual communications are everywhere. The designer has much competition for the viewer's attention. The more appropriate the design is to the message and the audience, the clearer will the content come through.

CHAPTER NINE

Concomitant Learning: An Anthropological Perspective on the Utilization of Media

Harry F. Wolcott

Cultural anthropologists study two complementary aspects of social behavior: ideal behavior and real behavior. One of the distinguishing characteristics of the anthropologist as a field worker is his attention to what people actually do as well as to what they say they do. While information about what people feel is ideal (preferred, best, proper, good), and can often be gathered with some ease through the use of interviewing or questionnaires, the anthropologist will make every at-

---

¹ The author wishes to acknowledge the support of the Center for the Advanced Study of Educational Administration, University of Oregon, during a portion of his time devoted to the preparation of this chapter.

217

tempt to observe real or actual behavior as well. His most important field technique is participant-observation; it provides the basis for his accounts of what "really is" as well as what people tell him "ought to be." The fact that ideal and real behavior are often disparate is not disconcerting to the anthropologist as long as he is satisfied that he has adequately described them both. He is not compelled to make judgments on discrepancies between real and ideal behavior any more than he is compelled to judge a culture as good or bad.

The purpose of this chapter is to take the perspective and methodology of the anthropologist to explore the real behavior of teachers and pupils in selecting, utilizing, and learning from instructional media.[2] The emphasis here is not on *ideal* or *normative* aspects of teacher behavior—how teachers should act, the kinds of goals or objectives towards which they should strive, the best ways to organize for instruction, or the right ways to select and use media—but rather on such questions as: What actually goes on in the classroom when teachers avail themselves of media? Are the only lessons learned the ones the teacher intends to teach? Are audiovisual aids and other media an unmitigated blessing? or can they also produce stress and conflict in teacher behavior and unintended lessons for pupils?

This discussion and the accompanying accounts of classroom behavior deal with instances in which instructional media, particularly the most frequently used audiovisual aids, are utilized. The implications of these comments are not limited only to such situations. Every classroom lesson, independent of whether the teacher supplements the instruction by using media, provides the opportunity for ideal behavior to be at variance with real behavior, for ideal teacher purposes to be pre-empted by accompanying learnings which provide a lesson of different consequences for the pupil.[3] A lesson never looks exactly the same to the learner as it looks to the teacher.

Actual classroom behavior is far more complex than phrases like "good teaching" or "proper use of instructional media" imply. There are

---

[2] Readers interested in other kinds of studies made by anthropologists concerned with educational problems are referred to an article summarizing such research— Harry F. Wolcott, "Anthropology and Education," *Review of Educational Research*, Vol. 37, No. 1, February, 1967, 82–95.

[3] Two anthropologists, Jules Henry and George Spindler, have discussed contrasts between intended and unintended learning in the school setting. See Jules Henry, "A Cross-Cultural Outline of Education," *Current Anthropology*, Vol. 1, July, 1960, 267–305, particularly his discussion between the intent and the results of education, pp. 301–302; and George Spindler, "The Transmission of American Culture," in Spindler, ed., *Education and Culture: Anthropological Approaches* (Holt, Rinehart & Winston, 1963), pp. 148–172.

aspects of instruction which are incidental to or even antithetical to the intended or ideal purposes. These incidental or unintended aspects are here called *concomitant learnings*.

Observing and recording protocols of the actual verbal behavior in classrooms is one of the assignments of a course titled "School in American Life" taught by this writer. Students practice the techniques of observation in the college classroom before proceeding to the public schools. From hundreds of protocols of classroom behavior made by students over a period of two years, examples have been selected which illustrate the concomitant aspects of intended and unintended consequences in classroom instruction where teachers happened to be using instructional media when students came to observe. The protocols are quoted verbatim in this chapter, as submitted by the students. While it is impossible to appraise the accuracy of any protocol, the very divergence among the students and their naïveté as classroom observers should preclude systematic biases or errors. The observations were not made in "demonstration" classrooms. Students were extended an invitation to observe in several schools each term, and they were also free to make arrangements for visits at other schools. Thus, most teachers did not know that they would be having an observer until a student entered the classroom.

INTENDED LEARNINGS

In his instructional role, at least part of a teacher's behavior is consciously directed toward producing some change in a learner, whether it be the acquisition of a new fact, a reorganization of existing information, or a reinforcement of or shift in values or attitudes. In its most formal aspect, such behavior by teachers reflects their intention as expressed in lesson plans, courses of study, and the whole concept of curriculum. In addition to any pre-planned and structured meting out of facts, concepts, and generalizations, teachers also consciously take the responsibility for instructing their pupils in attitudes and values as opportunities arise, particularly values concerning punctuality, cleanliness, courtesy, aesthetic appreciation, and love of learning— those which we often associate with the "middle-class bias" of schools. While we can easily think of some examples of intended learnings, it seems unlikely that a teacher can explicitly identify the totality of learnings he intends to impart. Each of us internalizes his "culture" to the extent that he takes for granted much of his own behavior, his reactions, and his expectations for others, including the expectations which teachers hold for their students.

Instruction in the classroom presents problems in the *selection and
accuracy of content* and in the determination of *how much information*
to introduce and *which information to emphasize.* In the following protocol of a fifth-grade class during a science lesson, for example, the
teacher appears to be getting the lesson across just as she intends it.
Further, she is using certain pedagogically approved techniques
(eliciting class response, developing an outline on the chalkboard,
relating discussion to experience). Yet, the scope of the lesson suggests
a superficiality in dealing with content which may not be as uncommon
in the classroom as we might like to imagine.

OBSERVATION NO. 1

T: What are some metals which we use every day? [*No response*] Let's start with some of those mentioned last time.
[*As the students answered she wrote the words on the chalkboard.*]

P: Quartz.

P: Gold.

P: Silver.

P: Copper.

T: And what do we use copper for?

P: Pennies.

T: Is there anything else we should add to our list?

P: Lead.

T: [*Pointing to list*] Do you know that our bodies contain all
of these? Using your element charts, what are some other things
we use?

P: Gases.

T: Which ones?

P: Oxygen to breathe with.

T: Do you see why these things are so valuable to us? It's their
properties. What are properties? [*No response*] Well, which
would you rather fall into, a tub of iron or a tub of cotton?

P: Cotton.

T: Why?

P: It's softer.

T: [*Writing "Soft" on board*] All right, what are some other properties of any matter then?

P: Hardness.

Other pupils, one after another: Sweetness. Cold. Sourness. Heavy.

[*Some time is devoted to a discussion of examples of matter which possessed the properties written on the board.*]

T: These properties are very important, then. Now, what are some other gases?

P: Helium.

T: What do we use helium for?

P: Weather balloons.

T: What else is important to us?

P: Iodine.

T: Why?

P: We need it in our bodies.

T: Any other thing?

P: Uranium which we use in bombs.

P: It kills with radiation.

T: Let's get off war. How do we use it for peace?

P: For power.

P: We can use it for power and not build dams.

This protocol illustrates that even when the lesson proceeds simply and directly in the way the teacher directs it, the problems of selecting and presenting content to accomplish teaching purposes are never simple. In this illustration, what the teacher intends to accomplish is not easily discernible. What the children *may* be learning includes not only a vague notion of properties, or the fact that we are surrounded by the elements, but also how to give the teacher the answer she wants, learning not to explore questions to any depth, or learning that to be a teacher all one has to do is write what pupils say on a blackboard.

The protocols which follow provide data for exploring classroom behavior in which the actual lesson perceived by the learner may be far removed from the ideal intent of the teacher.

Accuracy of the content presents a problem in intended instruction. In the following example from a high school biology class, the student observer, a former laboratory technician who had returned to the university to prepare for teaching high school science, included in her observation notes two parenthetical comments identifying misinformation in the teacher's instructions.

OBSERVATION NO. 2

T: What else might happen that could contaminate our cultures?

G: Dirty test tubes.

T: That's right, but ours were sterile. Open tubes and currents of air flowing in can sweep bacteria right into it. What else?

B: Coughing or sneezing on it.

T: That will do it, too. Remember how to hold the tube? Hold the open end down [*Teacher holds agar tube upside down. Observer shudders at technique!*] so air won't go in and stuff fall into it. [*Good trick if one can hack it. What you really do is hold it* **horizontally** *and* **not vertically!**]

T: Question number four: "How can contamination be prevented?" I think we've pretty well answered this. [*Teacher explains why it is necessary to flame loop after transplanting bacteria. Demonstrates loop and how to use it to students. Shows how students make mistake of laying loop down on table with bacteria still on it.*] Bacteria are all pathogenic, so remember that. [*Whoops! Error number two. I hope they don't remember* **that** *statement!*]

The observer's first comment calls attention to one of the most common assumptions regarding the use of instructional aids or equipment in classrooms—that teachers have the skills for using the materials with which they are provided. The observer's second comment questions the accuracy of the teacher's knowledge. Faced with the growing number of instructional aids for individual classrooms—the new "hardware" of educational technology—and the popular concept of an "explosion" of knowledge, we may suspect that it is the teacher's lack of ability or interest in acquiring new skills and knowledge that provides the major constraint in attempts at curriculum change. Further examples of this problem are provided later in the chapter.

Teachers are not required to be experts in all fields. In confronting problems in the scope of their studies and in providing accurate up-to-date information, teachers have the resources of both specialist personnel and specially developed media, with perhaps educational films firmly entrenched as the favorite source of instructional assistance. Yet, in the following protocol taken in a first- and second-grade classroom, the instructional value of the first of two films shown (a film presenting land and water forms) seems to have been negligible when evaluated by the discussion that followed it. The problem with the second film—that it was not the film originally ordered—has implications that will be discussed later concerning the unintended aspects of instruction.

Before the observer entered the classroom, children from two other first- and second-grade classes had come to the room to see the film on land formation and bodies of water. Children were watching the film when the observer arrived.

OBSERVATION NO. 3

[*Pupils are quietly watching film.*]

[*Film ends, pupils clap.*]

[*There is to be another film, so pupils sing a song about speckled frogs, waiting for the projector operator.*]

[*The teacher asks whether the children know anything about the name, Washington. I couldn't hear their replies.*]

[*The film is supposed to be about Washington but it is the wrong film. It is a film about service stations; it is shown anyway.*]

[*Film gets underway. The pupils whisper or giggle occasionally.*]

[*Special announcement over the intercom interrupts during the film: Would all cleanup members come to room five right now. Two pupils leave.*]

[*Film ends, pupils clap.*]

[*The two visiting classes line up at door and leave. Remaining children relocate furniture, raise blinds, and take down the screen.*]

[*The teacher goes to the front of the room, and the pupils gather around her.*]

[*Last of visiting teachers leaves with projector.*]

T: We don't have too much time left. We will talk about the film on land and water. What kind of land is a mountain?

P: It's rocky and steep.

T: Very good.

P: Land is dirt, and—

T: Yes, but what *kind* of land?

P: It is cold in the mountains.

T: Why?

P: Clouds and rain make it cold.

T: OK, good.

. . . .

T: And is a hill different from a mountain?

P: They aren't as steep and not as high.

P: They have a round top.

P: Hills are flatter.

P: Hills have grass and mountains don't.

[*Similar discussion takes place about valleys and plains.*]

. . . .

T: So what kinds of land have we talked about?

P: . . . [*Observer couldn't hear the reply.*]

P: Valleys, mountains, hills, and plains.

T: OK. [*Directs discussion to water.*] What else did you notice about a stream?

P: . . . smaller.

P: Streams are kinda heading down hill.

T: What kind of water stays in one place?

P: Mud puddles.

T: Good.

P: Lakes.

T: Yes.

. . . .

T: What lakes do you know of that we have around here?

P: Crater Lake.

P: Diamond Lake.

P: Pacific Lake.

P: Oh! That's an ocean.

T: I can tell that you did a good job today watching the movie.

From the teacher's closing comment, one might assume that the comments of the children reassured her that her instructional purposes were accomplished. Although the protocol of the discussion is not complete, the samples which the observer recorded suggest that the film provided little more than what some administrators refer to as a "time-killer," a suspicion supported by the showing of the second film.

Polyphasic Learning

Another aspect of intended instruction adds to the complexity of what teachers attempt to accomplish in class. This is a consequence of the tendency in formal education (more obvious in the lower grades but evident at all levels) to derive more than one lesson from any "learning experience." The anthropologist Jules Henry has suggested the term *polyphasic learning* to describe this process of learning more than one thing at a time. He contrasts polyphasic learning with mono-phasic learning, the hypothetical case in which only one thing is learned at one time. It is hypothetical, Henry insists, because it is a human inability. Henry describes the extent to which polyphasic learn-ing is emphasized or de-emphasized in an instructional setting as a cultural variable, and his observations in public schools lead him to conclude that American teachers *emphasize* the polyphasic aspects of learning. Here is Henry's discussion and a protocol he uses for illus-tration:

> Polyphasic learning is the process of learning more than one thing at a time. Normal human beings cannot learn only one thing at a time; rather they learn a pattern. This capacity to learn more than one thing at a time—to receive complex in-puts—is exploited in different ways in various periods in our own culture. The present tendency in elementary school education is to *exploit consciously such polyphasic learning capacities*. In simple societies the storage processes often handle but very little information at a time; and even when information is relatively complex, the in-put process is not spe-cifically developed with this complexity in the minds of the teachers. That is to say, for example, that while food-sharing among the Pilagá Indians ends up being not only the process of giving away one's food, but also a way of operating a scale of social distance, food-sharing *as information* is not consciously taught as a social distance scale. It is the difference between saying, "Give food to people," and saying, "Give food to your first cousins through your mother." In the first instance the individual simply learns that he has to share food, in the second he is required to master a social system in con-nection with the giving of food. It is the second instance that is polyphasic in *intent*.
>
> The present tendency in elementary school education in the United States is to exploit polyphasic learning capacities consciously. Thus a painting lesson becomes not only one in art, embodying the use of colors and brushes, learning the names of colors and how to mix them, and so on, but also a lesson in geography and human rela-tions. A painting of the Sahara Desert becomes a vehicle through which to communicate information about Africa, Arabs, and the Mohammedan religion *all at the same time*.
>
> The following extract from a protocol of observations in a fifth grade classroom will further illustrate the point:
>
> Teacher: What does art do for us?
> Student: It cheers us up.
> Teacher: It cheers us up. Yes, beautiful things will cheer you up when you're feeling bad. What else does it do?

Student: It expresses yourself—I mean it's not just copied.
Teacher: What does it express about yourself?
Student: How you feel.

Students go on to say that a happy artist draws bright colors, and unhappy artists use dark colors or gray. Teacher points out exceptions: when the artist is producing a scene in which the subject is dark or gray. She says, "If a person is not disturbed, mentally or nervously, he tends to like bright colors, doesn't he?" Teacher announces she is going to play records which a student has brought, and the class is to listen to them, get the feel and the rhythm —whether it is active, soft, soothing, or what—and then express themselves in a picture. She says, "You know, the more intriguing your picture is the more valuable it is. You may have a five-hundred dollar picture when you get through." [*Both sides of the record are waltzes.*]

Teacher stops the record, says, "Some of you are drawing before you feel the rhythm. You are bound to have a picture in your mind, but I'll make a bargain with you. Listen to the rhythm of the music, and then just cut loose and express yourself this time, and we'll draw the old-fashioned way another day this week." Teacher stops the music and says, "If you were in New York in an art class, you'd be paying ten dollars for this lesson, and if you talked, out you'd go. It's selfish to disturb your neighbor—now just be quiet." Plays more music.

From this example we see that what is ostensibly an art lesson is exploited, as a polyphasic learning experience for the purpose of attempting to teach among other things the following: (1) The immorality and even disease of being unhappy; (2) notions of economic life and the market; (3) the myth of the pot of gold at the end of the rainbow ("You may have a five-hundred dollar picture when you get through"); (4) the importance of "cutting loose," but under the proper circumstances; (5) the relationship (?) between music and painting on the one hand, and "self-expression" on the other. We observe also efforts to control children's spontaneous expressiveness (dark colors should not be used); and above all, we can see that this art lesson is used to maintain level or organization in the American culture as a whole.[4]

------

[4] Jules Henry, "Culture, Education, and Communications Theory." Reprinted from *Education and Anthropology*, edited by George D. Spindler with the permission of the author and of the publishers, Stanford University Press. Copyright 1955 by the Board of Trustees of the Leland Stanford Junior University.

Henry's discussion of polyphasic learning is included here because the utilization of any special media in a classroom introduces additional stimuli into the learning situation. External stimuli tend to increase the polyphasic nature of instruction; thus, the content of an educational film shown to a class may be only one facet of a complex lesson in which the teacher concomitantly gives (intended) instruction in courtesy ("Who remembers how we act when we watch a film?"), care, and use of equipment ("Be careful with that screen, boys"), allocation of privileges ("Who would like to take the film back to the office?"), management of time ("We'll have to hurry because another class needs the projector"), and so forth.

As the significance of the media increases (reflecting such criteria as uniqueness, duration, cost, relevance to the instructional program), there is a tendency to increase the polyphasic aspects of the lesson. Thus the amount of "readiness" instruction and the number of intended lessons which the teacher draws out of a regularly viewed TV program may seem minor when compared to the effort expended in preparation for a special visitor or for a classroom field trip. As an example, consider the following protocol taken in a fourth-grade class planning an ambitious field trip to explore tidepools at the distant seashore.

OBSERVATION NO. 4

T: Before we take our field trip, we have to get ourselves organized. [*The noise has not yet subsided.*] Class, I'm waiting on you. [*The class becomes quieter.*] Now, I think rather than having me tell you what we are going to do at the beach— which would make it my trip—I'll let you decide what we are going to do, so that it really will be your trip. So let's divide into committees, and each committee would be responsible for planning the action for one thing. For example, we would need a committee for clothing; the committee would then decide what kind of clothing we will need.

B: Swimming suit.

T: Mike, you had your hand raised.

B: No.

T: Can someone else think of another committee? Roger.

B: A committee for clothing and lunch. [*Teacher writes on blackboard: "1. Clothing and food."*]

T: What other committee?

B: Games.

T: Yes, activities. [*She writes: "2. Activities."*]

B: Can we run out in the water?

T: [*Evidently she didn't hear this question.*] Oh yes, before we
     forget, there is a law that says we can't take things out of the
     tidepools.

B: I'm gonna.

T: [*She ignores this remark.*] What other committee?

B: A committee to decide on behavior on the bus, because it's
     a long trip to the coast.

T: Very good, yes, behavior on the bus. [*She writes: "3. Stan-
     dards on bus."*]

G: Yea, a list on no-no's.

T: [*Laughing*] No-no's. I guess you might call them that.

B: We'll need some guys to keep order on the bus. [*The ma-
     jority of students start giving ideas all at once.*]

B: People don't push in lines on the bus.

T: Roger.

B: We could use the same people on the beach that are on the
     bus for standards.

T: Yes, very good Roger. We will need a committee for standards
     on the beach, too. [*She writes: "4. Standards on the beach."*]

G: Yes, I think we'll need two committees.

T: OK, now, we have four committees. I think that is enough.
     Number one is for clothing, what to take, wear, remember
     it might be raining. Number two, activities—this committee
     will think of things to do at the tidepools and on the beach.
     [*Students start yelling out things they think of like bats and
     balls, surfboards.*]

G: Can we take—

T: Why don't we let each committee decide for each thing? Now
     think for a minute about which committee you want to be on.
     [*Pause*] We will also need a chairman for each group. OK,
     who wants to work on clothing and food? [*Many hands come
     up.*] Steve, James, Cynthia, and Jimmie. Steve, will you be
     chairman? OK, for activities. [*Many hands come up.*] Mike,
     Brian and Dave. OK, standards on the bus. [*Two hands come
     up.*] Richard, Roger. We need a few more people.

B: Aren't there supposed to be two? Can we work on two com-
     mittees?

T: No, if you work on one that will be enough. Mark, why don't
     you be chairman. [*She points to the rest of the people to be*

on the committee.] You're going to want to meet in discussion groups. [*She points to certain places in the room and designates which committee will meet there.*]

[*Each group runs to its designated place, there is a great deal of noise. Two girls remain at their desks.*]

T: You have 15 minutes and then we'll meet back in our seats. [*She walks over to me and says: "You're now going to see the fourth grade at its peak in interaction."*]

It is hardly surprising to find extensive classroom attention in preparation for a field trip. The point is that the introduction of outside media may have a tendency to provide so many "teachable" aspects that the instructional impact of the lesson gets lost. Teachers are seldom conscious of their inclination to make complex lessons out of simple ones, drawing attention away from the intended lesson. In the classroom cited above, the presumed focus of the trip—the content of the tidepools—has at least temporarily been obscured by the extent of the other preparations.

Thus far we have considered classroom behavior concerning the use of media from the perspective of the teacher's intent. Henry's notion of polyphasic learning—that we learn more than one thing at a time—invites another consideration. The lesson as perceived by the learner is not restricted only to those elements which the teacher intends. In the same way that the introduction of instructional media creates a variety of learning situations on which the teacher may draw, so, too, the media create sometimes uncontrollable or unanticipated consequences that provide concomitant learnings.

UNINTENDED LEARNINGS

The teacher's intended or stated purpose for introducing educational media is usually to increase the basic information of the students or to help them reorganize information they already possess. We have already noted how ideal purposes can be compromised by problems related to the scope, accuracy, or relevance of introduced materials and by an inclination among teachers to overload or overwork educational experiences. These problems were introduced as functions of the intent and skill of the teacher; the educational consequences were related to the teacher's competence.

We now explore some possible stresses for the teacher who augments his instructional program by introducing media. The utilization of any media may force compromises in the way a teacher attempts to fulfill his ideal role. Media may become a variable external to the teacher and, therefore, not subject to his control. The result may be a learning that is incidental or antithetical to the intent in instruction.

MEDIA AS SOURCES OF STRESS IN THE TEACHER ROLE

The Preview Problem

Ideally, the teacher in the classroom is the instructional leader for his students. He is also responsible for their demeanor while in the classroom. Media can compromise him on both counts. For example, as instructional leader, a teacher is expected to be familiar with the material he presents to his class, so that he can select material that is appropriate and can guide his pupils in the use of the material. In the case of audiovisual materials, this necessitates previewing.

No teacher will argue against the desirability for previewing, but this is often impossible. The demands on a teacher's time are great, and the demands placed on the beginning teacher (the very teacher least likely to have prior information about available audiovisual material) are literally overwhelming. Even experienced teachers know the difficulties sometimes involved in coordinating a projector, a classroom, and a film along with the time to view it on just one occasion. Previewing requires this operation to be carried out twice. Consequently, beginning teachers either restrict their use of media to what they can examine beforehand or they use media in a way which has been described in their teacher-training courses as irresponsible. Seldom are aspiring teachers made aware of the idealistic nature of their training.

Media as Teacher Surrogate

If the teacher has not previewed the film, scouted a field trip, briefed himself on the TV lesson of the day, or conferred previously with a guest speaker, he abdicates his leadership—he puts his instructional program in someone else's hands and literally takes potluck on the outcome. The compromise may not be a comfortable one. The increasing use of TV instruction in classrooms, such as the short daily programs in foreign language instruction common in upper elementary grades in some areas, represents a case where the teacher abdicates his position as instructional leader of the classroom every day. The result is that the teacher is left with no role to perform or with only the role of disciplinarian. The following protocol from a sixth grade illustrates the passive role taken by one classroom teacher while the TV teacher "takes over" the class. One wonders if the remark of the teacher at the conclusion of the telecast is a reaction to pupil behavior or to the fact of the television itself.

OBSERVATION NO. 5

[*The teacher turns on the television and sits down in the back of the room. The TV instructor is a woman and is indicated by "TV." She uses a chalkboard.*]

TV: Today we're going to work on complete factorization. Does anyone know the difference between factoring and complete factorization?

T: Who knows?

P: Complete factorization is when you work the number clear down to its prime.

T: How many agree? [*The students' hands go up, and it looks as if everyone agrees.*]

TV: Can two times two to the second power (2×2^2) be reduced any farther?

T: Can it be?

P: No.

TV: Let's use the number 84 for practice. I want the boys to begin with 4×21, and the girls to begin with 6×14. I want both groups to work these down to their primes. [*The students are now busy working out the problem. They have all finished in two minutes.*]

TV: Okay now, you should all be about finished about now. We'll start with the boys first. We can factor 4 into 2×2 or 2 to the second power. We can factor 21 into 7×3. Our answer now should be 2 to the second power times 7 times 3. These are your primes. Okay girls. We can factor 6 into 3×2. Now we can factor 14 into 7×2. Our answer now should be 2 to the second power times 3 times 7. Now you can see that no matter how you go at it you always get the same primes if your answer is right. By dividing the class into boys on one side, and the girls on the other, we can get better arguments.

TV: Will the number 12 have more than one complete factorization?

T: Will it?

P: No.

TV: By now you should know that there is only one complete fac-
      torization. This is the Unique Factorization Property.

. . . .

TV: I want you now to try to complete this fraction. [*She writes
      the number 36/48. The students are busy working out the
      problem.*]

TV: You can reduce 36 down to 2×18: $2 \times 18 = 2 \times 2 \times 3 \times 3 = 2$ to the second power times 3 to the second power. We
      use the same unbrilliant approach to 48: $2 \times 24 = 2 \times 2 \times 2 \times 6 = 2 \times 2 \times 2 \times 2 \times 3 = 2$ to the fourth power times 3.
      [*The classroom teacher gets up from her seat to check on one
      of the pupil's work. The pupil has some pictures drawn on the
      paper, but there are no numbers written down. I couldn't
      hear what she said to him.*]

TV: For your assignment tomorrow, I want you to read exercises
      5-5, and do exercises 5-5c, 9-28. Practice up on your factori-
      zation at home tonight because we're going to have more of
      it tomorrow. Goodbye. [*The classroom teacher comes to the
      front of the room and turns off the television.*]

 T: I want you to be quieter for me than you were for her. Let's
      work 45/75 down to its prime. . . .

The recorded remarks of the classroom teacher during the telecast:
"Who knows?" "How many agree?" "Can it be?" and "Will it?" do not
provide the teacher with a very important instructional role in the
presence of the television instructor. Actually, the teacher has only
repeated the TV instructor's questions, presumably as a sort of self-
appointed audience prompter for the students. Whether pupils *need*
a prompt is questionable, although the protocol suggests that in the
classroom being observed pupils expect a prompt to precede any response they will make. Acting as a prompter is not a highly satisfying
task for most classroom teachers; rather, it is a potential source of role
stress and conflict.

Mechanical Problems

Studies of the adoption and rejection of new media provide interesting cases of persistence and change within the educational institution.[5] For many teachers, introducing audiovisual equipment into the
classroom also introduces an element of tension or excited confusion.

---

[5] References to two such studies, one by Gerhard Eichholz and Everett M.
Rogers, another by Louis Forsdale, are provided at the end of this chapter.

Some teachers refuse to incorporate newer media, particularly the electromechanical innovations, in their classrooms for this very reason. Other teachers accept new innovations as part of the inevitable march of progress, but they relegate the operation of equipment, frequently depending on their students for any prerequisite technical skills. Indeed, some teachers never learn to operate even the simplest of projectors or machines with any apparent confidence.

Coping with mechanical difficulties and breakdowns in equipment, or with organizational problems such as the sharing of equipment among colleagues, sometimes leads to unintended learnings because such situations catch the teacher off guard. Not every teacher reacts to mechanical difficulties with the calm observed in the following situation, but few teachers have as small a class as this one of seven students in an eighth-grade class in French. Note that the student observer included her personal reaction to the use of the film being presented, both for its content and its appropriateness in a language class.

OBSERVATION NO. 7

T: Is there anyone who would violently object to having the written dictée tomorrow so we can see a film today?

Class: [*In unison*]   NO!

T: Maintenant, le cinéma pour aujourd'hui est concernée de Monsieur De Gaulle. Il s'appelle *France and the French People*.

[*The film is black and white and it is in English. Most of the French is translated by the narrator of the film. I certainly feel that this particular film would be of much better use in a social studies class. It gives a fairly idealistic view of France under De Gaulle, but the worst part of the film is that it is entirely in English, thus not really benefiting those in the French class who want to extend their speaking and understanding abilities of the language. The film greatly exalts and glorifies De Gaulle.*]

[*All seven students seemed to be interested, because they were all watching the screen. The teacher got up from her desk after the first few minutes of the film and walked over to a file cabinet at the other end of the room by the sink. She remained there for 5 minutes and then left the room via the back door.*]

[*The boys suddenly burst into laughter when someone discovered that the takeup reel was not operating. The takeup reel had*]

*been put on the wrong way, and there was a huge pile of
film on the floor beneath the projector. The girls started
to laugh too.*]

P: I guess we had better do something about it.

[*The student got up from his desk and walked over to the projector. Since he couldn't find the off-on switch, he pulled
the cord out of the socket on the wall. Just then the teacher
came back into the room, noticed all the students out of
their seats surrounding the projector, and she turned on the
lights in the room.*]

T: Oh, no. What's happened? Oh, why do these things always
happen to me? [*All the students help to put the film back
on the reel correctly.*]

P₂: Wouldn't it be awful if the film was all over the room?

T: We are going to have two more films tomorrow. I certainly
hope that this doesn't happen again.

The Problem of Availability

Frequently, the use of media compromises the teacher's efforts to
provide continuity in his organization for instruction. The teacher does
not necessarily have access to people, transportation, or materials when
he needs them. Conversely, the availability of resources such as a special exhibit or a frequently requested item from an instructional materials center often dictates the time and conditions when media can
be used. The compromise arises because teachers attempt to organize
learning experiences systematically, building on experience through a
planned "scope and sequence" of curriculum organization. The seem-
ingly capricious way in which orders for instructional aids sometimes
arrive at the classroom finds teachers faced with a dilemma. They can
fragment one lesson with vestiges of an earlier one, or they can elect
not to introduce some additional source of information with the rationale that if it is not available at an appropriate time in an instructional sequence, then there is no point in using it at all. In the
following example, a teacher has just concluded a science lesson with
his ninth-grade class and he has explained to the student observer why
he felt the lesson (about snakes) had not been successful.

OBSERVATION NO. 8

[*After class I talked with the teacher who had by this time taken
out the snake and put it around his arm again. He indicated
that the class which I had just observed had been completely*

unprepared in that they were not due to discuss snakes for about a week. But another teacher from another school had brought the snakes over to him that morning, so he decided to use them for the class, as he would only have them for that one day.]

In a comparable illustration, a sixth-grade social studies lesson about Rio de Janiero (T: Don't you think Rio de Janiero is pretty after looking at the picture on page 40?) is interrupted when a pupil comes to the classroom to announce the arrival at the school of an exhibit of live farm animals sponsored by a local dairy company. As the observer notes, the exhibit is visited by every classroom in the school. Teachers do not customarily decline "invitations" for instructional experiences, regardless of the immediate relevance of such experiences.

OBSERVATION NO. 9

[*There is a knock at the door during the discussion of Rio de Janiero. One of the pupils gets up and goes to the door.*]

T: I'll get it. [*The teacher goes to the door and then returns to the room after talking to the messenger.*] The Dairy Display is here and we've been invited to go through it. This is the [name of local milk company] Story Book Barn. Shut your books and line up at the door. [*The students, teacher and observer leave the room and go outside to the display. The display consists of a pick-up truck pulling a trailer. Inside the trailer are two pigs, a rabbit, a rooster, a horse, a cow, and a goat. Every classroom in the school visits the display.*]

T: When you get through the display go back to the room and start work on your social studies. [To observer]: These kids are real good about keeping busy when I'm gone.

The Problem of Advertising

A display such as the free one sponsored by the local dairy presents yet another dilemma for the teacher. The dilemma pits pragmatism against idealism, for in the use of "free and inexpensive materials" in class (a practice of such scope that it supports the publication and sale of an annual catalog of materials), the teacher must measure his comments about the material between the extreme of endorsing the blatant advertising motives of the industries that provide them, and that of failing to extend the courtesy of recognition and appreciation for useful instructional material. From the teacher's point of view, the problem does not have an easy solution unless district policy provides strict

guidelines for the use of free materials (in which case the school-board
members have had to argue whether free materials handed out by the
Bell Telephone Company differ from those handed out by the Red
Cross or the Audubon Society). If the school board does have a policy,
the teacher is compromised because he is denied the right to use his
professional judgment in a matter which he may feel is properly within
his domain.

The relationships between the teacher and the profit-making, political and religious activities of the community are tenuous. School people
as a group are careful not to aggravate either local norms or national
stereotypes in this regard; the evidence suggests that professional educators continue to act more conservatively in regard to community expectations than the members of the community actually feel they
should.[6] Thereby, pupils are witness, at least indirectly, to a kind of
"don't rock the boat" behavior which reinforces another unintended
lesson—that teachers are relatively cautious, conservative, sometimes
peripheral members of the profit- and issue-making activities of the
adult community.

The Teacher as a Learner

Another source of stress introduced through the utilization of media
derives from the ideal that the teacher be both well informed and a
disciple of learning. The ideal teacher is thought of as one who brings
knowledge to his pupils at the same time that he, himself, is forever
an enthusiastic seeker of knowledge. Classroom observations suggest
that teacher behavior as it relates to the utilization of media can teach
other lessons instead, for not every teacher can juggle the role of hum-
ble, inquiring learner with the all-knowing role of sage. Not all pupils
recognize that one reason their teachers appear to be so knowledgeable
is that the teacher controls both the content and direction of class activity. The teacher teaches that which he can—that which he knows.

The teacher who includes external sources of information in his instructional program risks losing control of the content and direction in
the lesson. The content has been pre-packaged for him in the video-
tape, the film, or even in the comments which an uncoached resource
person may make in speaking to a group of students. The teacher's reaction to information which he does not control and which is unfamiliar to him may teach a love of inquiry, but it may also teach that

---

[6] See, for example, John M. Foskett and Harry F. Wolcott, "Self Images and
Community Images of the Elementary School Principal: Findings and Implications
of a Sociological Inquiry," University of Oregon, Eugene: Center for the Advanced
Study of Educational Administration, 1966 (36 pp., mimeographed).

learning requires too much effort, is too time-consuming, too boring, too difficult, or that it is an activity suitable for children but of no consequence for adults.

In the following protocol, a fourth-grade teacher demonstrating with slide projections may be teaching far different attitudes toward learning in general, and specifically toward scientific names, than those she intends to teach.

OBSERVATION NO. 10

[*During the showing of the slides it was hard to take notes since the teacher was showing me things and then sometimes the other teacher would ask her questions. But here is an excerpt from the slides while the teacher was narrating.*]

T: Myitods [?] do thousands of dollars worth of damage each year.

Pinworms are found on fresh fruits. So don't eat fresh fruits and vegetables from the market without washing them.

Tom, would you please shut the door and sit down?

Horsehair worms—Now you kids probably have never been around this but when I was a girl someone told me to put a horsehair in water and we would get a horsehair worm. So we went out where the horse was kept and got a horsehair. We put the hair in water, but after several days of waiting and watching, we found out they had played a joke on us. [*The children laughed.*] But now this is a true story. [*The teacher read the background of the horsehair worm—the story was printed on the slide which showed on the screen.*] In the barnyard we used to find them 15 inches long but this says the average length is 6 inches.

This one, the Arrow Worm, Phylum. . . . Wow, I can't pronounce this one kids [a long Latin name that I didn't get copied down] is a free swimmer among the plankton we studied about.

[*Two boys walk around the room. Three boys talk together in a little group. One girl plays with the window-shade string.*]

T: You know, if some of you kids were quiet back there, I wouldn't need to read as loud.

These look like cherries, but they are lamp shells. I won't even try to pronounce this word [Latin name], because I won't put the accent in the right place.

Whether the teacher should have read these particular Latin names in this particular class is moot. The important point is that the way in which teachers confront new or unfamiliar information becomes a part of what they teach. Not all teachers even subject themselves to the same instructional program that they provide for their pupils. One wonders what concomitant learning results when teachers turn the attention of the class to a telecast, broadcast, or film and then *leave the classroom.* In the following example from a fourth grade, the teacher did not return to the classroom until the conclusion of a fifteen-minute radio broadcast turned on at the office after recess.

OBSERVATION NO. 11

[*It is recess time. The teacher leaves the back of the room, where she has been talking to me, and walks to the front of the room to get her purse.*]

T: [*To observer*] Would you like to go for coffee? [*I said I would stay in the classroom. She left the room. Some children remained in the classroom during recess in order to work on arithmetic papers.*]

Time: 10:15

[*The rest of the class comes in from recess and promptly takes seats. One girl does not head for her seat but instead walks up to the teacher's desk and picks up a stack of papers. From observing, I guessed the papers were the corrected math assignment from the previous day.*]

Time: 10:18

[*The intercom now comes on in the classroom with a radio broadcast. Four different voices are heard. These are the voices of a frontier man and wife and their two children. I would estimate the age of the boy to be 9-12 and the age of the girl to be 5-8. About half of the students lay down their pencils and turn towards the intercom while the other half seem to be listening but continue to write. The story is about frontier life and the problems the early settlers were likely to encounter. In the story, the husband is forced to leave his family because of his participation in battles outside the settlement. The young boy has been given directions by his father to take care of the family and the farm. One day his little sister disappears. With the aid of an Indian boy, they find her safely. This incident reduces the tension between the two fighting groups, the settlers and the Indians. The radio then goes off. Shortly thereafter the teacher walks in.*]

T: OK class, hand in those math papers. | *The students get out of their seats to deposit their papers at a common point on the side of the room.*]

Administrative policy varies between districts and schools as to whether a classroom can be left without supervision. In schools where the teacher may not leave the class unsupervised, he can still escape by not subjecting himself to the message of the media. Thus, we observe teachers who use the running time of a film or broadcast to dust the room, arrange bulletin boards, correct papers, or handle administrative details. Such behavior on the teacher's part does not necessarily teach pupils anything antithetical to the teacher's stated purposes, but a teacher who ignores the instructional content of the media he introduces would do well to consider the question: What does my behavior in the classroom teach my pupils about learning? Curiously, when it is the pupil who ignores the media, teachers have a host of labels by which they characterize him: daydreamer, disinterested, inattentive, reluctant learner, and so forth.

Media as Moralists

As a final example of how media produce compromises in the ideal teacher role, consider the normative content of much school instruction, the "shoulds" and "oughts" through which models of proper behavior are presented to the young. Through the place he allocates to various normative aspects of behavior, the teacher can circumvent discussion about those norms with which his own behavior conflicts. Thus, a teacher who "smokes and drinks" may be less inclined to speak out against such practices than the teacher who abstains, even though providing at least token instruction in health, safety, and morals is mandatory in most school districts. The health, safety, conservation, and patriotic films available for classrooms are typically hortative. While they are consistent with a moralizing tradition characteristic in American education, they may compromise the teacher as a model of good behavior, with the unintended consequence of making him less effective in other aspects of the instructional program. Not all teachers are able to find themselves guilty as easily as the eighth-grade teacher in the following illustration from a class in health and safety.

OBSERVATION NO. 12

[*The teacher arises and walks over to the overhead projector. He removes the paper he had previously laid there.*]

T: You have five minutes to complete the assignment. If you don't finish, come in the first thing in the morning. The books will be here for you. [*The teacher walks to the side of the room and picks up a podium and sets it down near the overhead pro-*

jector. He inserts a paper into the machine and turns it on. On seeing that it works, he immediately turns it off. The teacher then walks out through the open door into the hall where he talks to a fellow teacher two or three minutes. The teacher enters the room.]

T: OK, let's put the books away. [*The students leave their seats and take their books back to the bookshelf.*]

T: Get your notes out. Today we have a picture on the overhead that is a little elementary, but it has four important points that are worth remembering. OK, let's look at it. What's wrong in this picture?

P: That broken ladder rung.

T: OK, we should keep equipment in repair. How many of you can think of an example of equipment at home that is being used but is in need of repair? [*Two boys reply by raising hand.*] I don't think we thought about that one long enough. [*He shows the next picture.*]

P: That man is getting out of the car on the wrong side of the road.

T: How many of your parents are guilty here? [*About half of the class respond by raising their hands.*] Good, because I'm guilty of it, too. Here I am trying to teach you something that I don't even do myself.

Several concomitant learnings may result from this or from any of the other protocols. Here, the eighth-graders may have learned that they should not get out of a car on the "wrong side of the road." They may have also learned that many adults, including their teacher, engage in such unsafe behavior. Or they may have learned, instead, that safety discussions, like the pictures teachers use to initiate them, are a "little elementary."

SOME NON-INSTRUCTIONAL ASPECTS OF MEDIA USE

Instruction or Entertainment: The Delicate Compromise

Particularly in selecting and using films, teachers face another compromise of their ideal self-image. They ask themselves the rhetorical question: Are we teachers, or are we just babysitters? The "right" answer is, of course, that teachers are specialists who blend their knowledge of the universe with their knowledge of human beings as learners to produce desired changes in the behaviors and attitudes of their students. A teacher is not a paid entertainer who does from Monday through Friday what TV and "real" movies do on the weekend. Yet, we argue that school should not be dull. We search for variety in lessons, for more effective ways to extend children's experiences, and for ways to win and reinforce their allegiance to school. The question of just how pleasant and "fun" to make school is crystallized for many teachers in the question: How many films shall I show, and how relevant do they have to be? If a film is entertaining but not very instructional, is it shown anyway? The answer is often Yes. Recall an observer's comment cited at the beginning of the chapter: "The film is supposed to be about Washington but it is the wrong film. It is a film about service stations; it is shown anyway." In the following protocol, the instructional value of both short films which these seven- and eight-year-olds had come to watch seemed questionable to the observer.

OBSERVATION NO. 13

T: You boys and girls are to line up and go to Room Two for a movie. Table One may go. Jennifer, you can do that later. Put the glue down.

Time: 12:55

[They went into the next room and sat in a semicircle. There were sixty-five children. Thirty-two of them sat in chairs, and the others sat on the floor in front of the chairs.]

T_2:   This is a film called "Snuffy, Smokey Bear's Pal."

[Two girls walked in after the film started. The teacher, who was sitting next to me, said the children had been learning about conservation. Snuffy was a dog that spoke to the children about building fires and leaving a clean camp. The dog was watching some children on a picnic. In this five-minute movie Snuffy said four times that he liked children who were good woodsmen and good campers, who would never be careless and let a fire start in the woods.]

P: Do we have another one?

T: That was fast. We have two.

[There were three teachers in the room. One of them tried to quiet the students.]

T_3:   Boys and girls! *[The room got a little quieter.]* All boys and girls! *[She waited for quiet.]* I think you can help Mrs. _____ most by talking softly, because when your voices get very big and loud, it bothers. We have a second film, and if you will talk softly, Mrs. _____ will have it ready in just a minute. The next film is from the Forestry Department. Do you remember when we had Smokey the Bear?

> [*The second film started just as this teacher finished speaking. The film was titled, "Junior Raindrop." It was a cartoon about a raindrop that started out as a nice little boy, but became a juvenile delinquent, then a gangster, when he was mixed with other raindrops in a flood. The narrator spoke too fast, and the sound was fuzzy. Five or six students in the back of the room were stretching and twisting. The movie was over at 1:15, and the children went outside for recess.*]

The conservation theme of both films may have justified their classroom use, although the observer seemed unimpressed by the content of either one. With the questionable educational value of many classroom films, it is not surprising that some educators dogmatically insist that teachers refer to such media as films rather than as "movies," hoping to minimize the association with entertainment. It is not too easy to enlist every member of the school staff in this linguistic plot. I recently overheard a school custodian explain that a classroom that appeared to be unoccupied was not deserted at all. "They're just havin' a show," he explained.

While audiovisual departments in large school districts try to devise ways to inform teachers of their *other* services and resources, the use of classroom films is so frequent in some schools and classrooms that it causes administrative uneasiness. In addition, upper-grade elementary school teachers disapprove of a practice of some primary-grade teachers who show all the films that come to the school, creating for the upper-grade teacher the frustrating moment when pupils make the comment that is the epitome of audiovisual sophistication: "Oh, we've already seen this."

Media in the Reward-Punishment System of the Classroom

Media can also be viewed as part of the reward-punishment system of the classroom. Filmstrips, field trips, records, films—all are intricately involved not only with instructional content, but also with pupil-teacher interaction. Because of the popularity of films, literally any film has value as a reward which a teacher can confer and as a weapon with which to counter pupil misbehavior or lack of endeavor: "If we have time" (i.e.; if class assignments are completed), or "If you are 'especially good' this afternoon," then the conditions have been met for the film.

In some classrooms, the good behavior that is a condition for seeing a film includes student acceptance of the film (or speaker, or exhibit) as a favor or privilege granted by the teacher rather than as an instructional source to be weighed and considered. In the following protocol from a high school class in economics, the class had just seen a film on international trade. The three-word appraisal of a student ("It was dumb") provoked a diatribe by the teacher in defense of the film, rather than a probing for the meaning of his comment.

OBSERVATION NO. 14

[*A film has just been shown.*]

T: All right, what did you think of that film?

Richard: It was dumb.

Girl: It was pretty color.

T: [*Addressing Richard*] You said it was dumb?

Richard: I did.

T: Why?

Richard: I don't know, it was just—

T: I thought it was a good film for economics. It was [good] because it showed . . . [*Observer could not keep up with the teacher*] and because of international trade. It was easy to see why we can't live without one another now. We actually can't. We need the things in foreign countries. [*Teacher started listing all the things she could think of from foreign countries. We started checking things up to see just how many things we had—my sweater that I had on from Hong Kong; the coffee that we were drinking that came to us from South America; etc.*] This was a real good picture. The magnesium from Norway that goes into the making of suitcases—the Volkswagen from Germany coming to America. . . . This was a good story in economics had you tried to get this out of the picture; and it didn't make you realize it at all, Richard? And isn't that strange, I thought you would enjoy it.

The teacher's response suggests that she regarded Richard's remark as an affront to her personally. She did not let Richard explain his reaction, and he may be less inclined to comment next time a film is shown in that class—that is, of course, if another film *is* shown.

Pupils generally recognize the reward element of media, especially films ("Oh boy, a movie") used in class, and teachers take advantage of peer group pressures to keep everyone in class well behaved in order to "earn" an audiovisual reward. Students often react with such enthusiasm that the effect is disconcerting to the teacher who interprets the response as a lack of commitment to the customary classroom tasks. Not every possible instructional aid elicits an overwhelming response, however. Opaque projectors seem low on the popularity scale, and the excitement generated over the use of recordings of music or of filmstrips varies widely among schools.

Students are aware that the introduction of an instructional medium often has a "cost" in terms of consequent pupil effort. The use of a film may presuppose a subsequent assignment, frequently a written one, and particularly if there has been no prior bargaining for good behavior. These assignments are often efforts, on the part of the teachers, to keep students from identifying films and television used at school with commercial movies and commercial television; suspicious pupils may try to assess the terms under which the reward is being bestowed. ("Are we gonna' hafta' make a story about it after?") An extreme example of this is suggested by the remark of a sixth-grade boy attending a week-long camp in outdoor education, a regular part of the sixth-grade curriculum in that school district. As a group of pupils and their adult leader approached the top of a ridge on a morning nature walk, the boy advised his friends, "Don't look at it. If you do, you'll have to write about it."

Media as Vehicles for Conveying
Cultural Stereotypes

Some media, particularly artifacts and films concerning peoples in other parts of the world, provide the stimulus for another kind of concomitant learning. These learnings, usually unintended, reflect the attitude that our own way of life is the only right and proper way, and that the way any other people live is inferior. This attitude may be accompanied by the concession that no one is really at fault because not everyone has access to all our advantages. Anthropologists refer to this as ethnocentricism.[7] It is an attitude that is antithetical to many stated teaching objectives, particularly in the social studies, concerning intergroup understanding, the dignity of all human beings, and the concept that there are countless variations in meeting and resolving the problems of human societies. The unintended aspect of instruction arises when teachers introduce artifacts from other cultures and present them

---

[7] For a discussion on ethnocentricism in the high school social studies curriculum see Rachel Sady, "Teaching About Ethnocentricism," Occasional Paper No. 3, Anthropology Curriculum Study Project Chicago: the Project, 5632 Kimbark Avenue, n.d. (15 pp., mimeographed).

to students out of cultural context, and with the expressed or implied notion that the culture under discussion is exotic but, at the same time, impractical and second-rate. For example, in one ninth-grade social studies class, the teacher opened with the following comment:

> The afternoon class is very fortunate in having two students whose relatives have travelled all over the world. In the back of the room are several artifacts from Egypt and India. In the middle of the room are things from Iraq brought to Dave by an exchange student who is living with his family while he attends the University. We have some jewelry and bowls. Here is a light fixture which they put over lights. We tried it yesterday in my afternoon class and it is just beautiful. Do you know what these are? They're camel bells. [*She rings them.*] Wouldn't they make a beautiful sound around a camel's neck. Here we have a beautiful Egyptian tray. Dave asked us to be especially careful with it. And do you know what this is? It's a camel saddle. Isn't it funny looking? Dave said his little brother has so much fun sitting on it and pretending he's riding a camel. [*A few students laugh.*] Now if any of you have interesting things to show please bring them.

By her comment, "Isn't it funny looking?", the teacher added a tiny increment on the side of cultural stereotyping. She lost an opportunity for her students to explore form and function which she might have fostered by asking such questions as, "Why do you think this saddle is shaped as it is?" or "What would be some of the problems to overcome in designing a saddle for riding a camel?"

The tendency toward ethnocentricism is as prevalent in the content of many of the commercially prepared instructional media as it is in the incidental comments made by teachers.

CONCLUSION

In this chapter, the instructional content of the classroom has been considered from the perspective of the learner as well as from that of the teacher. While we can discuss, with some certainty, at least part of what the teacher intends to accomplish (we can both ask him to describe his intent and observe his behavior in implementing it), we cannot do more than conjecture on all the possible dimensions of the lesson as perceived by the learner. The purpose of the discussion has been to alert the teacher or prospective teacher to the fact that the end product of the human teaching-learning interaction is seldom restricted to a unilateral transmission of an isolated unit of information. Lessons contain both intended and unintended elements, regardless of the sincerity, effort, dedication, or skill on the part of the teacher. Indeed, if teacher and pupil do not share a similar cultural heritage, there may be no intended learning at all.[8]

We have used the term *concomitant learnings* to include all the learnings other than the central purpose of the lesson as intended by the teacher. They also include the incidental lessons which a teacher would acknowledge as consistent with his intent, but which are not the focus of the lesson.

A lesson looks different from the bottom up than it does from the top down. From his point of view at the "top" of the lesson, the teacher asks, "What did I intend to accomplish in this lesson?" and "How well did I succeed?" The teacher who seeks an awareness of his impact must also contemplate the lesson from the perspective of the learner. This leads him to ask: "How did my pupils perceive this lesson?" "What are the possible unintended consequences of my instruction?" With this approach, the teacher should be able to utilize educational media more effectively in the instructional process.

REFERENCES

Eichholz, Gerhard, and Everett M. Rogers. "Resistance to the Adoption of Audio-Visual Aids by Elementary School Teachers: Contrasts and Similarities to Agricultural Innovation," in Matthew B. Miles, ed., *Innovation in Education,* Teachers College, Columbia University: Bureau of Publications, 1964.

Fordsdale, Louis. "8 mm Motion Pictures in Education: Incipient Innovation," in Matthew B. Miles, ed., *Innovation in Education,* Teachers College, Columbia University: Bureau of Publications, 1964.

Henry, Jules. "A Cross-Cultural Outline of Education," *Current Anthropology,* Vol. 1, July 1960, 267–305.

————. "Culture, Education, and Communications Theory," in George Spindler, ed., *Education and Anthropology,* Stanford University Press, 1955.

---

[8] Students interested in educational problems in cross-cultural settings are referred to the series, CASE STUDIES IN EDUCATION AND CULTURE, under the general editorship of George and Louise Spindler. Two studies dealing specifically with problems of introducing a Western-oriented curriculum in traditional cultures are John Gay and Michael Cole, *The New Mathematics and an Old Culture,* and Harry F. Wolcott, *A Kwakiutl Village and School* (New York: Holt, Rinehart & Winston, 1967).

Sady, Rachel. "Teaching About Ethnocentricism," Occasional Paper No. 3, Anthropology Curriculum Study Project, Chicago: the Project, 5632 Kimbark Avenue, n.d,. 15 pp., mimeographed.

Spindler, George, "The Transmission of American Culture," in George Spindler, ed., *Education and Culture—Anthropological Approaches,* New York: Holt, Rinehart & Winston, 1963.

SECTION 4.

IMPLEMENTING ELEMENTS AND SUMMARY

The *Thigh-bone*, 14. the foremost, 16. and the hindmost Bone, in the Leg, 17.	*Tibia*, 14. *Fibula*, 16. anterior, & posterior, 17.
The Bones of the Hand, 18. are thirty-four, and of the Foot, 19. thirty.	Ossa Manûs, 18. sunt triginta quatuor, Pedis, 19. triginta.
The *Marrow* is in the Bones.	*Medulla* est in Ossibus,

XLII.
The Outward and Inward Senses.

Sensus externi & interni.

There are five outward *Senses ;*	Sunt quinque externi *Sensus ;*
The *Eye*, 1. seeth Colours, what is white or black, green or blew, red or yellow.	*Oculus*, 1. videt *Colores*, quid album vel atrum, viride vel cœruleum, rubrum aut luteum, sit.
The *Ear*, 2. heareth *Sounds*, both natural, Voices and Words; and artificial,	*Auris*, 2. audit *Sonos*, tum naturales, Voces & Verba ; tum artificiales,

Introduction

An examination of the preceding chapters compels one to face the fact that there is need in education for a broad and comprehensive continuum of instructional resources ranging from print to non-print materials in all of their forms. Both the teacher and the student must be well equipped.

In the chapter by Richard L. Darling, the fundamental philosophy developed is that resources must be available at the school building and classroom levels if the most favorable environment for learning is to be present. Darling describes a new type of organization called a "media center" to provide these learning resources. The media center contains or makes available all types of learning resources which will be used by the students, teachers and, increasingly, by the families living in the neighborhood of the school. Without the kind of school media center which Darling describes, many of the exciting learning opportunities presented in the earlier chapters would be impossible.

The final chapter by Wesley C. Meierhenry is a synthesis of those preceding, in order to give some understanding as to where we are in education and some suggestions as to where we seem to be going.

CHAPTER TEN

Media Centers

Richard L. Darling

Educational media, to exert an effective influence on instruction, must be organized in such a way that teachers and students have access to them. Wherever media may be used as an instructional tool, it is essential that they relate to one another, complementing each other in the learning process and supporting both group instruction and individual study. To achieve this objective, each school must have a media center where teachers may procure a wide variety of instructional materials and equipment and organize them for use. These materials must also be made available to students for individual study. When the school media center cannot provide certain types of materials, services, and equipment, the individual school should be backed

253

up by a system or area-wide cooperative media center whose function is to supply instructional media not normally found in the school.

The ideal school media center combines into one integrated service the facilities and services of traditional libraries and audiovisual programs. The best aspects of both of the older services and the added benefits derived from the combination of the two, results in a media center that is more than a combined library and audiovisual program. It is geared to the best in modern learning theory and takes advantage of the most recent developments in the application of technology to education.

Effective support of the curriculum requires that the media center house large and varied collections of instructional materials as well as the appropriate equipment for their use. Its facilities, designed to accommodate a wide range of services and activities and a staff of media specialists and clerical and technical supporting personnel adequate to administer the media program, are a primary requisite if the center is to give meaningful assistance to teachers and students.

THE MEDIA COLLECTION

The most striking characteristic of a good educational media center is the diversity of its collections which include both printed and non-print materials, each accepted for its own integrity and its value to education. Materials for reading, for listening, and for viewing are all a part of the collection, and are used because of their contribution to the study of a topic in the classroom or by individuals studying in the media center. All instructional materials in the center are organized

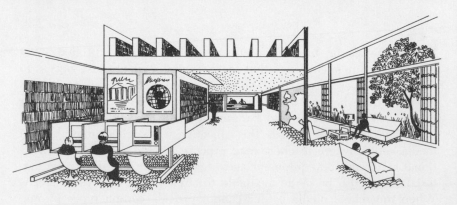

FIGURE 10-1

into an integrated catalog, providing teachers with an opportunity to determine what is available and to consider various media for possible contributions in meeting specific instructional needs. In addition, this catalog provides students with a wide variety of instructional materials from which to choose as they pursue their studies.

The largest single portion of the media collection consists of printed materials. The book collection, if it is to meet the requirements of individual study and research, is, in fact, larger than in traditional, book-oriented school libraries, but it is more directly related to units of instruction. The old idea that the collection should represent all subjects according to a percentage formula has no place in a media center whose function is instructional support. Each item justifies its place in the collection by its role in supporting a broadly conceived curriculum. Teachers and media specialists work together to select materials concerned with instructional units, or closely related groups of units that will challenge both the rapid learner and the slower learner. The book collection includes special and advanced reference works, varied indexes, bibliographies and multi-media lists, so that students and teachers may obtain more detailed knowledge of the contents of the center's collection than is provided by the catalog.

Paperbound books, less expensive than casebound, are used to expand collections quickly and inexpensively when schools introduce new courses, or when extensive duplication of a title is necessary. "Paperbacks" are often used as supplementary textbooks.

In order to make the current information in science, government, and other rapidly changing fields available, and to acquaint students with the diversity of magazine and newspaper publications, expanded periodical collections are necessary in both elementary and secondary schools. Increasing emphasis on independent study and research makes it necessary for the center to provide long runs of back issues and the necessary periodical indexes. Since space for such materials is always difficult to find, microfilm-readers and reader-printers are rapidly becoming standard equipment so that instructional media centers can store back volumes of useful periodicals and other materials on microfilm. Some large school district and area media centers have purchased microfilm cameras in order to preserve teacher-prepared materials, rare items of state and local history, and other uncopyrighted materials for student use.

Programed books, teaching machines, and programed materials for use in teaching machines have also become a part of the media center collection to meet special needs for independent and remedial study.

FIGURE 10-2

In addition to a varied collection of printed materials, media centers also provide auditory, visual, and other types of learning materials. The following partial list of non-book media administered by the center indicates the scope of the media center activities and variety of materials available in such a center:

art prints	models
bulletin board materials	motion pictures, both 8-mm and 16-mm
charts	photographs
community resource file	posters
display materials	radio and television schedules
exhibits	realia
felt materials	recordings, both disc and tape
8-mm film loops	scripts
filmstrips	specimens
globes	stereoscopic materials
kits	study prints
maps	transparencies and overlays

In order to provide services involving all types of materials, the media center must also be prepared to provide and maintain the necessary equipment. In addition to such standard items of equipment as 16-mm motion picture projectors, 8-mm projectors, filmstrip projectors, record players, and tape recorders, for classroom instruction, provisions must also be made for listening stations, individual viewers, micro-film-readers and reader-printers, and other equipment and facilities so that students can use materials individually. The center's equipment should make it possible for students to study as easily with non-print materials as they can with books, and should facilitate bringing different media together for the exploration of a topic.

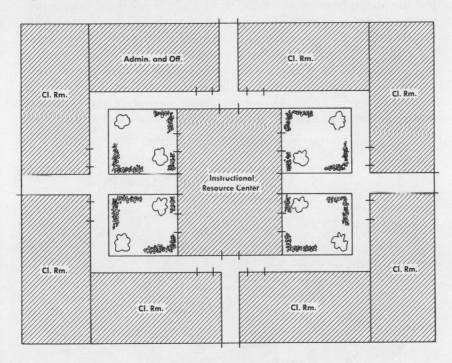

FIGURE 10-3

PHYSICAL FACILITIES

If students are to use this multi-media approach in individual learning, the physical facilities of the media center must be planned and administered so that both materials and equipment are readily accessible. Because of the recent emphasis on independent study, many school planners are experimenting with media centers quite different from the traditional school libraries they are replacing. The old-fashioned school library is characterized by a large study-reading room equipped with rows of rectangular or round multi-student tables. All too often, the library is used as a study hall, not as a library. The media center, on the other hand, is more likely to have a number of small study areas, equipped so that students may study individually with a variety of media. Some schools, especially those planned for team teaching, have located satellite resource centers near specific subject areas within the school.

To achieve the effect of small, intimate study areas where students feel the atmosphere more conducive to study, schools are now experimenting with a variety of arrangements and designs. Some media centers utilize a number of relatively small study rooms. Other break up a large area with bookstacks and furniture, giving the effect of separate rooms, but preserving flexibility for future modification. Individual study carrels, arranged so that each student will have considerable privacy as he works, are beginning to replace the traditional reading tables. Some carrels contain electrical outlets so that students

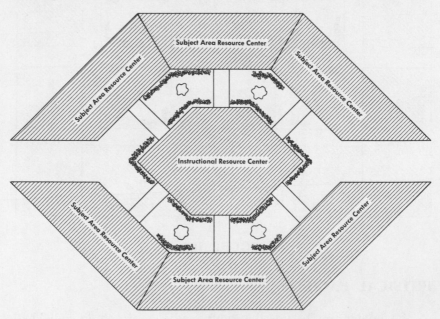

FIGURE 10-4

may use audiovisual equipment for listening and viewing. As dial-access information retrieval systems are installed in school and school system media centers, carrels will need to be equipped with built-in audio and video equipment.

The media center should be equally well planned for reading, listening, and viewing. These activities may be housed in separate areas of the media center, but if students are to be encouraged to use all media, it is probably more desirable to combine such activities. A primary consideration in planning a media center is the provision for adequate conduits for electrical outlets and audio and video transmission lines so that students may read, listen to, or view pertinent media as they study. To meet teacher needs, the center should also incorporate a viewing room where several teachers or small groups may preview television programs, listen to audio tapes and engage in small-group activities related to study or instructional preparation. In other words, in addition to supplying materials and equipment for large-group activities, the media center should also provide facilities

FIGURE 10-5

and equipment required to support both individual and small-group use of media.

MEDIA PRODUCTION

Media production is also within the province of the center, and facilities for this activity must be carefully planned. It is here that the media specialist and teacher can design and produce instructional materials to meet specific needs.

This area will likely be one of the busiest in the center. The staff (and perhaps the students) will make slides, transparencies, recordings, displays, bulletin boards, video tapes, charts, posters, or duplicated materials as needed. The production area, therefore should be liberally provided with work space, counters and tables, and storage space. If possible, a sound-proofed recording room and a photographic dark-room should also be provided in the production area.

The center will necessarily include other areas as well, such as conference rooms, storage areas, rooms to house the dial-access storage system and console, administrative office, and materials and equipment maintainence. The media center is not just a room, but a suite of rooms or areas carefully planned for each of its services.

MEDIA PERSONNEL

Effective service from the media center requires a special kind of professional and supporting staff. In order to assist teachers in curriculum planning and implementation, professional media specialists, whose training differs significantly from that of traditional librarians or audiovisual coordinators, are necessary. These specialists must undergo an extensive and unique program of preparation that will enable them to participate in curriculum making as well as implementation. This implies that the media specialist receives training as a teacher, with a thorough background in psychology, learning theory, and teaching methods, as well as the in educational value and use of media. The media center staff should include generalists who know all media, as well as specialists in the different media, and subject specialists who know the range of media as they relate to a subject discipline.

Trained aides, clerks, and technicians perform those duties in the center not requiring professional skills. They can prepare materials for use; assemble collections for teachers; prepare recordings, slides, and transparencies; handle the instructional equipment; and do the many clerical jobs related to ordering, circulation, and use of materials and equipment. The head media specialist, with imagination and administrative ability, can weld the staff into an effective team to aid teachers in improving instruction. Without an adequate staff, the media center can make, at best, only a minimum contribution to education. With it, the center can offer a range of services making it a most vital element in the school program.

SERVICES OF THE MEDIA CENTER

Whereas the traditional school library frequently provides a rigidly scheduled program in which entire classes are sent to the library, and the audiovisual program provides only for whole-class activities, a media center program encourages teachers to send individual pupils and small groups to the center as they need to use materials. Entire classes are brought to the center only for specific purposes.

The media specialists work with each teacher as well as with subject-and grade-level groups to plan teaching units. Together, they construct bibliographies related to the unit, with provision for the slow learner, the average, and the advanced. They evaluate materials, identify topics for which more materials are needed, and develop an overall outline for use of media. They determine the materials to be used, and the necessary skills involved; they decide which media will be used in class and which individually in the center. At times, media specialists may assist teachers with materials in the classroom. The media specialist, having worked with the teacher in planning, is well prepared to help individual children and small groups who come to the center as classroom activities dictate. Students seeking the media center for identified learning needs find media specialists prepared to give them the close individual guidance in reading, listening, and viewing that is essential for maximum benefit from these activities.

Books, films, filmstrips, slides, recordings, and other materials are all available for student use. After data has been collected, students can use the center's production facilities in preparing reports, utilizing transparencies, recordings, and other materials to supplement or take the place of a written report. The production of graphics has an important reinforcing effect on learning, since data must be thoroughly analyzed and understood before translation into visual form.

To meet student needs, flexible procedures and extended services are also necessary. Lengths of loans are geared to student assignments and classroom units. Because so many materials require equipment, media centers may need to be open evenings, Saturdays, and during vacation periods, or perhaps students may be permitted to check out equipment along with materials for home use.

Media services geared to classroom needs make the media center an extension of the classroom. The media specialists are involved as part of a team in planning and implementing instruction. The media center is the foundation which supports the school's curriculum.

THE DISTRICT OR REGIONAL MEDIA CENTER

Numerous large school systems have developed central media centers to supplement and support sattelite media centers in each school. Other school systems, too small to develop an adequate media center, have joined forces with their neighbors to provide a regional media center which serves several systems. The regional media center does not replace media centers in small schools; rather it provides materials and services to supplement those which the schools cannot supply for themselves.

The district center can relieve the building media specialist of a number of tasks, and can assist the school in improving the caliber of its program. For instance, regional media centers can take over routine and repetitive tasks which can be done more efficiently in a central location, such as the preparation of materials for use. The district center can establish processing services to order, catalog, and physically prepare materials essential to a modern instructional program. With centralized technical services, it becomes economically feasible to use modern, labor-saving equipment and data-processing equipment for card reproduction and other tasks which make it possible for materials to arrive at the school ready for immediate use with cards printed and prepared for filing in the card catalog. With the use of computers to produce a media catalog in book form, professional personnel may be relieved even of the tedious job of filing cards in the catalog.

Centralized processing certainly enables media specialists to function more effectively by increasing their availability to both faculty and students. Centralized processing is available for books from commercial sources; however, processing of non-print materials by private enterprise is still in its infancy, and, in any case, will not be adequate in quantity to serve the needs of most schools for some time.

Another important service of media centers involves the design, production, and reproduction of instructional materials. Though production should be done in individual schools to meet immediate needs, mass production of transparencies, prerecorded tapes, and other materials used by a number of schools, can be done in the main center saving both time and money. The center can produce high-quality materials at less cost because it can afford to use sophisticated production equipment that the individual school cannot afford. In addition, locally produced materials can then be made available precataloged, processed, and ready for use.

Another vital role of the central media center is to provide an inventory of instructional materials not usually owned by every school. Though there is no question that materials are more frequently used if readily available, and that the basic collection of instructional materials should be housed permanently within the school, there are, however, some types of materials better placed in central inventories. These include:

1. materials too expensive for individual schools to own;
2. materials too infrequently used for individual schools to own;
3. materials requiring constant care and maintenance impractical in individual schools.

Application of these criteria enables a school district to establish fairly readily the kinds of materials which the district media center should stock in order to support the instructional program of the schools. Sixteen-millimeter motion picture films, for instance, fit all three categories. They are expensive, infrequently used, and must be inspected and maintained if their usefulness is to continue. Other types of materials regularly used in the instructional program, but infrequently enough that many schools can share them, are museum materials, talking books for the blind, large-type books for the visually handicapped, models, and video tapes which may be played on individual school, video-tape playback equipment.

It is also the responsibility of the center to keep teachers informed of the availability of both services and media. One method of making materials easily accessible from central inventory and of relating them to the instructional materials owned by the individual school is to catalog all central inventory materials on cards which can be interfiled into the school catalog. A card catalog in this case becomes a *media catalog* in which teacher, student, and media specialist may locate all available materials on a given subject no matter where they are located in the district.

An effective distribution system requires immediate confirmation of requests and a delivery schedule that will enable schools to obtain items on short notice. In some centers, immediate confirmation of requests is accomplished through a telephone booking service. With daily delivery service, it is possible to request an item one day and have it delivered the next. Rapid service and adequate information provided to each school encourages teachers to make more use of media available in the center.

A district or regional media center also becomes the repository for professional materials, both print and non-print, in quantities impossible for one school to house. These resources enable professional personnel to engage in extended research and study either at the center or in their own school. Center services also extend to in-service education activities related to the design, production, and utilization of instructional media. Again, these activities can be carried on either in the center or in individual schools.

In addition to providing in-service education activities for the professional staff, the central office should assist the school by providing activities for the technical and clerical staff. Workshops for non-professional personnel include instruction in finding and making instructional materials, and in assisting the media specialists and teachers.

School systems which are experimenting with new and innovative kinds of programs should be identified, and arrangements made for both teachers and media specialists to visit and observe activities which may be adapted to improve their own programs. Perhaps the most important service of the center is its consultant and supervisory assistance to schools in their efforts to develop exciting and imaginative programs.

Planning new or remodeled facilities for school media centers represents another area of the media specialist's responsibility. School planners and media specialists must work together in order to be sure that adequate facilities to accommodate media programs are included when remodeling or building a new school. Supervisors can provide information on current trends in media service, on the way media centers operate in the instructional program of the school, and how these facilities will implement the instructional program.

As the school facilities and program grow, center personnel should take an active role in recruiting specialists, technicians, and clerks; assist the personnel department in interviewing candidates for positions; and in advising principals in assigning successful candidates to positions.

BUDGET AND PROGRAM

Program planning at the school-system level provides the framework in which local planning can proceed. One helpful element in such system-wide planning is the development of standards for local-school media services. Local standards designed to meet local needs or problems provide specific short-term goals and assistance in developing budgets. The district media center staff should prepare a staffing formula to meet local needs and to provide for a growing program. Such standards provide guidelines for developing the program, and they also serve to inform the local superintendent and board of education of the needs of the media program.

The preparation of regular progress reports for presentation to the superintendent and board are necessary to keep them informed about the development of school media services in both the district and in individual schools. When needed, the district center should prepare special reports in order to inform the school board and the general public of the importance of the media program or to develop and justify the annual budget.

The center's media supervisors should visit schools frequently to assist media specialists, teachers, and principals in developing long-range plans for improving media services and the instructional program itself. Supervisors should meet with the faculty members in individual schools to assist in solving problems in their programs and to remind them of the services available from the school system media center. These consultation visits give the supervisors a further opportunity to discuss new developments in instructional media and help local building personnel increase their competencies in teaching and in the use of instructional materials and equipment.

With the great growth in the production of instructional materials in recent years, especially since the passage of the Elementary and Secondary Education Act of 1965, the volume of new materials issued annually has grown so fast that no teacher or school faculty can hope to examine all of them. The regional media center can assist the local school in identifying useful materials for instruction by setting up a review and examination service through the center. Teachers and media specialists, working with instructional supervisors, can examine, subject by subject, the materials needed in the various programs. They can eliminate for the whole school system those which are *obviously* not worthy of consideration by the individual schools. The district media center can then assemble requested materials for preview and examination by all of the schools.

Using the evaluations provided by small groups of teachers and media specialists, the district media center can issue lists of recommended materials which have been identified as useful in supporting the school-district curriculum. These materials provide both media specialists and teachers an opportunity to examine materials of known value in order to select those which will prove useful in meeting the needs of individual students and of specific school programs. In order to do this, teachers will need released time for this work.

The district materials center may provide even more complex services, such as radio and television and dial-access retrieval services. These services should supplement those of the individual school. In effect, the district media center bears the same relationship to the school media center that the school media center does to the classroom.

Whether local or regional, media centers exist for only one purpose: to promote more effective teaching and learning. They supply the materials and equipment which support instruction, facilities for their use, and most important of all, competent media personnel to assist students and teachers in using media as they study and teach. The media center provides the organizational unit through which the varied media of communication can have impact on the educational program.

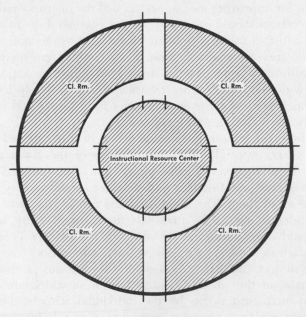

FIGURE 10-6

ADDITIONAL READING

American Association of School Librarians. *Standards for School Library Programs*. Chicago: American Library Association, 1960. 132 pp.

American Association of School Librarians and National Commission for Teacher Education and Professional Standards. *The Teachers' Library: How to Organize It and What to Include*. Washington, D.C.: National Education Association, 1966. 204 pp.

Brown, James W. and Kenneth D. Norberg. *Administering Educational Media*. New York: McGraw-Hill, 1965. 363 pp.

Darling, Richard L. "Is Central Processing for You?" *School Library Journal*, XIII (December, 1966), 15–18.

_____. "School Library Processing Centers," *Library Trends*, XVI (July, 1967), 58–65.

Ellsworth, Ralph E. and Hobart D. Wagener. *The School Library, Facilities for Independent Study in the Secondary School*. New York: Educational Facilities Laboratory, 1963. 143 pp.

Department of Audiovisual Instruction, NEA. *Quantitative Standards for Audiovisual Personnel, Equipment and Materials*. Washington, D.C.: Department of Audiovisual Instruction, 1966.

Henne, Frances. "Learning to Learn in School Libraries," *School Libraries*, XV (May, 1966), 15–23.

_____. "Toward Excellence in School Library Programs," in *New Definitions of School Library Service*. University of Chicago Press, 1960, pp. 84–87.

Jacobs, James W. "Inservice Education of Teachers in the Use of a School Library as a Materials Center," in Mary Helen Mahar, ed., *The School Library as a Materials Center*. Washington, D.C.: U.S. Department of Health, Education, and Welfare, Office of Education, 1963, pp. 49–52.

Miller, Robert H. "The Media Specialist," *Audiovisual Instruction*, XII (February, 1967), 133–37.

Nicholsen, Margaret E. "The IMC," *School Libraries*, XIII (March, 1964), 39–43.

Taylor, James L., Mary Helen Mahar, and Richard L. Darling. *Library Facilities for Elementary and Secondary Schools*. Washington, D.C.: U.S. Department of Health, Education, and Welfare, Office of Education, 1965.

CHAPTER ELEVEN

A Look Ahead

W. C. Meierhenry

As we reflect upon the present and future of American society, we are led to the unalterable conclusion that the solutions of its many problems depend upon education. Among the major factors affecting the kind and quality of education offered are the resources and programs developed to help students to learn, and the educational personnel who administer, supervise, and present the curriculum.

The purpose of this book has been to consider some of the skills and attitudes to which teachers, both now and in the future, must be exposed, and, where appropriate, developed. The authors and editors of this text believe that some of the roles of educational personnel will continue to be traditional, while others will be either new or applied in a changed setting.

CHANGES IN THE EDUCATIONAL SCENE

An examination of traditional educational practices discloses that throughout most of his school life the student has found himself reacting to a rigid set of circumstances, physical facilities, and curricular materials. The era of education characterized by such practices is ending. No longer will a student be the recipient of a teacher's presentation only when that teacher stands before him. The time is at hand when students will not be required to assemble in groups of twenty-five to thirty. The rigidity of requiring a class of such a size, sitting at desks arranged in rows facing a teacher at the front of the room, is disappearing.

It is now evident that how much space a student should occupy in a classroom, in a media center, or on the playground, are all relative matters. Further, some educators are insisting that such factors as permanent furniture limit what students can do. As a consequence, we are moving into a period when disposable classroom furniture may become commonplace.

We are also moving away from a reliance on certain fixed time relationships; for instance, school sessions beginning at nine and ending at three-thirty with a recess at ten-thirty and two, and the idea that school should be in session from Monday to Friday and from September to June. Likewise, the idea that the period of formal school attendance should begin at five or six years of age and end when the student reaches sixteen to eighteen years is also being questioned. Is age five too late for certain important edcuational experiences to occur? Can sixteen-or eighteen-year-old students profit from experiences that come before they are old enough to appreciate them? The traditional number of years now devoted to formal education seems far too limiting. Education is rapidly becoming a "cradle to the grave" activity.

The idea that the student should respond positively and appropriately in an artificial environment, the classroom, is also being examined. In order to secure effective learning, evidence indicates that it is necessary for the environment to be a rich and exciting one from the standpoint of both physical and human resources. Therefore, teachers, both present and future, will be confronted with a situation where much more emphasis is placed on the student, on the manipulation of his environment, physical facilities, time schedule, and even on his cultural background. There is a current search for flexibility and adaptability in meeting individual learner needs. We are groping to personalize what happens to the learner and humanize him during the very time when technology assumes an ever-increasing dimension in our lives.

NEW APPROACHES DUE TO TECHNOLOGY

The very reason that an opportunity exists to develop the flexibility which is required is due to technological developments in all fields, including education. The existence of media and new technological devices makes it possible to modify and adapt our past patterns of instruction and education to meet the needs of a contemporary society.

Educators are now seeking new configurations or patterns that will improve the educational setting. In some areas, entire systems of instruction are beginning to develop for a particular subject matter. The systems approach to instruction usually begins with a subject at a particular grade level and may later be extended to other grade levels.

We do not yet have specific solutions to the problems of course and curriculum development. Activities, however, may vary widely and include the manipulation of instructional bits by teachers, by students, or by both. Many technological devices lend themselves to such manipulation, based on the assumption that first the student and then the teacher are in the best position to know individual learning needs.

Some instructional strategists believe strongly that it will be possible to develop complete packages of instructional materials on a subject which can be presented via technological equipment of one kind or another. These instructional packages would be validated on certain classes of students and then utilized with other students who possess characteristics similar to the first group—all with a minimum of teacher involvement. Under such circumstances, the teacher functions as a counselor rather than as a purveyor of a body of knowledge.

A number of education developments occurring at the present time need to be examined in the light of what the teacher of the future must expect. First of all, there will be much more emphasis upon purposes and objectives, and their translation into behavioral terms. The manner of achieving such behavioral objectives may depend upon the presentation of a number of differentiated alternatives. A portion of the alternatives may be presented in the instructional packages themselves. Additional adaptations will take place at the local level, depending upon the type of student, his age, sex, socio-economic background, and other similar factors.

The word "teacher" is being interpreted much more broadly than it once was, varying all the way from the live teacher in the classroom to the "mediated" teacher, who is a teacher recorded in some type of medium. This approach does not rule out the live teacher; however, in some situations, the mediated teacher may serve equally well—or better. The alternatives available and the purposes to be served determine the choice.

Schools are being organized so that the fixed time schedule is giving way to a situation characterized by "no bells shall ring." It is now possible, through dial-access and other electronic devices for storing and retrieving information, to make learning experiences readily available at any time, in school or at home. Obviously, there are still certain educational tasks which must be accomplished during the usual school day, but their functions must be spelled out more explicitly than they have been in the past.

The traditional classroom walls are giving way to no walls at all or, in some cases, low partitions separating one classroom from another and separating classroom from the media center. Although physical walls may be required around the outside of the school for climate control, no longer is there a boundary between the schoolhouse, the playhouse, or the neighborhood in which the school is located. The fact is that the school is now being considered in terms of its relationship to the state, the nation, and the world at large. The use of television, the possible use of satellites or lasers for transmission, as well as other new developments, will make possible the integration of the "school" with the total world community.

DIFFERENTIATED STAFF COMPETENCIES

It is evident that teaching assignments will be on a new and differentiated basis. Some years ago, Walter K. Beggs proposed a new model which put the teacher in the center of the teaching act. He outlined the situation as follows:

> The teacher is still at the center of the process, but the function is changed, and the relationship to the dynamic is altered. He may be likened to a master of ceremonies or to the producer, rather than to the main actor. He is equipped with the ability to use effectively the techniques and devices that are available, and his responsibility is to focus these—along with his own talents—on a given learning

situation. Graphically, the design would place the teacher in position as a sort of central sun, which controls certain satellite processes.

Five such satellites may be suggested here: (1) *the teaching media,* including television, films, radio, projection devices, and various types of audio treatment; (2) *the teaching team,* which presupposes breaking the teaching act into related but specialized functions, such as design, communication, research, and presentation; (3) *programmed teaching devices* for individualized learning and immediate reinforcement of learner responses; (4) *the teaching system,* which is a preplanned and articulated design for teaching an entire discipline from its elementary beginning to the point where the learner is self-sufficient; (5) *the research complex* that is building up around learning theory, teaching technique, and learner growth.[1]

More recently, the National Commission on Teacher Education and Professional Standards (TEPS) has been giving a great deal of attention to this area. In a publication entitled "Man, Media, and Machines," Bruce R. Joyce indicated the following:

> The means for creating such an education are coming within our grasp. Advancing technology and new understanding are about to make it possible to prescribe for each child the learning materials and teaching strategies which closely match his achievements, ability, and learning style. We are beginning to have learning materials prepared by advanced scholars. We have it within our capacity to develop continuous materials development systems which through motion pictures and television tapes and written materials will allow each child to have contact with the thinking of advanced scholars and those who reflect on the course of our society. New knowledge is emerging about the dynamics of the social system of the school, about ways of creating a social climate that fosters reflective thinking and supports the individual as he seeks for meaning. Special techniques are being developed to help teachers improve their capacity to work with children supportively and to evolve new teaching strategies.

> . . . .

> Inroads are being made into the complex of problems that must be solved in order to develop a fully personal, intellectual, and humanistic education. Schools everywhere must search for methods of organization so that exciting teachers can orchestrate the many resources available to them and to the children they teach.

---

[1] W. K. Beggs in a speech given at the DAVI National Convention, Kansas City, Missouri, March 28, 1962.

This publication proposes an organizational model or structure for the school—a structure that places human teachers at the center of the decision-making process and provides them with the supportive staff to help work with children, individualize instruction, and personalize education. The structure also makes available to the teacher many persons who can bring scholarship, special human relations training, and technological know-how to the learning situation.[2]

In order to accomplish such publications, Joyce has divided instruction into "personal inquiry," "independent study," and "group inquiry." He proposes that staff members be chosen in order to expedite each of these types of educational activities. Each specialist will be called upon to assist in the development of instructional procedures for all phases of instructional endeavor, whatever form it takes. Even though specialists in these areas will be available, it is necessary for the teachers to understand the contributions media can make when presented in a meaningful combination. These experiences frequently lead to what scientists report as the "syntergystic" effect which suggests that the whole is equal to more than the individual parts. Thus, the skillful intermingling of various kinds of resources leads to an overall impact much greater than any one resource would have singly.

Other TEPS publications by Bernard McKenna and Dwight Allen[3] project a staffing arrangement on a vertical continuum rather than on the satellite basis as envisioned by Beggs and Joyce. In this kind of staffing arrangement, the emphasis is upon learner outcomes, and *then* relating staff competencies to the desired learning objectives. Such ways of looking at the staff might include a person adept in inquiry procedures, someone in attitude and value development, and another in the development of skills. Each of these teacher-specialists must be acquainted with the preparation and utilization of media.

---

[2] Bruce R. Joyce, "The Teacher and His Staff—Man, Media and Machines." Pamphlet published by National Commission on Teacher Education and Professional Standards and Center for the Study of Instruction, NEA, 1967, pp. 8–9.

[3] See for example: Bernard H. McKenna, "School Staffing Patterns and Pupil Interpersonal Behavior: Implications for Teacher Education," pamphlet published by California Teachers Association, Burlingame, California, 1967; Dwight W. Allen, "A Differentiated Staff: Putting Teaching Talent to Work," Occasional Papers No. 1 published by National Commission on Teacher Education and Professional Standards, NEA, December, 1967; and Kevin A. Ryan, "A Plan for a New Type of Professional Training for A New Type of Teaching Staff," Occasional Papers No. 2 published by National Commission on Teacher Education and Professional Standards, NEA, February, 1968.

SUMMARY

It is not enough to know how to operate machines—perhaps in the near future, such knowledge will not be necessary at all. Equipment operation is becoming more and more simplified and, eventually, teachers will manipulate media via buttons. Equipment is only an instrument for the transmission of information—a delivery boy, so to speak. It would seem that our primary efforts should be directed toward developing a more thorough knowledge of how to design instructional messages so that they can be understood and interpreted correctly by their receivers.

A current activity, identified by a variety of terms, is the preparation of instructional packages. Across the country, business and industry, school systems, teacher committees, and individual teachers are at work on such packages. They are stimulated by the desire to enable students to achieve specific objectives through the individualization of instruction. The instructional packages generally include a variety of media from which the teachers and/or students may choose the combination which best fits their learning needs and styles.

Fortunately, there are some new intellectual and conceptual tools available to assist in the design process. One is to examine the total learning situation by means of communication models. Early models were concerned primarily with the development of the message alone, without regard to the nature of the message, the kind of environment in which it was received, or the reactions of the receiver. Increasingly, however, communication specialists have become aware that a communicator (teacher) must understand and respond to the total situation. Messages often fail because some aspect of the total situation has been overlooked or ignored by the person desiring to communicate.

A second powerful conceptual device to assist teachers in the design of instructional messages to achieve specific behavioral objectives is the systems approach. The usefulness of a systems approach is that, like the communications approach, it calls attention to a multiplicity of factors and interrelationships which retard or expedite desired changes in behavior. Further, the concept of the system and subsystems is very useful in helping to break down a course into smaller parts and then suggesting appropriate scope and sequence relationships among the various topics or units.

Both the communication and systems approach have made it obvious that it is impossible to develop identical and universal messages which can be understood and reacted to by all students of a certain age or grade level. The students of a community, of an attendance unit, of a classroom, and each individual student must be recognized as unique. It is possible that generalized materials developed nationally can be used to a certain extent, but each teacher will be required to make individualized applications. Just because various media utilize different modes of presentation and appeal to the senses does not mean the message presented by them can be understood without some personalization.

Among the factors which play a very significant role in the lives of all persons today are the mass media. Almost all homes have access to such a mass communicative device as TV, and the fact that TV sets are operating in many of these homes from morning till night, seven days a week, has obvious implications for both materials, as well as methods, used in the schools. In addition to TV, radio, newspapers, and other mass media greatly condition the lives of all individuals—including those of school age.

After the teacher has taken into account some of the factors identified and discussed above, he is then ready to begin to develop objectives, first for an entire course, and later for the units or topics within that course. Here again, teachers have much more assistance now than they did a few years ago.

It is at *this* stage that decisions are made as to the kind of media which will be required in order to produce the desired student behavior. Such questions as whether reality exists in experiences, or only in the mind of the learner, condition the selection of materials, the extent to which on-the-shelf materials need to be modified and adapted, and the extent to which it is necessary to develop new materials. If new materials are required, the teacher again needs to understand the place and use of such facilitators of learning as cues, colors, and other similar design factors which are known to graphic-arts specialists.

A final step for the educator is to try out the materials, obtain feedback information, and to evaluate the success of the instructional design in terms of meeting predetermined objectives. When success has not been achieved, it is often difficult to isolate and identify the factors which inhibited the desired learning. Communication models and/or systems analysis often prove helpful in identifying the weak elements and suggesting means of improvement.

In assembling and producing the media to meet specifications, adequate support facilities and personnel must be readily available. A media program is necessary to provide all types of extant resources along with a wide range of production capabilities. Appropriately prepared media specialists are required to adequately service the needs of teachers and students.

The ideal teaching-learning situation can no longer be typified as "Mark Hopkins on one end of a log and a student on the other." Nor can teaching be considered in the traditional setting of a room, a book, a teacher, and a group of students. As our world becomes more complex, the body of knowledge grows so quickly that the growth is almost beyond comprehension. The teaching-learning situation must react to these changes. If the premise that "education is communication" is true, then it follows that both the quality and quantity of education can be upgraded through the use of technological advances and, more important, through what we know about the communication process itself. If "education is communication," then all members of the educational establishment must become better acquainted with the various disciplines that contribute to a deeper understanding of communication and of the teaching-learning process. Psychology, mass media, instructional systems, visual design, philosophy, communications theory, teaching strategies, and educational anthropology are some of the major contributors. Such knowledge is critical when it comes to the important job of designing instructional materials that will contribute most effectively and efficiently to a given learning situation. Even now, the role of the teacher is shifting from one that was basically custodial to that of a catalyst in the educational process. Emphasis is being placed not so much upon teaching as upon learning. The teacher is more a person who selects, evaluates, interprets, and guides students, rather than one who teaches facts and transmits information.

This text has been designed so that the reader is carried back and forth between theory and philosophy on the one hand, and practical experience and application on the other. There is no substitute for practice, but that practice *must*, in the final analysis, be based on sound theory.

Index

Author Index

Subject Index

Alphabet, 9
Belief congruence (*see* Message systems)
Communication
  evaluation, 182, 183
  instruction, 94, 100, 101, 111
  categories of learning, 97, 98, 99
  conditions for learning, 99, 100
  reality, 118, 119, 120
  barriers, 188
  belief systems (*see* Message systems)
  code systems (*see* Message systems)
  interference, 187
  levels, 140
  one-way communication, 140, 183, 185
  methods, 179
Communication models
  development, 60
  for analyzing the complex media, 67
  Gerbner model, 64–65
  Hovland model, 62–64
  Morris semiotic model, 69, 70
  Osgood model, 80–81
  perceptual input, 64
  Shannon-Weaver model, 61, 62

Communication models (continued)
  S-M-C-R model (Berlo), 65, 66, 67, 84, 141
  Westley-MacLean model, 67, 68
  two-way communication, 141, 183
Visual
  design, 197
  grouping processes, 211, 212
  information, 197, 198, 199
  responses to visual environment, 197
  ordering, 200, 202
  focusing on information points, 208
  figure and ground, 209
  proximity, 204
  simularities, 202
  closure, 206
  design principles, 205
  continuation, 207
  visual perception, 198
Conformity, 7
Diffusion of information, 31, 37, 39
Ethnocentricism, 244, 245
Gestalt theory, 197, 201, 202
Great Didactic, The, 12, 18-20
Gresham's Law, 50
Gutenberg, 9
Human understanding, 13, 22